D1562475

21ST-CENTURY
TV DRAMAS

21ST-CENTURY TV DRAMAS

Exploring the New Golden Age

AMY M. DAMICO AND SARA E. QUAY

 PRAEGER™

An Imprint of ABC-CLIO, LLC
Santa Barbara, California • Denver, Colorado

Library of Congress Cataloging-in-Publication Data

Damico, Amy M.
  21st-century tv dramas : exploring the new golden age / Amy M. Damico and Sara E. Quay.
     pages cm
  Includes bibliographical references and index.
  ISBN 978-1-4408-3344-1 (hardcopy : alk. paper)—ISBN 978-1-4408-3345-8 (ebook)
  1. Television series—21st century—History and criticism.   2. Television programs—History—21st century.   I. Quay, Sara E.   II. Title.   III. Title: Twenty-first century tv dramas.
  PN1992.8.S4D36 2016
  791.45'6—dc23   2015036000

ISBN: 978-1-4408-3344-1
EISBN: 978-1-4408-3345-8

20 19 18 17 16   1 2 3 4 5

This book is also available on the World Wide Web as an eBook.
Visit www.abc-clio.com for details.

Praeger
An Imprint of ABC-CLIO, LLC

ABC-CLIO, LLC
130 Cremona Drive, P.O. Box 1911
Santa Barbara, California 93116-1911

This book is printed on acid-free paper ∞

Manufactured in the United States of America

Contents

Introduction

What Is a Golden Age?

When applied to popular culture, and specifically television, a "golden age" refers to a period of years, and sometimes decades, during which the medium is changed in significant ways. The nature of these changes can vary, including the creation of such new storytelling genres as the television drama, the innovation of new technologies like cable networks, and shifts in certain viewing practices as online streaming. The first "golden age" of television began in 1949 and ended around 1960.[1] The era was defined to a large extent by the anthology drama, a form of entertainment that engaged the growing number of Americans whose homes now included a television set. Using a rotating, rather than constant, cast, anthology dramas showcased diverse storytelling, talented actors, and exemplary use of the new television format. Their production "resulted in a creative firmament for television that many television historians consider as yet unsurpassed."[2] Anthology dramas of the first golden age included *Kraft Television Theater* (1947–1958), *Studio One* (1948–1958), *Armstrong Circle Theater* (1950–1963), *The Hallmark Hall of Fame* (1951–present), and *Alfred Hitchcock Presents* (1955–1962).[3] These classic shows, and others like them, were marked as shining stars of the time period. Not all programs during these years were so favorably reviewed, however. In 1961, the then chairperson of the Federal Communication Commission (FCC), Newton Minow, expressed a more critical sentiment about television content when he delivered what is commonly referred to as the "vast wasteland" speech to the National Association of Broadcasters. Although Minow highlighted a few worthy programs in his address, his chief argument was that the majority of television programming was poor in quality. His remarks struck a chord and many historians use the time period around his speech to mark the end of the first golden age.[4]

It was not until the 1980s that television entered another period of transformation. In *Television's Second Golden Age: From Hill Street Blues to ER*, Robert Thompson argues that a surge in "quality television"—well written, novel television programs with high-quality production value—took place in the 1980s to early 1990s, marking what he calls television's "second golden age."[5] With the establishment of MTM Enterprises, and the company's development of such shows as *Hill Street Blues* (1981–1987) and *St. Elsewhere* (1982–1988), a new standard for television drama was set. These series, along with *Cagney and Lacey* (1982–1988), *Miami Vice* (1984–1989), *Moonlighting* (1985–1989), and *L.A. Law* (1986–1994), to name a few, broke with convention, integrated complex story lines, and used the workplace as a television setting in new ways.[6] The creation and broadcasting of these second golden age shows corresponded with, and was a partial response to, changes in the television industry, specifically the increasing availability and popularity of cable television, which broadened the types of shows available to viewers. The ever-expanding slate of program offerings, however, coupled with the introduction of such home-recording devices as the VCR, began to fragment viewing audiences. As Thompson suggests, a common element among second golden age programs was their "aggressively controversial story topics, behind-the-scenes battles between producers and networks over content, scheduling and often imminent cancelations."[7] He points out that "the general adoration of critics resulted in press coverage of these shows that was sometimes out of proportion to the size of the audience watching them."[8] In other words, the second golden age was defined by the quality of the programs overall, rather than the size of any single program's audience.

At the turn of the 21st century, a new era of television began to be recognized, characterized by the emergence of highly regarded, well-crafted programs offered by a variety of providers ranging from traditional television networks to online streaming services. Some critics refer to this most recent period in television history as a "second golden age," perhaps because they are unaware of, or dismiss, Thompson's argument about the 1980s and 1990s.[9] Others simply call the first decades of the 21st century the "new golden age," pointing to the large variety of high-quality programs available.[10] For still others, the early 21st century is called "the third golden age" of television, part of a continuing evolution of the medium.[11] Whatever the moniker, since around the turn of the century, distinct changes have taken place in the realm of television, including the rise of HBO, home to such acclaimed series as *The Sopranos* (1999–2007), *Six Feet Under* (2001–2005), *The Wire* (2002–2008), and *Deadwood* (2004–2006), as a television producer. Although HBO had been operating since the early 1970s, in the 1990s, it began to create original programs that ultimately changed the television landscape and made HBO a household name. In *Difficult Men*, Brett Martin suggests that HBO's novel forms of television production inspired new ways of creating programming for other network and cable companies.[12] Similarly, in *The HBO Effect*, Dean DeFino documents how the premium cable network established itself and ultimately influenced the landscape of television in the 21st century with its production of noteworthy television dramas.[13] Although HBO may have led the way in new types of television production, other networks followed, resulting in a plethora of award-winning shows from sources as diverse as FX, Sundance, Showtime, ABC, CW, and BBC America.

As occurred during the second golden age, developments in technology have played a part in the current diversity of television offerings. As programming and viewing have shifted to such online platforms as Netflix, Hulu, and Amazon, these businesses, known for distributing content, began to produce their own original series. Such enterprises quickly proved successful. Not only did original programs like *House of Cards* (2013–present) and *Transparent* (2014–present) win awards, they were also well received by fans and critics alike. This broadening definition of who can create television, not to mention how television can be viewed, confirmed that the 21st-century world of "TV" would never be the same. Matt Smith, a television industry professional, offers his insight in an *Adweek* blog: "This revolution in content production has been largely driven and enabled by a sea change in how consumers access programming. The first wave came as the proliferation of TV channels available via cable/satellite/telco subscriptions. The second wave is the on-demand availability of content through streaming services like Amazon Prime, Hulu Plus and Netflix, powered by over-the-top devices like Roku, Apple TV, Amazon Fire TV and gaming consoles like Xbox. Standalone niche networks that are available 24/7 in a channel format via apps and online—like the Tennis Channel and WWE Network—are also part of this wave."[14]

21st-Century TV Dramas examines the landscape of the current golden age from a variety of perspectives, including recurrent themes, connections with contemporary culture, and forms of audience engagement. Although the phrase "new golden age" may include such genres as situation comedies, miniseries, and documentaries, this book focuses on the wide array of television dramas that have appeared in the first decade or so of the current century. Some of those dramas are highly regarded by critics, have won awards, and engage large and active fan bases. Others—award winners and not—have smaller, niche audiences who are just as loyal to shows that may get less media attention than their blockbuster counterparts. Some of the dramas discussed in the book break new ground in terms of television content, whereas others add new and nuanced interpretations of familiar themes. Choosing which television shows to write about in depth is always a challenge, and surely, there are programs that merit more attention than this book can provide. In addition, although such shows as *The Sopranos, The Wire,* and *Six Feet Under,* as along with ABC's *Lost* (2004–2010) and Showtime's *Dexter* (2006–2013), form the foundation on which the new golden age rests, these are discussed in less detail here because they have been written about so widely elsewhere.

Why television dramas? Television content is best understood as deeply embedded in its historical moment: Programs, and television dramas particularly, can push against the status quo, explicitly (or implicitly) advocate for social change, frame challenges citizens are facing in new ways, or highlight flaws in institutions that govern viewers' lives. And although television audiences have become increasingly fragmented, the cultural medium of television remains a powerful force in U.S. culture, engaging viewers with social issues, registering their hopes and fears, and asking them to consider lifestyles that might be different from their own. *21st-Century TV Dramas* makes connections between cultural patterns and trends present during the first 15 years of the 21st century and the content of the television dramas running during this time. We are not alone in this enterprise. Twenty-first-century culture thrives on the practice of readily engaging with, and responding to, popular texts. Indeed, avenues for expression are constantly being developed, allowing more voices to contribute to timely, often sophisticated, discussions of television content. In acknowledgment of this fact, the references cited and sources consulted throughout the book come directly from the popular discourse around the shows discussed, including, among others, the ideas of journalists, cultural critics, bloggers, and fans.

How to Read This Book

21st-Century TV Dramas: Exploring the New Golden Age examines the connection between contemporary culture and a selection of notable 21st-century television dramas. Each chapter title identifies two complementary themes that set the context for the dramas discussed in that chapter. Introductions to each chapter provide an overview of the theme pairings, how the themes connect to contemporary culture, how some examples of dramas engage with those themes, and, when appropriate, how the themes have taken shape during earlier periods in television history. Specific 21st-century dramas related to those themes are then explored in depth. Although readers may choose to read this book from start to finish, the book's structure does not make this mandatory. The chapter introductions provide context, however the in-depth examinations of specific dramas and themes stand alone as individual components and can be read in any order.

Chapter 1, "Stories and Audiences," looks at how new ways of storytelling have emerged in a connected digital environment that has seen the landscape of television production and viewership change dramatically. Chapter 2, "Safe and Unsafe," considers how dramas have integrated aspects of living in a post–September 11 world into their narratives. Chapter 3, "Women and Men," examines new representations and constructions of gender that have played out in contemporary culture and have become increasingly common fare for television programming. Chapter 4, "Home and Work," explores televised representations of contemporary family and workplace environments contextualized by new understandings of both arenas. Finally, Chapter 5, "Fact and Fiction," discusses how 21st-century social issues connect to popular dramatic programming.

On a final note, we are television fans. Furthermore, we are not alone. In the classroom, we enjoy engaging in energetic exchanges with our students about the programs they are watching. In our academic careers, and in completing research for this book, we have encountered many scholarly articles, essays, television reviews, water cooler conversations, blog posts, fan sites, books, and feature articles written by other television viewers clearly invested in having conversations about television series, episodes, and showrunners. We hope this book adds to these conversations.

CHAPTER 1

Stories and Audiences

There was a time when television dramas were considered less sophisticated and lower quality than their cinematic counterparts. In the early part of the 21st century, this is not the case. Many television dramas are widely celebrated for their complicated and developed story lines, high production value, and diverse casts of talented actors. The distinction between television and film dramas has been blurred, as actors and directors typically associated with movie making are also engaged in television projects. For example, Martin Scorsese directed an episode of *Boardwalk Empire* (2010–2014), Gus Van Zant applied his directing talent to *Boss* (2011–2012), and Steven Soderbergh produced and directed the entire first season of *The Knick* (2014–present). In addition, actors with established film careers like Kevin Spacey, Robin Wright, Halle Berry, William H. Macy, Laura Dern, Matthew McConaughey, and Viola Davis, are starring on such television dramas as *House of Cards* (2013–present), *Extant* (2014–present), *Shameless* (2011–present), *Enlightened* (2011–2013), *True Detective* (2014–present), and *How to Get Away with Murder* (2014–2015).

The new crossovers between the television and film industries can be attributed to changes in television production practices and the success of particular programs, many of them produced by the premium cable channel HBO, at the turn of the 21st century. HBO turned its attention to the television format in the late 1990s with its highly regarded prison drama *Oz* (1997–2003). The premium network's comedy *Sex and the City* (1998–2004) followed, and in 1999, *The Sopranos* (1999–2007), a violent, gritty drama about mafia leader Tony Soprano, his colleagues, therapist, and family in New Jersey debuted. In his book *Difficult Men*, Brett Martin connects the success of the now iconic *Sopranos* to programs that include *The Wire* (2002–2008), *The Shield* (2002–2008), *Rescue Me* (2004–2011), *Mad Men* (2007–2015), and *Breaking Bad* (2008–2013), all shows with complicated, flawed, and unlikable men as lead protagonists.[1] Martin argues that: "this new generation of shows would feature stories far more ambiguous and complicated than anything that television, always concerned with pleasing the widest possible audience and group of advertisers, had ever seen. They would be narratively ruthless: brooking no quarter for which might be the audience's favorite characters, offering little in the way of catharsis or the easy resolution in which television had traditionally traded."[2]

Others state that cable programming "has become more innovative in recent years, with deeper character development and edgier story lines, while the major movie studios largely have abandoned intricate, character-driven stories for superheroes and pirates."[3] The cable television production model requires a lower number of episodes per season (12 or 13) than network television (22 or more), and within this time frame, some showrunners and writers choose to tell stories where the primary narrative was not wrapped up within a season. Martin writes: "The open-ended, twelve- or thirteen-episode serialized drama was maturing into its own, distinct art form. What's more, it had become the signature American art form of the first decade of the twenty-first century, the equivalent of what the films of Scorsese, Altman, Coppola, and others had been to the 1970s or the novels of Updike, Roth and Mailer had been to the 1960s."[4] Not all critically celebrated cable dramas are "open-ended," however. *Dexter* (2006–2013) and *Damages* (2007–2012) tell complete narratives within a season, for example, and *The Killing* (2011–2014) used two seasons to solve its first primary mystery. Regardless, in the 21st century, cable dramatic programming emerged as a high-quality storyteller, inspiring such network and other television programming producers as Netflix to compete.

Some of the best television of the early 21st-century television landscape offers nuanced, thematic explorations of humanity. For example, the HBO family drama, *Six Feet Under* (2001–2005), tells the story of the Fisher family, managing their family-owned funeral business after the sudden death of the family patriarch. The show's focus on death is complemented by characters—often in dysfunctional relationships—trying to figure out how to get the most out of their lives before their own time is up. As scholars Kim Akass and Janet McCabe point out, the show pushes against a conservative status quo vision of cultural institutions. They claim: "Structurally it deals with the space between death and burial; thematically it focuses on cultural taboos—homosexuality, mental illness, old age, sickness, drug addiction, adolescence, race and class—which in turn are used to revisit traditional cultural certainties like religion, marriage and the family; and ultimately it questions who we are."[5] For its part, the cop drama *The Wire* questions social and political issues connected to institutions in Baltimore, MD. Culture critic John Hendel points out that the early 21st-century setting of *The Wire* makes the program an important artifact of the time period, arguing: "[Director] David Simon brings a historian's sword in his analysis of urban decay, and the blade is very much one that befits the years 2002 to 2008. The era carried a specificity to its history that is worth noting and is memorialized in this iconic HBO show. The drama is a portrait of its time in the same way a show like AMC's *Mad Men* strives to capture the 1960s."[6]

One of the most popular dramas of the first decade of the 21st century was ABC's unique network drama, *Lost* (2004–2010), which integrated a storytelling technique that used developed backstories, and later flash forwards, to elaborate on the characters' lives in ways that wove together the show's central narrative—a story that begins when Oceanic flight 815, full of passengers, crashes on an unknown island. One of *Lost*'s key characteristics was the audience involvement in the series storytelling, a practice that increased as *Lost*'s content extended to multiplatform outlets and fans created content of their own. In his analysis of *Lost* transmedia, the term for storytelling that takes place outside of the actual television program, Carlos Scolari points out that the popularity of the show did not entirely capture what made *Lost* original.[7] He writes: "the fictional world of *Lost* does not end with these television products: it has spread to other media and communication spaces to become of the most comprehensive and interesting transmedia narratives of the first decade of the twenty-first century."[8]

Although serious themes are a staple, dramatic storytelling can also be funny and humorous elements are present in many of today's dramas. Some showrunners use a hybrid form of drama and comedy, known as dramedy, to tell their stories. Such programs as *Nurse Jackie* (2009–present), *Enlightened* (2011–2013), and *Shameless* (2011–present) use the 30-minute episode format, a length usually reserved for situation comedies. Although comedic at times, these shows are not straight comedies. On *Nurse Jackie*, nurse Jackie Peyton struggles with drug addiction while the show's hospital setting is the backdrop for more serious narratives. *Enlightened* follows a self-destructive corporate executive, Amy Jellicoe, who, after a very public breakdown, returns to her job with newfound insight she is intent on sharing with her less-than-receptive colleagues. *Shameless* tells the story of a family living on the poverty line in Chicago. Although the plot twists and character actions are frequently exaggerated, and may elicit laughter from viewers, one of the series' central themes is how to survive in a dysfunctional family faced with economic hardship. *Desperate Housewives* (2004–2012) combines soap opera story lines with comedy in an hour-long format that offers a behind-the-scenes look at a perfectly manicured U.S. suburb. Similarly, *Jane the Virgin* (2014–present), in its 60-minute time slot, leans more toward the comedic than the dramatic. By mimicking the melodramatic characteristics of the telenovela genre, popular in Latin America, the show integrates numerous witty moments.

Advances in technology, including the creation of digital connections between television creators and consumers, have played an important role in the development of dramatic storytelling into higher quality television viewing experiences. Given the cultural pervasiveness of the Internet, the television industry has developed an online presence, taking into consideration audiences' use of streaming video, expectation of extra show content, and reliance on social media. With their ability to respond instantly to the TV content, audiences share their ideas about programs in online environments, participate in program extras, and create content of their own based on the television dramas they watch. New forms of storytelling have also emerged as the shifts in premium cable, basic cable, and online streaming services allow for a diverse slate of programming to emerge. Producers have become committed to using digital tools to develop interest in their show and cultivate strong and committed fan bases.

The essays in this chapter examine different elements of 21st-century television storytelling and audience responses. "Storytelling in the Age of Convergence Culture" provides an overview of how transmedia storytelling and second screen use have altered the experience of engaging with television narratives. "Literary TV" examines how some television dramas, in particular *True Detective*, can be considered a new form of literature. A Side Note on *Mad Men* highlights the drama's period piece storytelling technique and fan response. "Twenty-First-Century Television Viewing and Netflix's *House of Cards*" discusses how the program's success, with its fresh take on White House politics and power, broadened the way television programming is delivered, accessed, and consumed. "*Jane the Virgin*: The New Telenovela" explores the contemporary representation of a Catholic Latina family in a storytelling format that riffs on the popular Latin American genre, the telenovela. "Dual-Language Dramas" identifies how changing demographics in the United States are informing the choice to include more spoken Spanish on television dramas. Finally, "ASD on TV" summarizes the presentation of, and reaction to, representations of one widespread contemporary concern, autism spectrum disorders (ASDs), on television.

Storytelling in the Age of Convergence Culture

Beginning in the second season of the popular vampire drama *True Blood* (2008–2014), interested readers could check out the weekly updated blog titled "Baby Vamp Jessica: Confessions of a Good Girl Gone Vampire" at babyvamp-jessica.com. On *True Blood*, Jessica becomes a vampire at age 17; on her blog, she expresses her feelings as she adjusts to her new existence and manages relationships in the ever-changing supernatural world she inhabits in Bon Temps, LA. Her blog entries vary—she poses questions to readers, shares photos and videos of herself and other characters, and she reflects about aspects of her life in vlog format, directly addressing viewers. The blog includes a comment feature and many readers play along, writing to Jessica and sometimes eliciting a response. For example, in her vlog entry titled "A House is not a Home," Jessica shares her concerns about her inability to cook and make a comfortable home and wonders what to do saying at one point: "If you can think of anything that might help, you know, household tips or whatever, with me not having to do anything too nauseating, please share them?"[9] Viewers of this vlog responded with a number of suggestions, prompting Jessica to write the following week: "Hey folks. First, I'd like to thank y'all for your generous input. I didn't realize I had so many friends out there! This is a lot easier than just googling 'how to be a vampire housewife' and sifting through all the crap on the Internet. So many of you—including *Lisa Cheli, R.J., Andrew*, and *bite me*—came up with the brilliant idea of microwavable dinners. Why didn't I think of that?!"[10] Jessica also noted, "I might have to try *amber*'s[sic] suggestion: Bringing home leftovers from Merlotte's" and "we just don't have a crock pot like *Melinda* and *Dana Hilton* suggested."[11]

The Baby Vamp Jessica blog is just one example of how developments in technology and the evolution of convergence culture have changed the landscape of television storytelling and audience engagement. Television dramas do not simply exist in a single form; creators produce ancillary content connected to their shows including web sites, Facebook pages, Twitter accounts, blogs, video games, comic books, and webisodes. Fans also produce materials that explore or extend elements of the television show, including fan web sites, blogs, wikis, videos, and fan fiction. This creation of materials by media industries or by fans is not a new phenomenon. However, today's convergence culture provides producers and audience members with new ways of creating, sharing, and responding to content in online environments that allow for easy interacting with a large, geographically diverse audience. This advancement of digital technology has resulted in a large increase of participants who engage in activities online.[12] In addition, the experience of watching television is changing: viewers connect with others using social media while they are watching television and may also use a separate device to access additional program material. In short, the 21st-century television environment is complemented by transmedia storytelling and second screen experiences.

Transmedia storytelling is a process where "elements of a story are dispersed systematically across multiple media platforms, each making their own unique contribution to the whole. Each medium does what it does best—comics might provide back-story, games might allow you to explore the world, and the television series offers unfolding episodes."[13] Although multiple media platforms can certainly be used effectively to market television programs, not all multiplatform promotion is considered transmedia storytelling. Prolific convergence culture academic Henry Jenkins points out that, even though transmedia initiatives are often funded through marketing budgets and may promote the show: "the best transmedia is driven by creative impulse. Transmedia allows gifted storytellers to expand their canvas and share more of their vision with their most dedicated fans."[14] Often in transmedia, fans are invited to participate in the storytelling. For example, fans may comment on blog posts, as in the case of Baby Vamp Jessica, or they may participate in alternative reality games (ARGs) like "The Lost Experience Game" connected to TV's *Lost* (2004–2010).

Several television production teams use transmedia storytelling as a way to develop interest and deepen viewers' experiences with the television dramas they enjoy. For example, to supplement the superhero drama *Heroes* (2006–2010), NBC released webcomics each week that expanded on elements of the television show. Eventually, the comics were produced in book format and can now be purchased from retailers. Showtime featured animated *Dexter* (2006–2013) webisodes that corresponded with the drama's dark theme. In addition to the Baby Vamp Jessica blog, the *True Blood* team developed other transmedia content that included an ARG, mini episodes, and extensive web sites for communities seen on the program—The American Vampire League and The Fellowship of the

Light.[15] For its part, *Lost*'s six seasons of television were accompanied by four ARGs, four novels, and one video game, not to mention numerous online videos, DVD extras, and web sites. Television expert Jason Mittell describes *Lost*'s approach to transmedia storytelling as "expansionist, working to extend the narrative universe across media and introducing many new characters, settings, plotlines, time periods and mythological elements."[16] Transmedia content must be both separate from, and related to, the television show. Viewers of a television program who do not engage with transmedia content, for example, should still be able to view and understand each program's episode. At the same time, those who do engage in the show's transmedia content should believe they have experienced deeper aspects of the story.[17] Often, transmedia content relies on viewers' understanding of the main story, the television narrative.[18]

Not all transmedia content is produced by popular culture industries. Fans, too, engage in creating sophisticated texts that expand on the narrative world of a television show. For example, *Game of Thrones* (2011–present) fans spent three years creating a Minecraft version of the show's world in anticipation of it being used as a role playing game.[19] Many fans contribute to wiki sites that provide detailed information about shows and characters. Searching for fan fiction related to a favorite television drama on fanfiction.net, a popular web site that houses extensive fan fiction narratives, may yield numerous stories about that drama's characters or program narratives. As one scholar remarks: "if anything characterizes transmedia narratives it is that they tend to drag on into eternity and it is almost impossible to stop them. As much as J.J. Abrams and his team of writers have tried to finish it, *Lost*'s narrative engine is still working. Transmedia storytelling teaches us that *if producers don't want, don't know or can't generate new contents, prosumers will create and distribute them.* You don't like Lost's ending? Create your own The End."[20] Fan contributions are part of the extra-television landscape and can be solicited and celebrated by media industries. For example, in February 2015, AMC launched "Mad Men: The Fan Cut," a contest that invited viewers to recreate scenes from the show's pilot. The 47-minute fan-produced pilot is streaming on the contest's web site and represents a wide variety of interpretations of previously written content.[21]

Engaging with television-related content does not only happen in transmedia contexts. Television is known as the "second screen" in media history (film is the first), but the vernacular around how television viewing is discussed now uses the term to refer to how viewers are using a literal "second screen" like a tablet computer or smart phone while they are watching television. Activity on tablets or smart phones includes looking up content online, commenting on such social media platforms as Facebook, tweeting, and viewing what others are saying in online environments. In many instances, today's viewers are engaging with television programming in real time.

Collected data illustrate what this engagement looks like. A Pew Research Internet Project study (2012) reported that television viewers with cell phones use their phones while watching television to "keep themselves occupied during commercials or breaks," "check whether something they heard on television was true or not," "visit a website mentioned on TV," "exchange text messages with someone else who was watching the same program in a different location," "see what others were saying online about a program you were watching," "post your own comments online about a program you were watching," and "vote for a reality show contestant."[22] A Nielsen study revealed that 84 percent "of smartphones and tablet owners say they use their devices as second-screens while watching TV as the same time."[23] The 2nd Screen Society, an industry group focused on studying these practices and proposing ways to maximize their business potential, issues quarterly reports that show consumer engagement levels with "second screens" while watching television. For example, a 2012 2nd Screen Society report indicated that the Summer Olympics inspired 85 million social media comments on multiple platforms between July 27 and August 12, 2012, and that an episode of the teen drama *Pretty Little Liars* (2010–present) resulted in 1.6 million tweets.[24] In fact, tweeting about television has become a popular activity: Nielsen reports that about 1 million Americans discuss television on Twitter each day.[25]

One example of a drama where Twitter motivates second screen use among viewers is ABC's *Scandal* (2012–present). Created by Shonda Rhimes, *Scandal* is a nighttime soap opera that tells the story of a Washington D.C. crisis manager named Olivia Pope. Episodes include a range of narratives from the standard procedural to the over-the-top long form twists and the show thrives on the latter, especially on Twitter. In fact, some critics credit the show's Twitter use and the resulting fan base's use of Twitter as a key factor in the drama's success.[26] In 2013, as the number one drama that earned about 8 million viewers a week, *Scandal* socializing also included 190,000 tweets per episode.[27] A long list of hashtags is associated with the show. General ones range from #Scandal to #AskScandal to #Gladiators (what Pope's team calls themselves), whereas more specific hashtags are associated with such plot points as

#whoshotfitz or #whoisthemole. Other hashtags reference fashion, plot predictions, and scenes from the show fans are talking about. Rhimes is an active Twitter user and the cast is active on the platform as well. Also central to the social experience of *Scandal* is that the actors live tweet during the show's broadcast, a practice that results in a 65 percent increase in conversation about the show.[28] Because *Scandal* fans do not want to experience plot spoilers, their tremendous Twitter engagement has resulted in more of them watching the show at its actual broadcast time, something increasingly hard to do in today's converged world.

The Walking Dead (2010–present), *Agents of S.H.I.E.L.D.* (2013–present), *Empire* (2014–present), and *American Crime* (2015–present) also engage actors in using Twitter before, during, and after program broadcasts. In fact, when *American Crime* entered preproduction in 2014, the cast was required to take Twitter training.[29] Although this training was likely motivated by a number of factors, it highlights a shift in television drama production, suggesting that communicating with viewers and directly involving them in some aspect of the show are important. The *Pretty Little Liars* (2010–present) cast continuously engages with their audience through Twitter, Facebook, and Instagram. Finally, television program applications are also emerging as content providers that viewers can engage with as they watch TV. One example of this is Story Sync. AMC debuted the application in 2012. According to the cable channel's web site: "This web-based app provides a live, two-screen experience that allows you to vote in snap polls, answer cool trivia questions, and re-live tense moments via video clips during the initial broadcast of each week's episode."[30] AMC has Story Syncs for later seasons of *Breaking Bad* (2008–2013), *The Walking Dead* (2010–present), and *Turn* (2014–present). Because Story Sync is integrated with social media sites, viewers who use this platform can share their experiences with others if they choose too.

Twenty-First-century television storytelling is not confined to the televised narratives of popular dramas. Although the dramas themselves continue to offer rich story lines and characters, supplemental content is increasingly a part of each program's culture. Viewers can decide how much or how little to engage with transmedia associated with the show, potentially becoming part of the wider narrative landscape. Viewers can also make choices about methods of viewing the shows themselves and whether or not to engage with cast members, friends, fans, or program content. Descriptions of 21st-century television viewing are increasingly less like ones where a person sits on a couch and stares at a screen.

Literary TV

Twenty-first-century television dramas have been compared to literary novels, creating debate about "TV-as-Literature."[31] In an article on the topic, subtitled "How television is struggling—and often succeeding—at becoming a mature literary form," Michael Agresta describes the parallels:

> It's become commonplace lately to talk about the serial television show as the novelistic medium of the 21st century—*The Wire* as a modern-day Dickens novel, *Mad Men* our Cheever, *Friday Night Lights* our Steinbeck. One could continue down the line, with *Lost* as our Michael Crichton and *Desperate Housewives* our Jacqueline Susann, but the lowbrow serial has been entrenched for decades now; it's the higher-quality stuff that's new. Whereas feature films were always limited in comparison to literary novels by their brief and rigorous story arcs, TV is free, theoretically at least, to use a broad canvas and unfold over tens or even hundreds of hours of screen time.[32]

Agresta goes on to claim that, since *The Sopranos* (1999–2007) debuted, television has met the benchmarks "essential to any narrative medium's claim to broad cultural relevance—holding up a mirror to society, conveying characters' internal lives with depth and integrity, achieving new expressive styles that reflect the consciousness and felt reality of the time."[33] Claiming, "Cable [TV] is the New Novel," Thomas Doherty elaborates, saying that although 21st-century dramas are historically part of a history of television programming, their "real kinship is literary, not televisual. Like the bulky tomes of Dickens and Dreiser, Trollope and Wharton, the series are thick on character and dense in plot line, spanning generations and tribal networks and crisscrossing the currents of personal life and professional duty."[34]

The lines between literature and TV have been blurred in other ways as well. For example, in 2011, novelist Salman Rushdie announced he was switching from writing novels to writing TV series, a creative form he claimed allows the writer to be "the primary creative artist."[35] Conversely, TV has crossed into territory once reserved for great works of fiction. Just as literary novels have been traditionally studied in college courses, such TV dramas as *The Wire, The Sopranos,* and *Breaking Bad* are now routinely included on academic syllabi and written about in published scholarship. Television showrunners have been held up as creative forces worthy of media interviews and recognition, whereas TV series have been given more and more serious attention, not to mention sought-after space, in such highly regarded reviews and magazines as the *New York Review of Books*.[36] Even the TV recap, the brief summary of what has happened in previous episodes of a series, has risen in prestige, called by some "an art form."[37] Meant to help viewers remember increasingly complex plots from episode-to-episode, the recap has gained the attention of professional critics and fans alike who are interested in summarizing and analyzing episodes that have already been aired.[38]

The HBO crime series *True Detective*, released in 2014, exemplifies the relationship between television and the literary novel. Quickly recognized as a "revolutionary" show, the drama gained immediate attention for casting well-known actors Matthew McConaughey and Woody Harrelson in the first season.[39] Playing homicide detectives in rural Louisiana, Harrelson, as Martin Hart, and McConaughey, as Rust Cohle, received accolades for their performances of characters whose relationship spans 17 years, and whose pursuit of a serial murderer continues to connect them. More than the actors, however, the series' format, writing, and literary references captured the attention of critics and fans, raising the profile of the television detective crime drama to a new level.

Created by former literature professor and short story writer Nic Pizzolatto, *True Detective* was originally intended to be a novel.[40] Before his move to television, Pizzolatto worked as a college professor and technical writer. He also wrote and published short stories in respected magazines and journals, including *The Atlantic Monthly* and *The Iowa Review*.[41] Pizzolatto attributes his creativity as a fiction writer to the television shows he watched as a child. In an interview on the subject, he states television was his "first cultural window."[42] He goes on to describe how, while pursuing his MFA in graduate school: "*Deadwood, The Wire*, and *The Sopranos* were all on HBO. Those shows were actually filling my hunger for fiction as an audience more than the contemporary fiction that I was reading. They seemed very much like auteur works—but the auteur works of a writer, not the auteur works of a director. Then I learned what a showrunner was and I was like, 'Wow, that actually sounds like the perfect job for me.'"[43] Pizzolatto moved to the small screen when he was hired to write for AMC's crime show, *The Killing*. One of many writers, Pizzolatto did not find the job to be a good fit and left the series in search of more creative control over his writing. Reflecting his roots as a writer of literature, by definition a solitary process, he said: "I want to be the guiding vision. I don't do well serving someone else's vision."[44]

HBO's purchase of the script that became *True Detective* brought Pizzolatto's ideals to fruition. As the only writer on the series, Pizzolatto maintained complete control over the script rather than working with the more common team of writers. In *True Detective*, because Pizzolatto had the unusual opportunity to maintain such creative control over the series, he was more like an author than is typically possible in the more collaborative television process. The series did not follow the usual practice of employing several directors either, aiming to use just one, Cary Fukunaga, throughout the entire series. In addition to one writer and director, *True Detective* uses the anthology format: each season features a single, stand-alone story with different actors, further adding to the literary feel of the show, as if each season is a new novel by a single author. As one critic puts it: "The anthology format allows the creator and actors to give a more detailed, devoted run at a single story. It goes deep, rather than wide. As well, the tight-knitness of the constraint of an eight-episode project leads to a more novelistic approach to storytelling."[45] Other literary elements of the series include the "fragmented time periods," "unreliable narrators,"[46] and the "hyper-literate dialogue."[47]

The series has been compared to a wide range of literary genres as well. For some, the writing "calls to mind a Southern Gothic novel with a mythological twist."[48] Others compare the characters to those "in a fable or a heroic tale,"[49] and still others refer to the series as a "literary time-jumping crime story,"[50] a crime procedural, or akin to the novels of "William Faulkner and Gabriel Garcia Marquez."[51] The consistent attempt to describe *True Detective* in literary terms reflects the fact that "*True Detective* is a literary television show that makes full use of literary forms and specific references in its narrative and resulting mythology."[52]

True Detective is not the only 21st-century television drama to be compared to literary forms or to make reference to works of literature.[53] ABC's *Lost* (2004–2010) featured many works of fiction and nonfiction being read by characters, sitting on shelves, or referred to in episode titles. For instance, in only 1 of more than 70 books referenced in the series, in season one, Sawyer is shown reading Richard Adams's *Watership Down*, a novel about a community of rabbits in search of a safe place to live. Many of the books referenced in *Lost* were chosen because their themes resonated with the episode, season, or series. As executive producers and writers Damon Lindelof and Carlton Cuse explained: "We pick the books with a great deal of meticulous thought and specificity and talk about what the thematic implications of picking a certain book are, why we're using it in the scene and what we want the audience to deduce from that choice."[54] Viewers responded positively, creating *Lost* book clubs and blogs about the referenced titles and their link to the fate of the downed Oceanic Flight 815.

AMC's *Mad Men* (2007–2015) was also filled with literary references that, rather than providing clues about the plot, helped viewers gain insight into the series' cultural and historical setting of the 1950s–1970s. Such books as Frank O'Hara's *Meditations in an Emergency* (1957), John le Carré's *The Spy Who Came in from the Cold* (1963), and Philip Roth's *Portnoy's Complaint* (1969) reflect as much what people were reading at the time the show was set as the theme of any particular episode or insight into any single character.[55] Viewers of the show were so intrigued by the books being read and referenced on the series that the New York Public Library created official "*Mad Men* Reading Lists" organized by character and season.[56] Viewers could follow the Battery Park City Library *Mad Men* book discussion on Twitter #MadMen#Reading and links to the books on the show bring followers directly to the book in the online catalog.

FX's biker drama, *Sons of Anarchy* (2008–2015) written and produced by Kurt Sutter, was another literary-inspired series, this time by Shakespeare. As Sutter puts it: "I loosely based all my characters on ones from *Hamlet*. I winked at it with Gemma as Gertrude and Clay as Claudius. Opie was Horatio. And the ongoing question was: Would the prince find out? We take these sort of huge tragic turns at different points in the series that feel Shakespearean to me, and at times we veer a little bit more toward *Macbeth*."[57] The series finale emphasizes the Shakespearean influence on the narrative. When the main character Jax Teller sacrifices himself by riding to his death, the scene goes to black with just four lines from *Hamlet* on the screen: "Doubt the stars are fire; Doubt that the sun doth move; Doubt truth to be a liar; But never doubt I love."[58] As one viewer blogged: "The quote in question comes from Act 2, scene 2 of the play, in a letter Hamlet writes to Ophelia. The meaning is simple: You can question anything except for the fact that I love . . . While he may have lost his way at various points in seven seasons of 'Sons of Anarchy,' viewers can never doubt that Jax loves. After all, he's Hamlet."[59]

The link between literature and AMC's *Breaking Bad* (2008–2013) has also been written about at length. The series itself has been compared to literary texts as different as Shakespeare's plays, Herman Melville's *Moby Dick*, and the *Curious George* series.[60] There are also direct references to literature in the episodes, some extending over entire seasons. For instance, a reference to the poet Walt Whitman is used as a foil to distract law enforcement from connecting the main character, Walter White, to a murder. Because Whitman and White have the same initials, White is able to convince detectives that the initials W.W., found written in the victim's notebook, are a reference to the poet rather than to himself.

Ultimately, however, it is a copy of Whitman's book, *Leaves of Grass*, which gives White away when the inscription "To my *other* favorite W.W." is found written inside it. The third to last episode of the entire series, cited by some as the greatest episode in television history, takes a literary work as its title, and its theme, "Ozymandias."[61] For those familiar with the poem before watching the finale, or for those who looked it up afterward, the parallels drawn include that the "fallen kingpin Walter White's empire is turned just as much to dust and ash as things tumble horrifyingly, gut-wrenchingly out of control for every single character fans hold dear."[62]

Like its predecessors, *True Detective* incorporates literary references throughout the inaugural season, capturing viewers' imaginations and inciting theory after theory about the mystery at the center of the story. Although detectives Hart and Cohle try to identify the serial killer at the heart of their case, viewers paying close attention to the dialogue began to pick up on possible clues that could reveal who he or she is. The main references are to a 1985 collection of short stories titled *The King in Yellow*, a cult classic that influenced writers from Raymond Chandler to Robert Heinlein.[63] The book shot up the sales charts by 71 percent in a single day after the fifth episode, in which the title is explicitly discussed. Headlines in *Slate, The Atlantic, The New York Times,* and *The New Yorker* debated the significance of the literary reference under titles like "True Detective: Who Is The Yellow King?" "True Detective: Yellow King Theory," and "True Detective: Who The Hell Is The Yellow King?"[64] Before the mystery was revealed at the end of the season, it seemed that: "the whole world was unhealthily preoccupied with the show, and deliberately or not, it made detectives of us all, establishing a worldwide cult of mini Cohles . . . Even if you weren't actively Googling 'Yellow King' or immersing yourself in far-flung fan hypotheses, there was a rare enjoyment in simply witnessing detailed investigation by proxy."[65]

Unlike the other 21st-century dramas that could be classified as literary TV, however, in using its literary references to engage viewers, *True Detective* shifted the form of a television genre. Early in the season; "Blogging sleuths . . . uncovered important literary references in *True Detective*, and the game of decoding what appears to be a giant philosophical puzzle has begun. People are taking this very, very seriously: They are quoting pages of obscure, late-19th-century fiction and musing on the meaning of death, all in relation to a television drama about cops tracking a serial killer. . . . Its mix of horror and philosophy, its linguistic clues and puzzles, its poetic anti-hero, its complex non-linear chronology all make it both viscerally gripping and intellectually dense."[66]

The intellectual engagement of viewers is most interesting in *True Detective*'s reimagining of the detective genre. "The growing intellectual currency of television," says critic David Carr, "has altered the cultural conversation in fundamental ways. Water cooler chatter is now a high-minded pursuit, not just a way to pass the time at work. The three-camera sitcom with a laugh track has been replaced by television shows that are much more like books—intricate narratives full of text, subtext and clues."[67] When applied to a unique form like *Lost* or such historical drama as *Mad Men*, the "intellectual currency of television"[68] adds depth to the mystery or setting of the show. When applied to the tried and true genre of the detective show, the impact is significant.

Nic Pizzolatto seems intent on making this change. Perhaps reflecting his roots as a teacher and writer of literature, he says: "My idea was that those familiar tropes could act as a way to ground the viewer, before subverting them," going on to say that he planned on "telling a crime story to lure people in, then feeding them the vegetables [an exploration of character and morality] that they wouldn't otherwise eat."[69] Anne Billson claims that the show has had an effect not just on the industry but also on viewers. "Pizzolatto," she writes "is typical of a new breed of TV auteurs, instrumental in the 21st century un-dumbing of American TV, who are not just unafraid of inserting esoteric literary references that not everyone will have heard of, but who positively revel in them as a means of injecting cryptic and playful clues into their visions. It's a sort of interactive TV, enabling viewers to play a role not so far removed from that of the gamer. . . . They're no longer just passive observers—they're participating."[70]

Side Note: *Mad Men*

In the history of 21st-century television dramas, AMC's *Mad Men* (2007–2015) made its mark through its approach to storytelling, its visual depiction of mid-20th-century United States, and its influence on popular culture. Created by Matthew Weiner, the series has been called one of the best television shows of all time.[71] In addition to widespread critical acclaim for writing, acting, costume design, and historical accuracy, *Mad Men* won multiple awards throughout its eight-year run.[72] It was the first basic cable series to win the Outstanding Drama Series Emmy Award, marking an expansion of the new golden age of television dramas beyond such cable networks as HBO.[73]

Set in 1960s Manhattan, *Mad Men*—named for the Madison Avenue advertising men of the era—introduces viewers to the lives of the men and women of the Sterling Cooper advertising agency. The main character, gifted creative director Don Draper, belongs to the larger category of 21st-century antiheroes, as he moves through each season making decisions that appear to serve his personal desires more than his moral compass. For example, Don's attempts to create the stereotypical 1950s suburban household—including his wife, Betty, and their two children—to compensate for his own horrific upbringing in a brothel during the depression ultimately fail because he cannot control his womanizing, a pattern that continues throughout the series. Draper, like many of the show's characters, represents individuals who, at this particular moment in U.S. history, were affected by the changing culture of the period. Peggy Olsen, who in the first season is hired as a secretary after a shamelessly sexist interview, fights her way into a professional position as a copywriter and eventually a creative director, a journey that registers the changing roles of women at the time. Conversely, Draper's wife, Betty, despite some shifts in her character toward the end of the series, remains firmly in what feminist author of the time, Betty Friedan, called "the feminine mystique": a housewife and mother whose ambivalence toward her role can hardly be contained despite her determined commitment to it. Joan Holloway, the voluptuous office manager who is also having an affair with her boss in the first season, uses her sexuality to make professional gains while revealing herself, throughout the series, as one of the most business-savvy employees in the office.

Each *Mad Men* character shines a light on an earlier era in U.S. history, one that seems distant and yet familiar to some viewers. As Weiner puts it, the show is like science fiction, but it uses the past, rather than the future, to comment on aspects of contemporary life that are difficult to talk about, including racism, sexism, parenting, marriage, and work.[74] In season one's episode, "Ladies Room," for example, Don and Betty's daughter, Sally Draper, appears in front of her mother wearing a plastic dry cleaning bag over her head as part of a game she is playing. In the same season, entitled "The Gold Violin," the Drapers go on a picnic and leave their wrappers on the side of the road without a second thought. These scenes create distance between the past and the present by underscoring how much has changed since the 1960s. In doing so, *Mad Men* uses the past as an allegory for the present, suggesting that life in the 21st century is just as troubled as it was during the tumultuous years of the civil and women's rights movements.[75]

Viewers became fascinated with the series, hosting *Mad Men* season premiere—and finale—parties, buying *Mad Men*-inspired products, and playing *Mad Men* games on the AMC web site. Fans embraced the show's cross-platform marketing approaches and the *Mad Men* team collabo-rated with several companies to promote their series. In 2010, for instance, the clothing store Banana Republic created *Mad Men*-inspired window displays at stores across the country as well as a contest where the win-ner got a walk-on role in an episode. Retailer Brooks Brothers offered fans a "Mad-Men Edition" suit designed by the show's costume designer. Other *Mad Men*-inspired products included limited-edition Ken and Barbie dolls made to look like Joan, Don, Betty, and Don's boss, Roger, whereas lines of nail polish, cosmetics, and shaving gear reflected the *Mad Men* style. Online apps and interactive web sites included an iPhone app called *Mad Men* Cocktail Culture, which helped users create *Mad Men*-style drinks; a game where users could choose a *Mad Men* charac-ter and dress them in *Mad Men* clothing and accessories; and a "Which Mad Man Are You?" quiz game that would align one's personality with a character from the show.[76]

In keeping with the advertising theme of the series, *Mad Men* was rec-ognized for its product placement of various historically accurate items including Heineken beer, Lucky Strike, Maidenform, Clearasil, and American Airlines. Commercials that were aired during the series' epi-sodes sometimes capitalized on this unique form of product placement. For instance, Unilever aired commercials set in a fictional advertising agency to promote a range of its products.[77] The series was also known for its attention to authentic historical details, including the settings and furniture, as well as the ashtrays, martini glasses, books, and other period details. The attention to detail was so impressive and accurate that arti-facts from the series are now housed in the National Museum of Ameri-can History.[78] Books of the era—*Exodus, Atlas Shrugged, Confessions of an Advertising Man,* to name a few—became popular reading for view-ers. In fact, entire *Mad Men* reading lists like the one published by the New York Public Library were compiled and the literary references on the show were regularly commented on by critics and viewers in an attempt to deepen their understanding of the enigmatic series.[79]

Other promotional techniques are noteworthy. Life-size posters of the lead characters were hung in Grand Central Station to promote season two, and actors inside the station dressed in *Mad Men*-style clothes while handing out Sterling Cooper business cards.[80] Before the fifth season pre-miere, posters were hung from the sides of buildings in New York and Los Angeles, featuring the same image of a man falling from an office building that was featured in the opening credits. The image was controversial for the way it evoked the iconic photograph "Falling Man," taken on Septem-ber 11, 2001, of a man falling from the burning Twin Towers.[81]

AMC's *Mad Men* marked the golden age of 21st-century television by expanding award-winning dramas from premium to basic cable networks, capturing viewers' imagination with its historically accurate depictions of 20th-century U.S. culture, and reflecting back to audiences the complicated relationship between the past and the present. The series anchors the new golden age while setting the bar for cinematic, narrative storytelling that viewers found irresistible.

Twenty-First-Century Television Viewing and Netflix's *House of Cards*

In 2013, when the subscription media delivery company Netflix announced its intention to produce an original television drama, it marked "a bold attempt to remake the television landscape."[82] *House of Cards* (2013–present), the British-based drama adapted for U.S. audiences, would be "streamed online to laptops and beamed directly to flat-screens through set-top boxes and Internet-enabled devices"[83] rather than viewed through network or cable television. In addition, the entire series, all 13 episodes, would be released at once, allowing viewers to completely control where, when, and how much of the series they watched at any given time. As Ted Sarandos, head of Netflix content, stated: "When we got into original programming, I wanted it to be loud and deliberate . . . I wanted consumers to know that we were doing it and I wanted the industry to know that we were doing it so we could attract more interesting projects. Doing it in some half way, some small thing, it wasn't going to get us there."[84] The release of the U.S. version of *House of Cards* changed 21st-century viewing practices, shifted how TV dramas were produced and released, and reflected, in its plot and characters, contemporary perceptions of U.S. politics.

Before *House of Cards*, television viewing was part of the collective U.S. experience, in which shows were released by networks or cable operators in specific time slots during which they could be watched. This meant that viewers watched the same episodes at the same time and could share the anticipation, as well as the experience, of each newly released episode or series. Ratings were based on how many viewers tuned in to a specific program at the time it aired. As cable companies began to offer on-demand viewing and the service became popular, timeshifting—the practice of viewing a show after its airdate—became part of the show's ratings. The networks and cable companies, however, maintained control of when new episodes could be seen and for how long they were available, although some viewers would access episodes on web sites.

House of Cards changed that dynamic. Viewers were already familiar with binge-viewing, or watching multiple "re-runs" of a series' episodes for hours at a time, a practice originating with "marathons" offered by networks and then made more common with the release of entire already-aired seasons of series on DVD, on-demand services, and online streaming sites. With *House of Cards*, viewers could watch brand new programming the way they had watched those series that had already been aired. By releasing the entire series at once, viewers could watch as many, or as few, episodes as they wanted to in a single sitting.[85] The change meant that, rather than "feeding a collective identity with broadly appealing content, the streamers imagine a culture united by shared tastes rather then arbitrary time slots."[86]

In addition to altering how quickly and where a series could be watched, *House of Cards* also marked a shift in the way programming is tracked and evaluated. Due to its collection of data on how and what its subscribers watch, Netflix was able to predict the potential viewership for *House of Cards*. As Netflix chief communication officer Jonathan Friedland stated: "Because we have a direct relationship with consumers, we know what people like to watch and that helps us understand how big the interest is going to be for a given show. It gave us some confidence that we could find an audience for a show like 'House of Cards.' "[87] According-ing to *Forbes*, this was the first time that television producers used large data algorithms to shape decisions about what types of programming to distribute.[88] Data were also used to target potential *House of Cards* viewers, according to the other shows the data said they liked. As David Carr writes: "there was not one trailer for 'House of Cards,' there were many. Fans of Mr. Spacey saw trailers featuring him, women watching 'Thelma and Louise' saw trailers featuring the show's female characters, and seri-ous film buffs saw trailers that reflected Mr. Fincher's touch."[89] Netflix further bucked traditional TV practices by refusing to participate in rat-ings and not sharing details about how many viewers *House of Cards* has had since its release in 2013.[90]

House of Cards also transformed the way television programming is accessed. Although streaming shows over the Internet were available before *House of Cards*, through Netflix itself or other online providers like Hulu and Amazon, those subscription services offered viewers access to existing, rather than new, content. Netflix's production of an original series that was available only through Internet streaming meant viewers could stream new content. In addition, viewers could watch *House of Cards* on their laptops, tablets, and phones, but they could only watch the series on their traditional television set if it was hooked up to the

Internet. With the release of *House of Cards*, critics predicted that as more viewers look to the Internet for their television content, cable television would become less appealing as viewers cut their cable in favor of less expensive subscription models that gave them more control over cost and content. Since the release of *House of Cards* in 2013, Netflix has created other successful original programming for example *Orange Is the New Black*. Streaming providers like Amazon have followed suit, suggesting the shift from network and cable-driven programming is here to stay.

Although *House of Cards* marks a reinvention of television production and consumption, the subject of the series was anything but new. Starring Kevin Spacey as the House majority whip Frank Underwood, *House of Cards* follows the trajectory of a politician who, after being passed over as the next secretary of state, sets a determined course to rise in power whatever the cost. Flanked by his wife, Claire, who is as dedicated to her husband's goal as he is, the couple plot and scheme without emotion even when the price is the livelihood, or life, of those around them. *House of Cards* asks viewers to consider Underwood's belief in "ruthless pragmatism" as a moral code that justifies his choices.[91] Set in Washington, D.C., the show depicts a dark side of contemporary U.S. politics and the men and women who exemplify those traits.

House of Cards was an immediate hit with viewers and critics. Seasons one and two were nominated for multiple awards in a variety of categories, and the series won both Emmy and Golden Globe awards. In 2013, it was the first web-only television series to win an Emmy.[92] Beyond the novelty of the show's mode of delivery, the success of *House of Cards* may be at least partly a result of its political content, suggesting that the mode of delivery makes little difference if the program content is no good. According to Gallup polls released the same year as the series, only 33 percent of Americans said they believe government dysfunction was the biggest problem facing the country, up from less than 10 percent in 2009, whereas a Pew Research Report found that just 19 percent of Americans said they trusted the U.S. government.[93] *House of Cards'* dark look at Washington politics resonates with these sentiments. Spacey's character, Frank Underwood, embodies this mistrust with his brutal pursuit of power, regardless of the cost. The opening scene of the first season shows Underwood strangling a neighbor's dog that was hit by a car. His direct address to viewers—a technique used throughout the series in which Spacey looks into the camera as he speaks—sets the tone for Underwood's character in no uncertain terms: "Moments like this," he says, "require someone who will act, who will do the unpleasant thing, the necessary thing."[94] These sentiments capture general attitudes toward Washington and its politicians in the early 21st century. As Ari Melber of *The Atlantic* writes, Underwood "is a hopped-up version of a dominant archetype in national politics: People who enter the arena for the same reasons a big audience still watches it—the thrill, glory, and ambition. Policy and morality run a distant second and, even then, often serve as props to underscore 'the stakes' of the maneuvers involved, not as dimensions of independent substance."[95]

Throughout the series, Underwood and his wife, Claire, make choices in their own favor without concern for the impact. For viewers who see government leaders acting with apparent disregard for the lives of everyday citizens, supporting Wall Street over Main Street to use the language of the great recession, the Underwoods are stand-ins for all that is wrong in U.S. politics. A 2013 Pew Research report found that 30 percent said they were angry with the government over such issues as government shutdowns, dysfunction in Congress, and a perceived invasion of privacy.[96] Like other antiheroes of 21st-century dramas, including serial killer Dexter Morgan and drug dealer Walter White, Frank Underwood is despicable in his choices, yet oddly compelling nonetheless.[97]

The character of Claire has also struck a chord with viewers for her own antihero traits.[98] Set on supporting her husband's ambitions, in the first season, Claire, who runs an environmental nonprofit organization, does whatever it takes—for example fire half of her staff—to further his career. In season two, Claire's character is shown to be just as relentless as her husband when she turns her back on people who trust her. After wooing her colleague Gillian Cole away from a high-paying job offer, for example, Claire fires her and then threatens the health of Gillian's unborn child by terminating her health insurance. In one of her most chilling lines of the season, Claire tells Gillian: "I'm willing to let your child wither and die inside you if that's what's required."[99] In an emotionally laden plot during which Claire reveals she was the victim of rape, she proceeds to name her rapist during a live television interview. In doing so, she manages to put to rest long-standing rumors that she had had an abortion by saying that she was impregnated as a result of the rape and that she aborted the pregnancy because of the circumstances. The truth, viewers know from previous scenes, is that Claire was pregnant three times and the abortions were choices based on her ambition.[100]

The Underwoods stand as a unified front toward furthering their own interests, bound together by their desire for power in a marriage based on ambition rather than romance or a sense of family. One critics says: "the most commendable, groundbreaking aspect of 'House of Cards' [which] is not simply that Claire is Frank's backbone, it is that TV now has an antihero couple, a relationship founded on pure villainy that changes the way we look at evil in pop culture."[101] Whether we dislike them or root for them, as a couple, the Underwoods' presence in the 21st-century television drama also tells us something significant about how we see U.S. politics and the troubled behavior of U.S. politicians. As Conor Friedersdorf writes: "*House of Cards* reveals our alarming inability to resist or condemn the powerful *even when their depravity is revealed to us in the most unambiguous terms*. If any human beings are evil, then Frank and Claire Underwood are evil. A root cause of political corruption is our aversion to treating them as we would less powerful people who are equally evil."[102] From its transformative role in television-viewing practices to its reflection of 21st-century perceptions of U.S. politics, Netflix *House of Cards* has made its mark on TV drama.

Jane the Virgin: The New Telenovela

According to the Pew Hispanic Center, Latinos are the largest minority group in the United States.* In 2013, it is estimated that more than 54 million Latinos were living in the United States.[103] Two-thirds of this population is American, born in the United States and "descendants of the big, ongoing wave of Latin American immigrants who began coming to this country around 1965."[104] Despite the growing population of Latinos in the United States, representation of this group on U.S. television has been limited. An extensive Columbia University report found that the number of Latinos in U.S. television programming does not reflect the population of Latinos in the United States.[105] In addition, when Latinos do appear on U.S. television shows, they are most often portrayed in a limited number of roles, primarily as criminals, law enforcement officials, or blue-collar service workers.[106] One exception can be found on the CW dramedy *Jane the Virgin*, the story of Jane Villanueva, a 23-year-old member of a matriarchal Latino family consisting of Jane, her mother Xiomara (Xo), and her grandmother, Alba. Although the women are all bilingual, Alba speaks Spanish the most on the series. The show's storytelling format parodies the telenovela's emphasis on heightened and melodramatic narratives and features a narrator who speaks—often with witty commentary—to viewers as stories unfold.

---

*The terms Latino and Hispanic are used interchangeably here and refer to people who identify as being of Hispanic, Latino, or Spanish origin as defined by the 2010 U.S. Census.

The telenovela, the "tele" being short for television and "novela" meaning novel, or book, in Spanish, is a popular storytelling genre in Spanish and Latin American cultures. Telenovelas are often compared to U.S. soap operas but differ from them in several ways. Unlike an afternoon soap opera, "telenovelas in most Latin American countries are aired in prime-time six days a week, attract a broad audience across age and gender lines, and command the highest advertising rates. They last about six months and come to a cinematic close."[107] Telenovela narratives prioritize romantic relationships over the family relationships that drive U.S. soap operas, and also include social issues relevant to the program's country for instance class differences, migration, and race.[108] *Jane the Virgin* is loosely based on a Venezuelan telenovela called *Juana La Virgen*. Calling it "a telenovela for the modern age," NPR Code Switch writer Brenda Salinas points out that the program's storytelling technique relies simultaneously on adhering to, and satirizing, telenovela tropes, and that the show airs weekly, following the U.S. television season rather than the typical telenovela time frame.[109]

In the spirit of the telenovela, *Jane the Virgin* presents viewers with exaggerated scenarios during which the narrator chimes in with humorous comments directed to the audience. As the first season begins, Jane is engaged to Michael when, during a routine physical examination, she is accidentally artificially inseminated by a distracted female doctor. Jane becomes pregnant and finds out that the father, Rafael, is a man she had a crush on, and shared a kiss with, several years earlier, and for whom she now works. In a nod to telenovela tropes, the doctor whose mistake sets the narrative in motion is also Rafael's sister. *Jane the Virgin* focuses on how Jane deals with her unexpected pregnancy and how the choices she makes affect the direction of her life. As the season progresses, viewers are also introduced to several romantic narratives, an organized crime mystery, and the Villanueva family's reunion with Jane's father—long separated from Jane's mother—who just happens to be the star of a telenovela the family watches.

The series is more comedic than dramatic, despite its hour-long format, but the dramatic elements are seriously presented and the program's characters are well developed, offering an interesting and original representation of contemporary Latinos. *Jane the Virgin* takes place in Miami and features a diverse cast of Latino characters engaged in a variety of professions: Jane is studying to be a teacher, a career she is ambivalent about, works as a waitress, and is an aspiring writer. Her mother, Xo, is a fitness instructor. Rafael, the baby's father, runs a large hotel, and Jane's father, Rolegio, is a successful actor. Despite her young age, unexpected pregnancy, and indecision about what career to pursue, Jane is the most powerful character on the show. She models intelligence, thoughtfulness, and personal agency to the series' viewers, many of them presumably millennials themselves, as the show is on the CW, a network popular with teenagers and young adults.

In addition to depicting a strong, young female character, *Jane the Virgin* also offers a contemporary representation of Catholicism, the religion at the heart of the Villanueva family and, in many ways, central to various aspects of the plot. Research on how Catholicism is depicted on 21st-century television dramas is limited, but two studies offer some insight. First, Scott Clarke's 2005 analysis of religious characters on network programming revealed that out of 549 characters coded in the study, just 32 of them (5.8 percent) were religious. Of this religious character group, 25 characters were connected to a specific religion, none of whom was Catholic. Although Clarke points out that the omission of Catholic characters is a new trend (a 1994 study suggested that Catholics were the dominant group on television), he also notes that a number of religious characters in his research had major roles.[110] In later research, Erika Engstrom and Joseph Valenzano found that Catholicism is the dominantly privileged religion in the first three seasons of the fantasy/sci-fi drama *Supernatural*. The authors identified: "two main themes: (1) the depiction of Catholicism as 'good' and (2) the portrayal of other religions, including Protestantism, as evil."[111] Evidence to support these findings includes the use of Latin (the native Catholic Church language) to extract demons from the humans they inhabit, the positive portrayal of Catholic priests, and the power of such Catholic artifacts as crucifixes, rosary beads, and holy water. In contrast, the villains on *Supernatural* are largely associated with non-Christian religions, and characters associated with Christian religions who are not Catholic are "portrayed as fraudulent, sinful or evil."[112]

The presentation of Catholicism on *Jane the Virgin* is both novel and timely. Several characters are Catholic and religious imagery is an integral part of the setting. Jane and her grandmother Alba are often seen wearing crucifix necklaces, and religious pictures are present in the family home. All three Villanueva women are seen practicing their religion by attending church, occasionally praying, and referencing God in conversation. Although it is clear that Catholicism is important to Jane, Xo, and Alba, it is also clear that their religion resonates with each of them in different ways and is not always central to their decision making.

The depiction of Catholicism in *Jane the Virgin* is no more apparent than in the main narrative of the series, Jane's pregnancy. Despite the zany circumstances that lead to Jane becoming pregnant, the dilemma around

the pregnancy is handled seriously: viewers observe Jane's process of deciding whether she will keep the baby, give the baby up for adoption, or have
an abortion. That decision is not made in a vacuum, however, and Jane is
pulled in different directions by the people in her life. Her boyfriend Michael
wants her to have an abortion, Rafael wants to adopt the child and raise
it with his wife Petra, and Jane's grandmother Alba wants her to keep the
baby. Jane's mother, Xo, is clear that she will support Jane no matter
what she decides and tells her daughter that if she wants to have an abortion, it is okay. Although each person in her life has an opinion on what
Jane should do about her pregnancy, the choice and power to decide the
course of action are presented as Jane's and Jane's alone.

What is notable throughout these different conversations, as well as in
Jane's ultimate decision to keep the baby, is that the institution of Catholicism does not enter into the equation, especially because the Villanuevas
are established as practicing Catholics and because Catholicism has a
clear position on the subject. The conversation around what Jane should
do prioritizes the personal (Jane's life and how it will change) over the
religious (when life begins). Even Alba, the most religious of the Villanuevas, does not voice her opposition to abortion in religious terms. Instead,
she wants Jane to have the baby because, when Xo was pregnant with
Jane, Alba encouraged her to have an abortion, a choice that would have
meant Jane, whom she adores, would never have been born. In framing
Jane's choice in these ways, *Jane the Virgin* privileges a prochoice ideology, presenting abortion as a viable and implicitly moral option, a position
with which those opposed to abortion, including the Catholic Church,
disagree. However, because Jane elects to continue the pregnancy and
because her grandmother states so emotionally that she could not envision a life without Jane in it, the prolife narrative is acknowledged, and
contextualized, in a way that neutralizes a potentially contentious debate
the show might otherwise provoke on the subject of abortion.

In contrast to religion's absence from the discussion around whether
or not Jane will have the baby, Jane's decision to remain a virgin, despite
being tempted by her feelings for Michael, is clearly influenced by religious beliefs. Alba's voice is a factor here as well; it is her statements that
Jane recalls when she considers how intimate to be with her boyfriend.
Whereas religious symbolism does not enter into the pregnancy discussion,
"Chapter 3" of the first season is explicitly Catholic. While in church,
Jane imagines being scolded by the congregation and Virgin Mary statue
for having sex. This comedic, musical scene explicitly links Jane's choice not
to have sex before marriage with her Catholicism. The combined nar-
ratives around virginity and pregnancy—one registering religious belief,

the other not—result in a uniquely 21st-century construction of Jane as a young woman who is a complex product of her culture, religion, and upbringing. Perhaps like many 23-year-olds, Jane is revealed to be a young woman of faith who nonetheless does not subscribe to all of the church's teachings. In fact, this tendency is documented in the current population of U.S. millennials.[113]

Jane the Virgin walks another fine line in the representation of religion when it combines the ridiculous with the reverent. In doing so, however, the show manages to avoid making fun of Catholicism itself. In season one, "Chapter 4," for example, Jane and Michael attend pre-Cana sessions with her priest. The narrator humorously defines for the non-Catholic viewer what pre-Cana is while, on the screen, the following footnote appears: *Pre-Cana: Catholic marriage counseling led by a priest.* * *Who has never been married.* Despite this often pointed out irony of marriage counseling conducted by a man who is not allowed to be married, the priest and the conversation he has with Jane and Michael are not treated as unimportant or irrelevant. Similarly, in "Chapter 7," although the nuns at the school where Jane teaches know the details about how she became pregnant despite being a virgin, they call Jane's pregnancy a miracle to prompt infertile couples to believe that hugging Jane will assist them in conceiving. The nuns also craft and distribute a coin with Jane's face on it as a marketing gimmick to increase interest in the church. This modern framing of Jane as the Virgin Mary verges on ridiculous, but beneath the humor is a deep respect for Jane's pregnancy and the wish for other couples to conceive a child. Jane confronts the nuns about their antics and asks them to stop, but she cannot, and will not, challenge their faith, especially because Jane herself believes in divine intervention. In these instances, Jane again makes her own choices and engages with her religion in her own way. She challenges the nuns' assertion that her pregnancy was divine intervention, but does not challenge the idea of divine intervention itself.

In another story line, once humorous and poignant toward religion, Alba is in the hospital in a coma. An upset and worried Jane rushes home to get her rosary to pray by her grandmother's side. Later, she sits by Alba's bedside, rosary beads in hand. Xo, at a different moment at the hospital, kneels and prays to God for her mother's recovery, promising to be more conservative in her sexual practices if she recovers. Although Alba is conscious at this point and hears Xo's prayer, Xo is not aware of this and keeps her promise to God (sometimes with some manipulative prompting from Alba) because she believes God responded to her wishes. Moments like these demonstrate the faith Jane and Xo possess even if they do not practice Catholicism in the more traditional ways Alba does. Finally, when the family is preparing for Easter in "Chapter 18," flashback scenes show Jane as a girl having doubts about the veracity of the resurrection of Jesus on Easter Sunday. One of this episode's themes is faith and although it is never explicitly made clear what the adult Jane thinks about the resurrection, it is obvious how meaningful the religious holiday is to her.

In an adaptation of the telenovela format, *Jane the Virgin* broadens the representation of Latino characters on television dramas in original and contemporary ways. By including different levels of engagement with Catholicism as a part of one family's identity in the nuanced way that it does, the show highlights an element of cultural identity with which viewers may be able to connect. Through its various portrayals of different Latino characters, the show challenges previously documented stereotypes of Latinos on TV and ushers in a new form of representation. Finally, *Jane the Virgin*'s focus on a modern Latina protagonist as a woman guided by her own agency, intelligence, family, and religion provides a positive role model for young CW viewers.

Side Note: Dual-Language Dramas

Although it only ran for two seasons, FX Network's *The Bridge* (2013–2015) made its mark on the 21st-century drama landscape in several ways. Primarily, and most notably, it was the "first Spanglish TV drama on a premium American cable channel—or on any American channel for that matter."[114] The main language spoken on the show is English, however approximately 30 percent of the dialogue is in Spanish.[115] A crime procedural set on the border between Mexico and the United States, marked by a bridge that both connects and separates the two countries, *The Bridge* moves back and forth between the towns of El Paso, Texas, and Juarez, Mexico. When the scenes are set on the Mexican side of the bridge, the dialogue is in Spanish; when set in Texas, the characters speak in English.[116] Most, but not all, of the time English subtitles translate the Spanish dialogue for English-speaking viewers. Sometimes, however, the Spanish-speaking characters deliberately speak in Spanish to prevent the U.S. characters from understanding what they are saying. In those instances, subtitles are often eliminated, preventing non-Spanish-speaking viewers from understanding as well. As executive producer and writer Elwood Reid describes: "If two people are speaking and there's a gringo there and they switch over to Spanish, it creates this cool narrative tension . . . You lean in to the screen: 'What's going on?'"[117]

The rationale behind the dual-language dialogue in *The Bridge* is not just the plot. Tapping into the Latino market with a television drama that would not only depict Latino characters but also use their language was of great interest to the FX Network. Sally Daws, FX's senior vice president of marketing at the time *The Bridge* was released, said the series "had a huge potential opportunity with the Hispanic audience."[118] Hispanic audiences gravitate toward shows on such Spanish networks as Telemundo and Univision and therefore "offering this kind of premium cable experience" to those audiences is a new venture.[119] As actor Demian Bichir, who plays the main lead male, detective Marco Ruiz, explains, speaking in Spanish had a positive impact on Latino viewers. "We're giving those 33 million Hispanics in the U.S. un punto de encuentro—a point where they can actually identify themselves," Bichir said in an interview. "We are blessed to be able to show characters from Mexico that have never been portrayed on American TV."[120] In addition, with its border location, the drama was able to put a new spin on the crime and serial killer formula that is so popular in other 21st-century shows. By integrating the topics of deportation, immigration, and border crossings into its plot, *The Bridge* marries politics with murder in a unique merging of genres.[121]

It is the subtitles that are most frequently commented on by U.S. audiences, however. In earlier U.S. television shows, if a character was supposed to speak a language other than English, the actor would have a limited number of choices: either he or she would start speaking in that language with subtitles, and then suddenly switch over to English for the duration of the show, or the actor would simply speak in English with an accent in an effort to emphasize that the character's native language was not English. The shift seen in *The Bridge* honors the native language of the characters and asks viewers to adapt to different dialects, marking a transitional moment in television history. *The Bridge* is not the first, or only, 21st-century drama to include characters who do not speak English, however; other shows have explored how to move away from the standard practices of depicting non-English-speaking characters. In 2004, *Lost* (2004–2010) featured a Korean couple who initially spoke only Korean. Not only could English-speaking audiences not understand what they were saying without subtitles neither could the other characters, making for an effective plot device in a series filled with suspicion and distrust. FX's *The Americans* (2013–present), about Soviet spies living in the United States during the Cold War, includes Russian language scenes. *Homeland* includes scenes spoken entirely in Middle Eastern languages, ABC Family's *Switched at Birth* (2011–present) uses American Sign Language, and *Game of Thrones* (2011–present) includes a fictional language of Valyrian and Dothraki.

Perhaps the drama most akin to *The Bridge*, at least in terms of language, is the CW's *Jane the Virgin* (2014–present), which also features actors who routinely speak English, or Spanish with subtitles, depending on the character and the subject being discussed. HBO's *American Crime* (2015–present) and Netflix's *Bloodline* (2015–present) follow suit, including scenes shot in Spanish with, and sometimes without, English subtitles.

Whether the motivation for these shifts in language aims to capture a more global viewing audience, reflects a changing demographic within the United States, or suggests an increased level of sophistication in the dramas themselves, it is clear that English-speaking audiences will continue to see a variety of languages on the small screen in the years to come.

ASD on TV

In 2011, the Theater Development Fund, a nonprofit organization that supports performing arts, unveiled the Autism Theater Initiative, a program designed to make live theater accessible to families where a member—a child or adult—may fall on the autism spectrum. These shows are modified for the audience, leaving out components that might be difficult for this population such as strobe lights. In addition, performances include quiet spaces in the theater lobby that are staffed by autism specialists.[122] Major theme parks Universal Studios and Walt Disney World offer services for guests with cognitive disabilities, including guests on the autism spectrum, which may include special break areas and service cards that, among other things, permit those on the spectrum who cannot tolerate long lines to be able to minimize their wait time for attractions.[123] Another program, Wings for Autism, allows children on the spectrum to participate in a mock flight experience, where families walk their child through the procedures of getting to the airport, obtaining boarding passes, checking luggage, going through security, and boarding a plane.[124] These programs, and many others, represent a heightened awareness of ASD that is part of a national conversation in the 21st century. This conversation takes place on television dramas as well, as characters with ASD appear on popular shows.

According to the Centers for Disease Control and Prevention, ASD is "a group of developmental disabilities that can cause significant social, communication and behavioral challenges."[125] The current diagnosis of ASD includes the conditions of autistic disorder, pervasive developmental disorder not otherwise specified (PDD-NOS), and Asperger syndrome, conditions that were previously diagnosed separately. Those who are "on the spectrum" may face challenges with social, emotional, and communication skills and vary in their abilities to function independently, think, problem-solve, and learn.[126] In March 2014, the Centers for Disease Control and Prevention estimated that 1 in 68 children has ASD—a number that is 30 percent higher than previous estimations arrived at in 2012. The 2014 report also notes that ASD is about five times more likely in boys than in girls and that intellectual ability varies among individuals although almost half of the diagnosed children in the study had "average or above average intellectual ability."[127]

More heightened societal awareness of ASD might also be traced back to a now debunked study that suggested autism was linked to the vaccines babies are given as part of wellness visits. *Lancet*, the journal that initially published the research, retracted the work and issued statements emphasizing that the connection was unfounded and the author was unethical in his research.[128] However, some still believe in the link and have publicly advocated against vaccinations. Actress Jenny McCarthy, for instance, received significant media coverage by asserting that vaccinations caused autism. Given that the scientific community does not see any causal link between vaccinations and autism, her views were revisited again in 2013 when she was hired to be a host of *The View*.[129] Other media attention around ASD has contributed to public awareness as well. The advocacy organization, Autism Speaks, has become better well known and HBO's film *Temple Grandin* (2010) resulted in more media attention directed to Grandin herself, an adult woman with autism who, in interviews and a TED Talk, has become a recognizable spokesperson about how being on the spectrum has positively informed her work with animals.

The film and television industries have a history of including characters on the spectrum in their narratives. In the 21st century, several television dramas feature characters who exhibit characteristics reflective of ASD in both home and work settings. This trend has not escaped the notice of popular culture writers, and several have discussed the trend itself while musing over which characters fall on the spectrum. For example, *Huffington Post*'s Maggie Furlong wonders whether the trend suggests "an effort to embrace and personify a disorder that has become more and more prevalent."[130] *MacLean*'s Brian Bethune evokes Susan Sontag's suggestion that in each historical moment, there is an "illness" that mirrors a particular fear and wonders whether the prevalence of ASD-oriented story lines in popular culture is the most recent version of this.[131] Others suggest that the inclusion of these characters contributes to interesting television. As *Salon*'s Emily Shire points out, this is "not surprising considering that some traits associated with autism can make for colorful characters that are obsessively logical and unusually blunt or comically awkward and completely unaware of social cues."[132]

Characters on television dramas who have ASD traits are diverse and range from young Max Braverman on *Parenthood* (2010–2015) and lawyer Jerry Epstein on *Boston Legal* (2004–2008) to doctor Virginia Dixon on *Grey's Anatomy* (2005–present), accountant Edgar Roy on *King and Maxwell* (2013), and detective Sonya Cross on *The Bridge* (2013–2014). Although these characters have been acknowledged by their show-runners as being on the spectrum, other characters are not "officially" diagnosed even when their character traits are closely aligned with those associated with an ASD diagnosis. For example, some have pointed to Temperance Brennan (*Bones*), Gregory House (*House, M.D.*), Spencer Reid (*Criminal Minds*), Jake Bohm (*Touch*), Will Graham (*Hannibal*), Astrid Farnsworth (*Fringe*), and Sherlock Holmes (*Sherlock*) as displaying characteristics associated with ASD, although these characters are not officially diagnosed. The reasons for this vary. For example, the creator of *Bones* (2005–present), Hart Hanson, indicated that, although he based Brennan on a friend who had Asperger syndrome, he did not want to name her as such because he wanted the show to recruit a large broadcast network audience. Hanson and other producers including popular situation comedy *Big Bang Theory*'s Chuck Lorre and *Parenthood*'s Jason Katims also articulate the importance of portraying a character on the spectrum in an accurate way if they are identified as being on the spectrum on the show.[133]

Katims, whose son has Asperger's, has tried to achieve this with the construction of Max on the family drama *Parenthood*. One of the ongoing story lines on *Parenthood* centers on Max as a child with Asperger's syndrome. Max is identified as having Asperger's at the beginning of the series and plotlines revolve around the family's response to his diagnosis. Max Burkholder, the actor who plays Max Braverman, works with a medical professional to help him with character development and to assist him in understanding what someone with Asperger's syndrome may be thinking or feeling.[134] Katims has stated that he hopes the Asperger's story line on *Parenthood* will help "normalize" the condition and demystify it.[135] Other shows have also tried to create realistic Asperger's characters by hiring consultants. For example, UCLA neuroscience professor, Dr. Susan Brookheimer, provided advice for the high-functioning autistic character Gary on Syfy's *Alphas* (2011–2012) and Alex Plank of WrongPlanet.net, an online ASD community, was hired to be a consultant on FX's *The Bridge*, where the show's detective Sonya Cross is on the spectrum.[136,137]

In this convergence culture, an interesting component of the proliferation of characters who exhibit ASD qualities on television is the response to these portrayals by bloggers and other writers who are themselves on the spectrum. One of the unique qualities of media convergence is that it allows for anyone to create and participate in online communities, allowing for marginalized groups to have a voice. The communities also provide spaces of support and connection among people with similar thoughts, challenges, and lifestyles. There are many ASD communities ranging from those created by individuals to those sponsored by nonprofit organizations, medical organizations, or journalistic publications. Within this ever-expanding collection of voices from those on the spectrum, a number of thoughtful posts and articles reflect on, challenge, and celebrate the various portrayals of characters who exhibit ASD characteristics. Other members of the ASD community—parents, experts, and caregivers—have also joined in this conversation, articulating their feelings and ideas about these television depictions.

The representation of characters on the spectrum is complicated. On one hand, these television depictions model some positive examples of adults and children as functioning, integrated members of a community and workplace. On the other hand, because these characters are high functioning, only part of the spectrum is being shown. In fact, the characteristics of a large percentage of those on the spectrum are not shown on television.[138] Beth Arky of the Child Mind Institute provides a nice example of the complexities of ASD portrayals in her discussion of how members of the ASD community reacted to the portrayal of Jake on *Touch* (2012–2013). Although some members of the ASD community believed the show conveyed information about the father–son relationship nicely, providing an accurate picture of difficult situations parents and children face when managing a disability, others challenged the construction of a seemingly autistic child who had superpowers and were upset because difference in a person does not always arrive with exceptional talents or abilities.[139] These types of discussions about character portrayals of those with ASD are pervasive in online environments.

For example, Lynne Soraya, the *Psychology Today* writer of the publication's blog titled "Asperger's Diary: Life through the lens of Asperger's Syndrome" offers a detailed critique of *Grey's Anatomy*'s Virginia Dixon. Soraya suggests that Dixon is a stereotypical character and writes: "she has all the diagnostic criteria, all at once and all to the extreme. She overengages (sic) with her new colleagues, lecturing them on her subject area, jumping tangentially from subject to subject. She doesn't look anyone in the eye. She avoids physical contact. She struggles with any and all social subtext going on between her fellow doctors and their patients. She shows no feelings, and doesn't appear to appreciate them in others."[140] In addition, Soraya points out that Dixon's Asperger's characteristics are more male than female oriented and addresses several scenes where Dixon's character acts in ways that are inconsistent with how Asperger's manifests in people. Soraya argues that if the writers were being true to Dixon's character, they would have to acknowledge that a professional MD with Asperger's would have had to develop coping mechanisms to achieve such a position, strategies Dixon does not seem to have on the show.[141]

Landon Bryce of thAutcast.com, a spectrum-oriented blogazine, offered mixed reviews of *Parenthood*'s portrayal of Max. One of his critiques of the show is that viewers are not seeing the experience of Asperger's enough from Max's perspective, but rather through the family experiences. He also argues that the portrayal does not represent a clear picture of the condition. "This is TV autism—Max talks clearly and expressively, he never hurts himself or anyone else, he's only once (I think) told the people trying to help him that he hates them. He does not cry in his house about how everyone hates him. And he always looks perfect—no drool or snot or knots in the hair. He is the Doris Day of aspies."[142] In another post, however, Bryce writes that the depiction of Max over the series has improved and gives Jason Katims a place on his list of "Outstanding Neurotypical Media Allies of 2011," stating "because of Jason Katims, viewers have been given a window into our lives."[143] Bryce respects that Katims has committed to telling Max's story over the course of *Parenthood*'s run rather than simply addressing it in a one- or two-episode story arc.

Finally, many writers have commented on *The Bridge* and the construction of Sonya Cross, an El Paso detective. *Salon*'s Shire, who often writes about disabilities, argues that the character is realistic because Cross's spectrum traits do not define her but are rather part of who she is—a smart detective who has Asperger's. Although the show writers acknowledge her diagnosis, it is not explicitly stated on the program itself, and for Shire, this is a strength because it leaves "the viewer initially as puzzled by her behavior as her co-workers are."[144] Writer John Elder Robison who describes himself as a "free range Aspergerian" agrees and identifies Cross as a character he can identify with. He contrasts Cross to *Boston Legal*'s Jerry Epstein and *Criminal Minds*' Spencer Reid, characters Robison argues were poorly executed. He says about Cross: "She's serious. She's smart. She's beautiful. She's a hardworking, by-the-book Aspergian cop who is misunderstood by her peers yet genuinely confused when people are put off by her."[145] Not all are thrilled with the way Asperger's is presented on *The Bridge*, however. Raul Ojeda, host of the

Alien Ghost ASD online community, argues that Cross's Asperger's characteristics function more as comic relief on the show and argues that this presentation would encourage viewers to "consider an Aspie a problematic person." Ojeda echoes Soraya's concerns about Dr. Dixon and argues that a high-functioning character like Cross would have learned to adapt her behavior over time to conform to social norms in the workplace, something he does not see Cross doing.[146]

Clearly those on the spectrum and their families have a vested interest in how television represents the ASD experience. The ASD community members' thoughts about and analysis of TV portrayals provide an instant window into how such characterizations resonate with the lived experience of ASD. The ideas shared by members of these communities are valuable to the wider culture because they demonstrate—more so than the TV shows themselves have the potential to do—the intellect, diversity, humor, and smarts that challenge misconceptions of, and educates others about, being on the spectrum. Of course not everyone who has ASD is as high functioning as these writers, but even so, it is important that those who are have a voice.

CHAPTER 2

Safe and Unsafe

The terrorist attacks that took place on September 11, 2001, profoundly changed the sense of personal and national security in the United States. Television responded to the attacks with programming changes, new story lines, and, eventually, dramatic shows that reflect the post-9/11 world. For example, such criminal procedurals as *Law and Order* (1990–2010), *CSI* (2000–present), and *NCIS* (2003–present) integrated references to the terrorist attacks, and plots about terrorist threats, into their scripts.[1] In other dramas, 9/11 became a plot point. *Rescue Me* (2004–2010), for instance, centers around firefighters working in a post-9/11 New York, whereas *Brothers and Sisters* (2006–2011) opens with the main character returning to her family in Los Angeles after living in New York during the attacks. On the BBC's *Mistresses* (2008–2010), a woman mistakenly believes her husband died in the fall of the twin towers, only to find out he has run off with another woman.[2] The content of television dramas also mirrored a post-9/11 zeitgeist of fear and uncertainty. *Lost* (2004–2010) played on emotions of fear and exploited the unknown, whereas *Heroes* (2006–2010) reflected the desire to save a city from destruction. On the science fiction front, *Battlestar Galactica* (2003–2008) addressed contemporary political issues through its space world conflicts, and the military drama *The Unit* (2006–2009) highlighted the dangerous missions military operatives engaged in during war time while their families dealt with their absence and secrecy.[3]

September 11 also shifted what it meant to "keep Americans safe." Aimed at doing just that, The U.S.A. Patriot Act, or simply, The Patriot Act, became law on October 26, 2001. Initially positioned as legislation needed to keep the country secure from future attacks, debates around civil liberties ensued as The Patriot Act allowed for unprecedented government access to citizens' e-mails, library records, telephone calls, and financial documents. Another measure that aimed at the nation's security was the establishment of the Office of Homeland Security, charged with coordinating a strategy to protect the country against terrorism. Officially renamed the Department of Homeland Security (DHS) in 2002, DHS remains a cabinet-level department of the federal government to this day, operating with the overarching goal of "keeping America safe."[4] In his proposal to create DHS, President George W. Bush articulated the need for "a single department whose primary mission is to protect our homeland."[5] As DHS became integrated into the culture, so did other aspects of fighting what was soon familiarly called "the global war on terror." Such terms as "enemy combatants" and "detainees" became part of everyday discussions. According to the Council on Foreign Relations, enemy combatants (permitted detainees during war time) can be lawful (associated with a state military or action) or unlawful (not associated with a state-supported action).[6] Debates about the costs and benefits of "enhanced interrogation" or "torture" also emerged as journalists reported on detainee treatment, living conditions, and methods used by their captors to retrieve information. Those debates, including discussion of the practices that were reportedly taking place at the Guantanamo Bay Detention Camp and other sites around the world, continue even today. National dialogue around racial profiling and distinctions between Muslims and Islamic fundamentalists served to educate a U.S. populace who knew little about Islam before the attacks.

Aspects of the post-9/11 concern with safety and terrorism made their way quickly into television's dramatic narratives. In October 2001, just weeks after the attacks, The West Wing (1999–2006) aired a special episode that responded to the event and then went on to integrate terrorist-oriented story lines throughout the remainder of the show's run. The rescue drama Third Watch (1999–2005) responded first by editing out a story line, in which an Arab storekeeper shoots a shoplifter and second by producing three episodes that addressed the World Trade Center attacks directly.[7] NYPD Blue (1993–2005), Doc (2001–2004), Judging Amy (1999–2005), and Without a Trace (2002–2009) are just a few of the programs that integrated story lines referencing September 11 or featuring terrorist threats as a part of the story.[8] Among the most central changes to the post-9/11 television landscape were the updated appearances of counterterrorist plots on procedural dramas and the new face of counterterrorism dramas. *24* (2001–2010), *MI-5* (2002–2011), and *Homeland* (2011–present), for example, all tell stories of apprehending terrorists and preventing terrorist activity.

Although popular television story lines continue to feature components of safety and security in the post-9/11 era, the depictions may not accurately reflect the realities. A Norman Lear Center analysis of the highest viewed network television dramas that aired during the 2009–2010 season revealed how elements of the war on terror are seen on the small screen eight to nine years after the September 11 attacks. The study showed that in the 70 episodes viewed of *24, CSI, CSI: Miami, The Good Wife, House, Law and Order, Law and Order: Los Angeles, Law and Order: SVU, NCIS,* and *NCIS: Los Angeles,* 67 percent of terror suspects were white and 62 percent of these terror suspects were U.S. citizens or residents. Furthermore, the analysis notes that these dramas rarely depict torture, religious or racial profiling, or a clear legal process. Finally, the research showed that military force and government violence are portrayed as legal but ineffective.[9] Although such analysis cannot be generalized to similar themes on cable or premium channels, it helps to contextualize how network programming has tended to represent the war on terror during the 2009–2010 season.

Surveillance culture has also become part of the new normal after 9/11. Although the Patriot Act, and provisions of it, has been regularly debated in terms of the threats it may present to personal freedom and privacy, actions starting in 2013 by the National Security Agency (NSA) analyst Edward Snowden drastically changed these discussions. By releasing numerous classified NSA documents, Snowden revealed the extent to which the United States was engaged in surveillance, including the vast amounts of information being gathered on private citizens. For example, one program, PRISM, collects digital information from nine private Internet firms, including Google, Microsoft, Facebook, and Yahoo!. The NSA also breached privacy rules when it collected and searched phone call databases, monitored world leaders' phone calls, tracked cell phone locations, and tapped into data storage centers maintained by Google and Yahoo!.[10] Such surveillance is possible given the tremendous advances in 21st-century technology, a culture in which digital data collection, storage, and mining are ubiquitous and where fear of future is attacks is ever present.

Just as television showrunners have integrated new stories of terrorist threats into their programs, so have they incorporated elements of this surveillance society. Some programs, for instance *The Good Wife* (2009–present) and *The Newsroom* (2012–2014), feature story lines that address the pervasive reach of the NSA, whereas *Person of Interest* (2011–present) highlights the complications of citizen monitoring in a digital age. On crime-fighting dramas, these advances in technology and resulting heightened surveillance are often framed positively and are relied upon to track suspects and apprehend criminals. As Gregg Easterbrook of *The Atlantic* points out: "Post 9/11, audiences seem to prefer heroes with government authority. Federal agents based in secret facilities, elite crime fighting units with extralegal powers, fantastical technology, and commando-team backup are everywhere on primetime."[11]

The essays in this chapter highlight connections between 21st-century television dramas, the post-9/11 world, and the post-9/11 preoccupation with safety and security. "*Rescue Me* and Recovery from 9/11" claims that *Rescue Me* mapped uncharted territory by portraying a fictional group of New York City firefighters coping in the aftermath of September 11. "Terrorism, Torture, and Trust in Counterterrorism Narratives" surveys the complicated representations of terrorism, and terrorists, in post-9/11 dramas. In discussing *Homeland*'s first season, "Protecting the Homeland" explores how the show's lead female character, a CIA agent determined to prevent another terrorist attack, reflects a broader cultural longing for security. Two Side Notes, "The Russians in *The Americans*" and "Comic Book TV," suggest that television offers narratives about "keeping America safe" that are distinct from the global war on terror. The former looks at how the 21st-century renewal of tension between Russia and the United States allows for the re-emergence of a familiar popular culture villain, whereas the latter details the increasing presence of comic book and graphic novel narratives on the programming schedule. Finally, "You Are Being Watched: *Person of Interest* and Citizen Monitoring" explores how one show portrays the complexities of living in a surveillance society.

Rescue Me and Recovery from 9/11

In the months following the September 11, 2001, terrorist attacks on the United States, it was hard to imagine that a TV show would ever develop a fictional drama that appropriately addressed the day or its aftermath. The mood of the nation was subdued and filled with grief, as Americans sought ways to find comfort in the familiar, even as they adjusted to a new normal.[12] The first television programming related to 9/11 took the form of informational documentaries or fictionalized depictions of real events: the two planes flying into the Twin Towers, the impact of the crash and subsequent collapse of the Towers on people at the site, the inspiring revolt by passengers against the United 93 hijackers despite the ultimate tragedy in Shanksville, PA, and the devastation of large parts of the Pentagon where another plane hit. Some post-9/11 television dramas, for example *24* (2001–2010), made implicit allusions to torture and terrorism, both concerns related to the attacks, but no series explicitly referred to the actual day.[13] It was not until the FX Network aired *Rescue Me* (2004–2011) that 9/11 became an explicitly and continually mentioned event that served as the focus of an entire series. As "the only piece of popular entertainment to spring from 9/11,"[14] *Rescue Me* holds an important place in the post-9/11 television drama landscape.

Rescue Me follows New York City firefighters as they adjust to life after the September 11 attacks. The main character, Tommy Gavin, is a veteran firefighter who lost his cousin and best friend, along with 59 other firefighters he knew, when the Twin Towers collapsed. Tommy struggles throughout the series with the effects 9/11 has had on his life, including feelings of survivor guilt, anger, depression, and alcoholism. These difficulties affect him personally and professionally, disrupting his family life and friendships despite his skills as a firefighter. Starting in the first episode, and continuing throughout the series, Tommy sees ghosts of people who died on 9/11, including his cousin, along with other people who did not survive the many fires he has fought over the course of his career. As Tommy tells his wife: "O.K. I got news for you. There's no getting over it. Normal is dead and buried underneath ground zero. I'm just trying to make sense of what's left above ground."[15]

Created by actor Denis Leary and executive producer Peter Tolan, *Rescue Me*'s focus on the New York City Fire Department (FDNY) after 9/11 made the show compelling partly because the role the FDNY played in responding to the attacks was so highly regarded and widely publicized. The FDNY sustained more losses in the attacks than any other group of responders, with casualties totaling 341 firefighters and 2 paramedics. Firefighters were hailed as heroes in the days and months after 9/11 and stories of their bravery and courage were shared widely as a counterpoint to tragedy and heartbreak. Fire stations in New York City were overwhelmed with visitors thanking the men and women who worked there for their selfless contributions. Images of firefighters become popular throughout U.S. culture, from Halloween costumes to books and websites that idealized and memorialized "the brotherhood."[16] On the 10th anniversary of the attacks, one critic wrote that, in the aftermath, "it seemed impossible to imagine that just three years later, someone would try and make sense of the events of 9/11 by turning it into a television series."[17] That television series creators should try to do so through an irreverent focus on the nation's 9/11 heroes was even more surprising. The series resonated with post-9/11 audiences, however, for several reasons.

Rescue Me depicted New York firefighters as flawed individuals, challenging the narrow post-9/11 definition of them simply as heroes by giving the characters on the series complex, even negative characteristics. In the first episode, as Tommy challenges firefighters on probation to live up to the highest NYPD standards, he does not frame that goal in terms of heroism but in terms of commitment and skill: "I've been in the middle of shit that would make you piss your pants right now. Uptown, Downtown, Harlem, Brooklyn. But there ain't no medals on my chest, assholes, because I ain't no hero. I'm a fireman. And we aren't in the business of making heroes."[18] Shifting the focus from firefighters as heroes to firefighters as people struggling to process the impact of their work, including such tragedies as 9/11, offered viewers the chance to recognize some of their own difficulties in dealing with the aftermath of the attacks. The compelling contrast between heroic actions and troubled emotions reflected the conflicted feelings of the culture more generally.

In this light, one critic claimed the show was "the longest treatise on post-traumatic stress disorder that may ever have aired on American television"[19] and Leary's character, Tommy, is at the center of that story. In the first episode, a psychotherapist visits the fire station to talk with the men as part of a post-9/11 grief counseling effort. She tells Tommy: "We're finding that the effects of 9/11 are still being felt, especially among members of the police and fire department."[20] Although none of the men want to speak to her, the camera reveals to viewers that each member of the fire station is desperately seeking a way to cope with the effects of 9/11, from drinking alcohol to writing poetry. Despite initial concerns that no one would want to watch a show dealing with 9/11 so soon after the events occurred, *Rescue Me*'s unapologetic depiction of men struggling with posttraumatic stress actually gave viewers a way "to refract our national outrage and sadness over the 9/11 attacks through the lens of fictional television."[21] The series did so by creating a protagonist who represented the dichotomous responses people had to the attacks, the good and the bad, the outrage and the sadness.

The series was not only about the dark aspects of post-traumatic stress, however. Defined as a comedy-drama, *Rescue Me* also helped viewers lighten the heavy burden surrounding the horrifying nature of the attacks through humor—often irreverent, sexual, scatological humor—that contrasted sharply with the poignancy of how each firefighter is shown to be dealing with loss. More specifically, the show depicted "humor in sad situations and the sadness of lighter moments."[22] By combining laughter with serious subjects, *Rescue Me* struck a fine balance between humor and grief, making it okay to laugh, even in the face of loss. As series cocreator Peter Tolan stated, 9/11 "was an earth-shattering, life-changing event for so many people. But because there was so much humor in it, this is how we really deal with things. This is how people move forward."[23]

Another way that *Rescue Me* helped viewers navigate life after 9/11 was to extend itself beyond September 11 to include trauma in general. When a therapist visits the fire station, Tommy asks: "You want us to talk about our feelings?" The therapist replies: "Yes, I do." He responds by broadening the issue beyond that specific date: "Forget 9/11, all right?" he says, and goes on to describe the horrors of fighting fires, saving and losing people in fires, essentially expanding the scope of the show to include not just 9/11 but also loss of all kinds.[24] This inclusion of grief beyond 9/11 allows the series to remind viewers that loss is everywhere, is part of the human condition, and, although the 9/11 attacks were horrific, so are the other horrors encountered daily by men and women across the country. That Tommy is haunted not only by ghosts of men he lost in the Twin Towers but also by others who were lost in more typical fires reinforces this fact, reminding viewers of the larger context in which any loss is significant, not just loss as a result of a terrorist attack. As one critic put it, *Rescue Me* "handled its heavy questions without heavy-handedness or judgment," ultimately sending the message that "what helps us all survive: friendship, family and service to a cause greater than yourself."[25]

The first and last episodes of the series capture the essence of how and why *Rescue Me* is considered the "one successful America TV series based on its [9/11] aftermath."[26] The dialogue and the scenery in the two episodes are similar, but the differences are significant. The seventh season, and the series finale, aired on September 7, 2011, just days before the 10th anniversary of the attacks, a date marked with ceremonies and memorials across the country. The timing of the series finale was carefully thought through by the producers who "were conscious that where to end the series was a choice about where we as a society contextualize and place 9/11 on its anniversary."[27] In their words: "If we put it on the week of 9/11, we thought we ought to be saying something appropriate and meaningful to the occasion, and what it all means 10 years on, in terms of the landscape of the heart and how one deals with grief."[28] The result is a return to the beginning of the series that registers the heartbreak of the years immediately following 9/11 while also recording a forward movement in understanding, emotion, and faith.

The series begins and ends with parallel scenes in which Tommy addresses new firefighters—also known as "probies"—as they prepare to enter the department. Both scenes are set against the backdrop of lower Manhattan, where the Twin Towers are noticeably absent from the skyline. In both scenes, Tommy refers to the losses he has suffered personally and professionally on 9/11, and in both scenes, names and photos of firefighters lost in the attacks are visible behind him. Despite these similarities, there are important differences that mark not just Tommy's recovery over the years of the series, but the nation's recovery as well.

Tommy's speech to the probies marks one difference. In the first episode of the series, Tommy is aggressive and angry in his description of those he lost on 9/11. "I have seen it all," he says:

> I knew 60 men who gave their lives at Ground Zero. Sixty. Four of them from my house. Vito Costello. Found him almost whole. Ricky Davis. Found him almost whole, hugging a civilian woman. Bobby Vincent. Found his head. And my cousin Jimmy Keefe, my best friend. You know what they found of him? What I was able to bring back, give to his parents? A finger. That's all. A finger. These four men were better human beings and better firefighters than any of you will ever be.[29]

The derogatory words he uses toward the new firefighters, comparing them to "these four men" who "are better human beings and better firefighters than any of you will ever be," holds those who died in the 9/11 attacks as untouchable heroes. On a table behind him, there are individual photos of the four men he refers to in his speech. In this scene, the photos of these men, and therefore the men themselves, represent the firefighters lost on 9/11. This representation is personal specifically to Tommy—representing only those who were closest to him, those he chose to mention despite the fact that there are others he knew, and many he did not, who perished on that day.

Seven years later, in the same location during the series finale, Tommy addresses a new group of recruits. Instead of the photos and names of the four people closest to him, behind him now is an enormous flag with the names of all of the firefighters who died in the attacks. Tommy says:

> You are staring at the names of 343 heroes. Three hundred forty-three American heroes. Three hundred forty-three men who ran in while the entire world stood watching and waiting. First responders on the front line of a war that may never end. I want you to stare at these names. I want you to memorize them. Go home tonight. Get on the Internet and look up these names. Find out who these men

were and what they did on that day. And then you'll realize: This ain't a job. It ain't an occupation. It's a calling. A need.[30]

The shift in focus from the four firefighters he cared personally about to all of the firefighters lost that day suggests a broadening of Tommy's grief from the personal to the communal, from seeing the impact of 9/11 as what one person suffered to the suffering of an entire community. Also, the instructions to remember the names of the firefighters who were lost, to go home and research them, to understand who they were, suggests a shift from grieving the past to memorializing it, a remembering of those who have been lost as inspiration rather than a comparison of the living to the dead. Even the episode titles reflect the shift. The first episode of the entire series is titled "Guts," emphasizing the character of the dead heroes, compared to the final episode of the series, titled "Ashes," which mourns and makes final the death of those who were lost. As if to reinforce Tommy's own shift in thinking, in the background of the final scene, in the place of the clearly absent Twin Towers, the Freedom Tower, which is more than half-way built, can be seen on the skyline marking the difference between absence and presence.

A final yet poignant difference between the first and last episodes of *Rescue Me* is around the topic of God. In the first episode, when he finally says a few words about 9/11 to the therapist, Tommy is clearly angry and questioning the existence of God:

> We lost four guys from this house. One of 'em was my cousin Jimmy.
> My best friend. Best goddamn fireman I ever worked with, good family man.
> Dedicated American, blah, blah, blah, you know? And every day, I gotta drive to work. I drive through my neighborhood. I see guys, drunken assholes that I went to high school with, who stand on the corner, high, having a great time, and I gotta wonder why these assholes are still walking around when Jimmy Keefe ain't. My cousin, the priest, says it's because it's all part of God's plan, like God's got a plan. You know what? If there is a God he's got a whole shitload of explaining to do.[31]

These words suggest a crisis of faith, a questioning of not just God but also an anger toward God for the "plan" that needs a lot of "explaining." Tommy's words are understandable given the incomprehensible, senseless loss of life that occurred on 9/11 and doubtless many viewers had similar questions. In the series finale, however, while addressing the new recruits,

Tommy actively returns to the question of God with a softened perspective that reflects a wisdom and integration of 9/11 into who he is as a person and a firefighter. He tells the most recent batch of probies that when a fellow firefighter dies and they do not:

> you're gonna ask yourself why did I walk away, but not him? I'll tell you one thing the answer to that question is not at the bottom of a bottle. You can't drink or fight or screw your way to figuring out the answer to that question. People die. We're firefighters. We die a lot. I lost my buddy, my best friend, my cousin, my brother. Some people say it's God's will. I don't know. I don't even know if there is a God. I hope there is. Because that would mean one day all this shit is gonna make some sense.[32]

Although *Rescue Me* is not an explicitly religious TV drama, the change in language reflects a shift from anger and loss of faith to being open to the possibility that there is more than Tommy is able to understand. That Tommy "hopes" there is a God and that he hopes one day it will all "make some sense" is a change from his earlier position. He has not accepted God nor does he pretend to understand how God may relate to a tragedy like 9/11, but he is hopeful and open to the possibility of deeper understanding.

As Tommy walks away from the probies at the end of the series, turning them over to his lieutenant, he gets in his truck where he encounters another ghost, this one his friend Lou instead of his cousin Jimmy who haunted him in the first episode. This shift from the ghost of his cousin who died in 9/11 to the ghost of his friend who died in a recent fire further reflects the way *Rescue Me* moves from the trauma of 9/11 to the trauma of everyday life. In the background, viewers can hear the lieutenant assigning the new probies three names of firefighters who died on 9/11 to research: "These are some names you are never, ever gonna wanna forget. I am going to assign three names . . . Anderson, your three names of remembrance are Capt. Ryan Hickey, Lt., Timothy Higgins, and firefighter Jonathan Hohman. Black, your three names: Firefighter Thomas Holohan, firefighter Joseph Hunter . . ."[33] As the sound fades, viewers are left with the impression that, 10 years after September 11, we must remember and learn from those who lost their lives. Yet, we must not compare ourselves to them or waste our own lives trying to live up to them. The last image of the series is of a newly commissioned fireboat. Denis Leary describes the boat in detail: "The name on the hull of the boat is done in steel from the World Trade Center. It's a $27 million boat, and the only reason they have them is because they realized on 9/11 that they need that service from the water, right down by where the buildings went down. Watching the boat, which the department was kind enough to give us that day, roll in was pretty emotional for a lot of the real firefighters. So for better or worse, I think we did the right thing."[34] In the end, *Rescue Me* captured a decade of loss and recovery in a way other television dramas were unable to do. As commentator Randee Dawn states, "it seems unlikely that any series will ever be able to say they crawled inside the minds of those still mourning the tragic day more effectively then 'Rescue Me' did."[35]

Terrorism, Torture, and Trust in Counterterrorism Narratives

One of the longest running counterterrorism dramas of the early 21st century was already in production before the terrorist attacks of 2001. *24* (2001–2010), a dramatic action thriller where each episode takes place in the course of a single hour—and therefore each season is just a day long—was a popular program set in the U.S. government's Counterterrorism Unit, or CTU. The show's main character, Jack Bauer, leads a team of operatives in unravelling terrorist threats and saving lives in a manner that often breaks official protocols, rules, and laws. As the series progresses over its eight seasons, *24* explicitly reflects elements of the contemporary dialogue about the Global War on Terror.

In the years after 9/11, new counterterrorism shows emerged as well, with mixed success. *Threat Matrix* (2003), a show set in the then new DHS, lasted only a year. *The Grid* (2004), which explored narratives of the terrorist fighters and the terrorists themselves, also lasted a single season. *Sleeper Cell* (2005–2006), a drama about the inner workings of a terrorist cell in Los Angeles, was canceled after two seasons. *Intelligence* (2013–2014), a program revolving around agent Gabriel Vaughn who has a brain microchip and is under the direction of the U.S. Cyber Command Department, was also short-lived.

Other counterterrorism dramas have been more successful. The BBC show *Spooks* (2002–2011), called *MI-5* in the United States, was popular with U.S. audiences and offered a contextualized view of fighting terrorism from a U.K. perspective that relied heavily on referencing sometimes complicated international politics. A deeper exploration of international politics and relationships among nations is also central to *Homeland* (2011–present), the award-winning program that centers on CIA agent

Carrie Mathison and her work in counterterrorism initiatives. Narratives focusing on fighting terrorism also surface in other 21st-century dramas. For example, *The Blacklist* (2014–present) depicts agents working in the off book section of the FBI Counterterrorism Division assisted by a hyperconnected, high-profile criminal to catch other elusive high-profile criminals, some connected to terrorist activities, others less so. Collectively, these programs fictionalize elements of the Global War on Terror. Many commonly include multidimensional Arab and Muslim characters, represent Islam in complicated ways, include graphic torture scenes, and reflect the post-9/11 zeitgeist of uncertainty by using trust as a narrative device.

Three of these counterterrorism dramas, *24*, *Sleeper Cell*, and *Homeland*, include dominant story lines about preventing large-scale terrorist attacks on the United States. Because the people behind 9/11 were Middle Eastern members of Al Qaeda, an Islamic fundamentalist terrorist organization, it is not surprising that the enemies in counterterrorism television shows tend to have these characteristics. The perpetrators who plan the fictional attacks are often Muslim, and the implicit and explicit connections between the religion of Islam and terrorist activities are frequently explored. In the real post-9/11 world, Muslims were worried they would unfairly be linked with terrorist activities, especially in a climate where fear, uncertainty, and ignorance prompted backlash against Muslims and Arabs. These concerns were not without merit as the FBI reported that hate crimes against Muslims increased dramatically after the September 11 attacks.[36] In this climate, television portrayals of terrorists were more closely examined and, some argued, depictions of Arabs or Muslims on television furthered an unfair stereotype of the one-dimensional Arab terrorist—a caricature present in a multitude of popular culture texts before and after September 11, 2001. For example, *24*'s season-four plot centered on a series of terrorist cells composed of Middle Easterners living in the United States. Many were concerned that fictional representations of terrorists who exhibited Arabic or Islamic markers would further misunderstandings about, and hate crimes directed toward, these groups. Despite protests from several organizations, including The Council of American–Islamic Relations (CAIR), *24* revisited the use of ruthless terrorist characters of Middle Eastern descent several years later.[37]

However, as author Evelyn Alsultany points out, *24*'s representation of Arab characters is not a simple construction of American-hating terrorists. Although *24* depicts Arab terrorists as the main villains in two of its seasons, the show also includes a range of Arab and Muslim characters who are not terrorists. One is a government agent dedicated to fighting terrorism, others are sympathetic victims of hate crimes, and still others are civilians who willingly assist CTU agents. In addition, Alsultany points out that 24 gives the Arab/Muslim terrorists a back story in season four, which ultimately complicates viewers' understanding of terrorist motivations and takes the characters out of the one-dimensional mode of representation.[38]

In a similar way, Sleeper Cell introduces viewers to a diverse group of Muslims. Although some cell members, along with the cell leader, are from the Middle East (Saudi Arabia and Iraq), others in the cell are not. Cell members include a former gang member who converted to Islam in a U.S. prison, a Bosnian Muslim, an American co-ed, a closeted gay Iraqi, a French former skinhead, and a former Dutch prostitute. The undercover FBI operative, Darwyn al-Sayeed, who infiltrates the cell, is an American Muslim. The various homelands of Muslims on Sleeper Cell remind viewers that Muslims hail from many countries other than those in the Middle East. In fact, Steven Prothero, author of Religious Literary, points out that the majority of Muslims live in Indonesia, followed by Pakistan, Bangladesh, and India.[39] In addition, Sleeper Cell uses its terrifying story lines to highlight how fundamentalist interpretations of the Koran and the tenants of Islam differ from the average Muslim's. As Darwyn actively practices his faith, viewers are introduced to the rituals that are clearly comforting and important to him. In addition, at times Darwyn interprets passages from the Koran in ways that support peace, respect, and love, emphasizing the more common, nonviolent beliefs of Islam. Because cell leader Farik is an Islamic militant from Saudi Arabia, engages with Arab contacts, and returns to his home country, the show may implicitly reinforce a connection among Arabs, terrorists, and Muslims that does not always exist. However, the show's inclusion of an instructional element about Islam emphasizes the importance of the Islamic faith to viewers. The program also models how Muslims are unfairly treated; one of Darwyn's handlers is consistently disrespectful of his religion and these exchanges allow viewers to sympathize with Muslims who simply want to practice their faith.

Homeland's portrayal of Islam is also complicated. On one hand, the show makes the connection between Middle Eastern terrorists who practice Islam and features Muslims who use their religion to justify abhorrent actions. On the other hand, Homeland also features Muslims who work to prevent terrorism, specifically an informant, the wife of an imam, and a wrongly accused CIA analyst. The most complicated portrayal of the Islamic terrorist connection comes through the character of Nicholas Brody—a soldier who was captured and held by terrorists in the Middle East. There he was introduced to Islam and continues to practice the religion when he returns to the United States. Because viewers are not sure whether Brody is to be trusted as a U.S. soldier returned from captivity, or mistrusted as an American soldier who has been turned against his country, it is significant that his belief in Allah and religious practice does not change. As *The Atlantic*'s Yair Rosenberg points out: "[Brody's] Muslim faith remains constant throughout and is shown to be independent of his political allegiances. To be fair, *Homeland* walks a fine line by having Brody take up both terrorism and Islam, but in the end, it shows that the two are wholly distinct. Thus, after Brody assists the CIA in finding and killing Abu Nazir, he is shown in morning prayers—a sight that deters a black-ops U.S. government assassin from shooting him."[40]

Just as the representation of Arab and Muslim characters has shifted after September 11, so have the methods of extracting information. On counterterrorism dramas, and in fact many dramas with a criminal element, torture has become a mainstay of dramatic action. The number of torture scenes increased dramatically on television after the September 11, 2001 terrorist attacks. A Parents Television Council study shows that between 1995 and 2001 there were 110 scenes of torture on prime-time broadcast programming. The report documents "from 2002 to 2005, the number increased to 624 scenes of torture. Data from 2006 to 2007 showed that there were 212 scenes of torture."[41] *24*, *Homeland*, *Sleeper Cell*, *MI-5*, and *The Blacklist* all routinely display a variety of creatively grotesque torture scenes that include waterboarding, electric shocks, painful injections, and many other forms of physical brutality. Much attention has been given to *24*'s torture scenes in particular. The Parent's Television Council documented the presence of 67 torture scenes in *24*'s first five seasons.[42] The *New York Times*' arts writer Adam Green suggested that *24* was "normalizing torture."[43] Green points out that, on *24*, torture is readily accepted by the "good guys" as a necessary, even reasonable, action, and that innocent parties recover quickly—both emotionally and physically—from being tortured. These choices allow viewers to avoid having to consider the actual toll such actions would take.[44] In fact, in 2007, the U.S. military requested that the producers of *24* "tone down the torture scenes because of the impact they are having both on troops in the field and American's reputation abroad."[45] To emphasize the seriousness of this request, a West Point general traveled to California to ask *24*'s producers to stop promoting illegal behavior.[46]

In December 2014, a Senate Intelligence Committee report confirmed that CIA operatives had engaged in torturing prisoners as part of the war on terror. The report's findings show that the CIA engaged in interrogation techniques that were excessively brutal, yet not effective, in gathering "actionable evidence" despite CIA's claims to the contrary. The report also graphically describes the methods used in torturing detainees and the behavioral and psychological results of such treatment.[47] Although *24*—as a long running network program with mainstream popularity—has been criticized the most for its violent torture scenes, torture on television dramas is pervasive. On *MI-5*, agents are captured and tortured routinely. In fact, actor Richard Armitage made news when he agreed to be authentically water boarded for a scene in the show. After the controlled experience, the actor told *The Daily Mail*: "I realized that it really is a form of torture that shouldn't be used. I only lasted five to ten seconds and the voice crying out to stop isn't me acting."[48] *The Blacklist* has been called "odious torture porn" for its detailed portrayals of the ways the criminal of the week kills victims not to mention the variety of interrogation methods.[49] As Green observed in *24*, contemporary torture scenes on television do not reflect the reality of enhanced interrogation. For example, characters under physical and mental distress on being captured recover quickly with little psychological impact. This is especially evident on *The Blacklist*, where agents are routinely captured and physically hurt during an interrogation. One of many examples occurs in a season-two episode titled "Luther Braxton—The Conclusion," where Agent Keen is water boarded repeatedly in an attempt to gain information. Despite this trauma, Keen is able to recover from the experience quickly and report back to work the next episode. In addition, torturous methods on television routinely produce results, something the Senate Intelligence report does not confirm. As *The Washington Post*'s Catherine Rampell argues: "rarely do torture plot lines involve false leads and victims that 'enhanced interrogation' ensnares in real life; that might lead to messier denouements. Pretty much the only time torture *isn't* effective on TV—that it, when the one being tortured bravely guards his or her secrets despite unspeakable pain—are when it's the good guys getting tortured."[50]

In the second season of *Sleeper Cell*, the terrorist cell leader Farik is captured and ultimately extradited to Saudi Arabia, where he is tortured. Throughout the show, Farik is portrayed as an insidious, violent, and merciless Islamic fundamentalist and his capture provides viewers with a brief victory. In discussing the plot with *USA Today*'s reporter Bill Keveney, executive producer Ethan Reiff claims that *Sleeper Cell* does not take a political position on torture but instead asks: "Is it a good thing? Is it a bad thing? Does it help the cause or hurt the cause? Those questions have to be wrestled with."[51] On the first three seasons of *Homeland,* torture is not celebrated as a successful method of extracting information. Instead, operatives try to talk to and establish communicative relationships with their captives. In addition, the long-term psychological impact of being held captive and tortured is explored through the character of Nicholas Brody. Torture sequences are not absent from the program, however. Muslim enemies are primarily depicted as the aggressors, but in season four, this shifts to imply that the CIA is engaging in such tactics as well.

A final characteristic of counterterrorism programming is the use of trust as a dramatic element. On *24*, there is often a mole that viewers find out has been working against the agency they claim to serve, suggesting that even in institutions that should be the most trustworthy, traitors exist who are willing to sacrifice innocent lives for their own personal gain. On *Sleeper Cell*, viewers know terrorist cell members cannot trust Agent al-Sayeed and the fear he will be found out infuses the scenes with dramatic tension. *Homeland* is also driven by themes of trust: Carrie Mathison's mistrust in Nicholas Brody informs her actions and choices in the first two seasons. Once she is proven correct in her belief that Brody returned to the United States as a terrorist, the government is able to turn Brody's allegiances back to the United States, but Carrie and viewers wonder how sincere he is. Finally, on *The Blacklist*, Agent Elizabeth Keen must trust the elusive criminal Reddington as he provides the FBI team with intel to catch criminals, despite the fact that Keen knows he is holding secrets of his own while also pursuing a secret personal agenda. Reddington is also instrumental in convincing Keen not to trust her husband, a man who is ultimately revealed to be working for an international criminal leader.

Counterterrorism programming presents viewers with a frightening, violent world that reflects some of the nation's deepest post-9/11 fears and concerns about international terrorism and managing terrorist threats and terrorists themselves. In so doing, the programs present more complicated explications of Arab and Muslim characters, instructional information about Islam, a religion that is perhaps unfamiliar to many Americans, and graphic torture scenes that reflect the nation's heated discussion around enhanced interrogation. Central to many of these narratives is the theme of mistrust, which reflects a post-9/11 zeitgeist of wondering just how safe Americans really are.

Protecting the Homeland

Although the Showtime drama *Homeland* (2011–present) has been discussed in terms of its exploration of post-9/11 issues around patriotism, betrayal, and counterterrorism, it may be most original for its portrayal of Carrie Mathison, the lead female character.[52] Critics have had generally positive responses to the depiction of Carrie who, played by Clare Danes, is affected by manic-depressive illness.[53] Season one, in particular, asks viewers to consider whether Mathison's manic depression, for which she sporadically, and secretly, takes prescription medication to manage her moods and behavior, makes her a trustworthy heroine. This uncertainty registers the impact terrorist activities have left on the American psyche, which simultaneously seeks assurance that the homeland is safe, and recognizes that the methods for maintaining that safety are uncertain at best.

The opening sequence of the first three seasons of the series provides viewers with insight into both Carrie's childhood and the country's history, sealing the connection between the two. A girl in pigtails, presumably a young Carrie, is shown watching TV. The images she views are both specific and general: images of war and terrorist acts from the 1980s to the present, including attacks against Libya, the hijacking and crash of Pan Am Flight 103, the September 11 attack on the Twin Towers, as well as random images of people shouting and running, planes flying, and buildings falling.

Interspersed with those images, politicians, including Ronald Reagan, Bill Clinton, George Bush, Colin Powell, and Barack Obama, are shown and heard responding with such words and phrases as: "series of strikes against terrorist . . . acts of terror . . . this relentless pursuit . . . This was an act of terrorism. It was a despicable and cowardly act . . . Until something stops him . . . We must and we will remain vigilant at home and abroad."[54] The phrases and the choppy manner in which they are presented combine with the images to create an unsettled, chaotic, and dangerous feeling that reinforces the fact that terrorism must be stopped. Adding to that sense of insecurity, young Carrie sits absorbing all of the words and images, growing up in a world that has not been safe from terrorism in her lifetime despite ongoing efforts—rhetorical and actual—aimed at countering unpredictable attacks and violence.

As a product of this world, the adult Carrie, on whom the series is focused, has become a CIA agent absolutely intent on fighting for the safety and security of her country. In the Pilot episode, a conversation with Saul Berenson, Carrie's mentor at the CIA, captures how literally

Carrie takes her role.[55] When Saul confronts Carrie about her unortho-
dox methods for tracking the season's main suspect, Sergeant James Brody,
who was imprisoned in Iraq for eight years and now may have been turned
by Al Qaeda against the United States, the following exchange occurs:

> Carrie: I'm just making sure we don't get hit again.
> Saul: I'm glad someone is looking out for the country, Carrie.
> Carrie: I'm serious. I missed something once before. I won't, I can't,
> let that happen again.
> Saul: It was 10 years ago. Everyone missed something that day.
> Carrie: Yeah. Everyone is not me.[56]

The lines in this scene are so central to *Homeland* that they are included
in the opening credits sequence, the only fictional commentary among
the many historical clips of presidents and politicians responding to acts
of terrorism. The repetition—in the first episode and the opening credits—
reinforces the intensity with which the show represents Carrie's personal
mission to keep United States safe.

The event that happened "10 years ago," 10 years before the series premiered in 2011, is the September 11, 2001 terrorist attacks, an event that
is significant on several levels. If the opening sequence presents a timeline
not only of historical events but also of Carrie's life, 9/11 would have
been among the first terrorist attacks Carrie could have helped prevent
as a CIA agent. That she believes she "missed something" that allowed
the attacks to happen, and that she failed in her effort to protect the
country, makes her even more determined to prevent acts of terrorism in
the future. It also underscores her self-identified role as protector of the
nation. As she says in response to Saul's claim that "everyone missed
something that day": "Everyone is not me." Even the phrasing of this
statement—an odd inversion of the more familiar declaration "I'm not
everyone"—isolates Carrie from other people in her sense of responsibility for the country's safety. As Carrie's audience, we begin to hope she is,
in fact, different from those around her and hope that she is the one who
can save us from another attack, the person who watches over us, out-
smarts the bad guys, and keeps us safe.

Viewers had good reason to feel anxiety about the country's safety
after September 11, 2001. In the first 10 years alone, at least 45 jihad-
ist terror plots were prevented, many of them in the United States.
Among the most publicized were the December 2001 "shoe bomber,"
who planned to blow up a commercial airplane with explosives in his
shoes, and the 2009 "Christmas Day Bomber," who intended to blow

up a passenger plane with explosives in his underwear. Other plotted attacks focused on various sites around the country, including shopping malls in Columbus, Ohio, and Chicago, the Brooklyn Bridge, the Sears Tower, the New York City subway, the D.C. Metro, a car in Times Square, various synagogues, and military bases.[57] *Homeland*'s Season four opening credits reflect these expanded threats, including images and words about more recent terrorist activity in the Global War on Terror.

Despite Carrie's commitment to keeping the homeland safe, her heroism is complicated and unclear, characteristics that reflect U.S. culture's own anxiety and uncertainty around what it means to be safe in the early 21st century. More specifically, for viewers the reference to 9/11—a turning point in U.S. history for being the first major attack on U.S. soil—is emotionally laden. Indeed, *Homeland* "plays a brilliant game of chess with viewers still making sense of post-9/11 America 10 years later . . . tapping directly into our ongoing confusions over real vs. imagined threats and our eroding civil liberties."[58] After 9/11, a new awareness of being vulnerable to attack stunned the U.S. nation and created a longing for safety so deep it led to the creation of the Patriot Act and other counterterrorism measures, including the establishment of the DHS, a department that resonates with the series' title.[59]

All of these measures, however, cannot guarantee that no new act of terrorism will occur and it is in knowing this truth that Carrie's unique gifts and liabilities resonate the most. Carrie's dual role—as a gifted protector and an unstable individual—in the series begins immediately in the first episode with her unquestionably brave actions in Baghdad, where she sneaks into a prison and promises asylum to a potential source who could prevent an attack on U.S. soil.[60] She is shown in the war-torn city, paying off contacts, promising the captive that his family will be safe if he shares his information, and being forcefully removed from the jail by armed guards just as the information is whispered in ear.

The next scene in the episode is marked "Ten Months Later," where, back in Washington, the camera pans the inside of Carrie's home. An entire wall is devoted to articles, pictures, and information about Abu Nazir, an Al Qaeda leader meant to evoke Osama bin Laden, thought to be plotting further attacks against the United States. Carrie arrives home after a night of casual, anonymous sex, swallows a blue pill concealed in a bottle of aspirin, and quickly changes clothes. Minutes later she is seen arriving late for a meeting at the CIA and is reprimanded by the Director: "Nice of you to join us, Carrie. How is it that you are the only analyst in this section that can't get to a briefing on time?"[61]

The contrast between these two images of Carrie, competent, brave, and persistent on one hand, secretive, tardy, and careless on the other, propels the show into its first season. It is revealed, as the season unfolds, that the pills Carrie takes are for her manic-depressive illness, a condition she must hide from the CIA to keep her job. Defined by manic episodes where the person experiences exceptionally high energy and moods, followed often by incapacitating depression, manic depression "can cause sleeplessness, sometimes for days, along with hallucinations, psychosis, grandiose delusions, or paranoid rage."[62] These symptoms go expressly against the stability Carrie needs to do her job, yet they also give her unique insights into how things work that allow her to draw conclusions others might not see. As actress Claire Danes describes, the illness and the profession are "related in some ways. They both involve paranoia and when somebody's mind is susceptible to that, they're constantly questioning themselves and the world around them and that translates pretty easily to her work."[63]

The illness is revealed in an exchange between Carrie and Virgil, one of the men she hires to do unauthorized surveillance work for her.

> Virgil: Just tell me I'm not out here risking federal prison on behalf of a crazy person.
> Carrie: I am crazy.
> Virgil: It's not funny. If anybody at the agency finds out about this.
> Carrie: I've got a mood disorder, okay?
> Virgil: I looked it up Carrie. Clozapine's an anti-psychotic.
> Carrie: I'm dealing with it. I've been dealing with it since I was 22.
> Virgil: Does Saul know?
> Carrie: God no. Nobody does. Don't act so shocked. I mean it can't come as a complete surprise.
> Virgil: You know I love you Carrie. But I gotta be honest. None of this is making me feel any better.
> Carrie: What are you saying? That I'm making this shit up? Well maybe I am. You know, maybe it is all in my head. But you're in it now Virgil, up to your fucking neck.[64]

Although this exchange helps the plot move forward by giving viewers information about Carrie's mental health and her approach to managing it, the fact that neither Carrie nor Virgil is really sure that her ideas about Brody are accurate leaves the question of Carrie's trustworthiness completely unclear. In fact, the question of whether she is "making this shit up" continues to raise itself throughout the entire first season of the show.

As a result, viewers are never really sure what is true. Although we root for Carrie to be right, we never fully trust that she is. Although we want to believe she can keep everyone safe, we are not entirely certain that she can.

One of the most moving examples of this occurs in episode five, "Blind Spot." Carrie, informed that a member of Abu Nazir's group who was being held prisoner has committed suicide, arrives at Sal's house to show him a video in which she believes Brody passed the prisoner a razor blade. Sal sternly rebuffs her, saying there is no evidence that Brody did anything of the sort, telling Carrie to be prepared to "clean out her desk" if she moves forward with the accusation.[65] Although Carrie's mania is beginning to express itself, making her speech pressured and intense, she also has deep convictions about what she believes happened. Overwhelmed by Sal's rejection, Carrie goes to her sister's, a safe place for her that also represents the kind of all-American family that loves and supports each other in good times and bad. When her sister tells her she should spend the night in her guest room, Carrie agrees and her two young nieces, hearing that she is in the house, ask if they can spend the night in the guest room too.

Although all signs point to a quiet night, Carrie is unable to sleep. Instead, despite the fact that her nieces are snuggled down on either side of her, she lays awake in bed as if watching and waiting for something to happen to which she can respond. Unable to drift off, Carrie tries to sneak out of the room only to be asked by her younger niece, Josie, whose age approximates the age of Carrie in the opening credits, where she is going:

Josie: Auntie Carrie?
Carrie: Shhh. Close your eyes.
Josie: What are you doing?
Carrie: Nothing, pumpkin. I just can't sleep.
Josie: Are you worried about the bad guys?
Carrie: What bad guys, Josie?
Josie: You know, the ones who blow people up.
Carrie: Are you worried?
Josie: A little.
Carrie: Yeah, me too.
Josie: I have an idea. Come live with us. We'll protect you.
Carrie: No honey, you know what? That's my job. Go to sleep.[66]

In this scene, faced with the vulnerable girls whom Carrie clearly loves and wants to protect, we identify with her desire to do her job, to protect them and us. Yet, we are also acutely aware that Carrie does not seem well, her behavior has become erratic, and she may be paying attention to everything, or the wrong things; we are unable to tell which. She leaves their room, but ends up sitting on the stairs, head in hands, crying as if unsure what to do to keep her promise.

As much as we want to trust Carrie, *Homeland* gives us plenty of reasons to know we should be cautious about doing so. She is volatile, shows poor judgment in her personal life, takes her medication only sporadically, and puts not just her own life but also others at risk. Such behavior is aggravated when she is experiencing either end of the manic-depressive spectrum—highly erratic mania or immobilizing depression. It is at the juncture of our belief and doubt, of Carrie's far-fetched and brilliant insights that we begin to see the risk inherent in trusting her. Yet, *Homeland* continues to suggest that, despite our doubts, we would rather have Carrie doing her work on our behalf than not.

When she is manic, for example, she sees things that others do not and makes sense of the terrorist plot in ways she would miss if she were thinking like "everyone." In an episode called "The Vest," as her sister is bringing her home from the hospital in the midst of her manic episode, Carrie jumps out of the car at a stop light and runs to a nearby garden where she sees buds beginning to grow. From this observation, she draws what turns out to be accurate conclusions about Abu Nazir's behavior, even though those ideas are initially rejected by the CIA and considered the result of her illness. Even Dana, Brody's daughter who calls the police on Carrie at the end of the first season claiming Carrie is crazy, seems to recognize some truth in Carrie's request that Dana call her father and "talk him down" from detonating the bomb he has strapped to his chest.[67] Brody's plan, set in action long before he returned from captivity to the United States, is to kill the vice president in retaliation for the death of Abu Nazir's son, and Brody's charge during his captivity, the young Issa. "I didn't believe her at all," Dana tells her father about Carrie's suggestion that Brody needs to be stopped from taking the lethal step.[68] Yet, it is ultimately Dana's phone call, the call suggested by Carrie, which persuades Brody not to detonate the bomb. Despite seeming unstable or crazy, something in what Carrie says and does resonates with other characters in the show—a level of insight they cannot fully ignore, most likely because it is true.

In the final episode of the first season, Carrie decides to undergo electroconvulsive therapy (ECT) to manage her manic depression. Sal tries to stop her from doing so, suggesting there are alternatives to the shock treatment that has such side effects as short-term memory loss and a slowing down of the very mania that has helped her not "miss anything" this time around. Sal himself confirms this when he tells her, "You were wrong about Brody, but you were right about Nazir," reassuring her that the ideas she fought for turned out to be accurate, and that she did her job well.[69] Carrie's gift for her work is only further confirmed as she drifts off under the influence of anesthesia and, just as she is about to lose consciousness altogether, has a sudden memory of Brody calling out Nazir's son's name, Issa, in his sleep. Her eyes pop open and she says: "Issa. Issa, Issa, Nazir's son. Brody knew him. Don't let me forget."[70] The memory provides the missing link between Brody and Nazir telling Carrie, and us as viewers, that she was not wrong about Brody—he has been turned and is a danger to the United States. She did not miss anything, after all, and whereas no one else in the operating room understands what she is saying (her sister even asks "What did she say?" to which the nurse replies "nothing, it's the anesthetic. Everyone does it"[71]), viewers do because of the camera's close-up on her when she says those final lines. This insight will be forgotten, however, when she undergoes ECT: it will erase her short-term memory and make her "normal."

This closing sequence returns viewers to the original question about Carrie's ability to protect the homeland. On one hand, we know that she is right about Brody and that her mind, in particular its mania, makes her different from everyone else who is fighting to keep the country safe. We want her to have access to that mind, even its dysfunction, because we have been shown that it is the best weapon we have for fighting 21st-century terrorism. We want her to be there for us, not to lose her memory or change her brain chemistry. Yet, we also know that the risk inherent in an unpredictable ally is that protection will be sporadic, rather than steady, and stressful rather than calming.

Although Carrie Mathison's manic-depressive illness continues to play a role in the following seasons of *Homeland*, it is the representation of Carrie's mental state in the first season that speaks most directly to the show's resonance with 21st-century U.S. culture as it processes decades of terrorist activities that now endanger the country itself and the methods that have been developed to counter those threats. It is in the first season's episodes that Carrie's illness is revealed and explored, accepted and rejected. It is in this early story line that we first cheer on Carrie as a heroine, and cringe with doubt about her reliability. We want her to see things that others do not, to be intent on not missing anything, to keep us, like her nieces, safe while we sleep. And despite knowing that our faith in her ability can be shaken, we do not want her intensity dampened by such normative treatments as ECT. We want her to protect us, to protect the homeland, as uncertain as her ability to do so may be.

Side Note: The Russians in *The Americans*

In 2009, during a dinner in Geneva, Switzerland, then Secretary of State Hillary Clinton gave her counterpart, Russian foreign minister Sergey V. Lavrov, "a red plastic button emblazoned with the English word 'reset' and the Russian word 'peregruzka.' "[72] The gift referred to U.S. Vice President Biden's suggestion earlier in the year that the two countries "press the reset button" on their relationship that, he said, had recently seen a "dangerous drift."[73] There was some confusion about Clinton's gift— "peregruzka" means "overcharged" in Russian, not "reset"—and the awkward exchange between the two diplomatic leaders seemed to foreshadow the further disintegration of U.S.–Russian relations during the first two decades of the 21st century.

After the Berlin Wall came down in 1991, symbolically ending the decades old Cold War, the two superpowers had fallen into a relatively neutral, if not completely positive, alliance. When Russia invaded the nearby country of Georgia in 2008, those relations became more tenuous and additional events undermined trust between them. One of the most surprising incidents was the 2010 arrest of 10 deep-cover Russian spies living in the United States who had "allegedly buried stashes of money and wrote messages in invisible ink as they sought to collect tidbits about U.S. policy and secrets."[74] The spy ring was accused of being "engaged in what is known in the spy business as 'spotting and assessing'. They identified colleagues, friends, and others who might be vulnerable targets, and it is possible they were seeking to co-opt people" who might be turned against the United States[75] As one source put it, the Russian spies were in the United States "in case Russian intelligence ever needed anything . . . The idea was that they would become so Americanized that no one can ever find any connection between them and Russia."[76] The fact that Russian spies lived in the United States for 20 years after the end of the Cold War, and that they were working and raising families as "ordinary Americans" undetected by intelligence agents, caught the imagination of the country in general and of one man in particular.[77] Joseph Weisberg, showrunner and ex-CIA officer, took the story as the inspiration for FX's hit series *The Americans*.

Set in the 1980s in the midst of the Cold War, *The Americans* features two undercover Soviet spies, Elizabeth and Philip Jennings, who live in the Washington, D.C. suburbs with their two U.S.-born children. Trained by the Soviet intelligence agency, the KGB, the couple gathers top-secret U.S. government information through deception, determination, and whatever other means necessary to serve their country, Mother Russia. They regularly report back to their handlers who set them on course for their next mission. Despite their old-fashioned spy tactics—disguises, coded messages, and dead drops—the Jennings struck a chord with viewers in an era when drones and satellites are the standard weapons of espionage. Russian villains, long a mainstay of U.S. television, became less prominent after the Cold War ended, as new nationalities—Arabs, Muslims, and Koreans—leant themselves more readily to contemporary conceptions of the "bad guy."[78] Elizabeth and Philip, along with their Soviet colleagues, renew this presence on the small screen, but in doing so they also break some familiar stereotypes of Russian characters, primarily by being somewhat sympathetic as hardworking, small-business owners who are also struggling to sustain a marriage while raising two children. The Russian characters on *The Americans* also differ from their Cold War forerunners because the actors hired to play them are Russian, or at least speak Russian, adding a level of authenticity to the series. Finally, all of the characters—whether Russian or American—are given complex natures that combine good and bad choices and motivations, unlike their more one-dimensional predecessors.[79]

The series' uncanny alignment with actual developments in U.S.–Russian relations is perhaps the most intriguing. These parallels were a surprise to everyone, including Weisberg. In a 2015 interview he states:

> When we started out, one of the real goals of the show was to say look at the enemy and think about whether or not there's any reason to be so hostile toward people. At the time, things were really quite peaceful in our relationship with Russia. So it seemed like a good time to be able to re-examine how we thought about them. And almost as soon as the show went on the air, things started getting more and more hostile in our relations with Russia. And now they seem to be almost at an all-time low since the advent of the Cold War.[80]

Indeed, since *The Americans* aired, there have been even more signs that the age of U.S.–Russian rivalry has returned.[81] Disagreements over issues as diverse as nuclear arms, gay rights, human rights, and Syria's civil war have created more strain and less common ground between the two countries.[82] With Russia's re-election of Vladimir Putin in 2012, the asylum granted to Edward Snowden for leaking classified information about U.S. surveillance protocols in 2013, and the invasion of Ukraine in 2015, it is not surprising that Americans today feel less at ease with Russia than they have in recent decades. A 2015 Gallup poll found that

18 percent of Americans named "Russia as the United States' greatest enemy over any other country, including longstanding U.S. foes such as North Korea and Japan."[83] The Cold War appears to have re-emerged as an international conflict so potentially significant that it has been given such nicknames as Cold War Part II and Cold War 2.0.[84] The reset button Biden and Clinton called for has clearly not been pressed.

With this resurgence in international tensions, Russian villains have taken on increased significance in television dramas. A short-lived, 2015 drama *Allegiance* featured a newly minted CIA agent who is unaware that his family members are in fact part of a Russian sleeper cell. The U.S. Network's *Covert Affairs* featured Russian spy plots over its four-year run from 2010 to 2014. Season three of Netflix's *House of Cards* (2013–present) includes a story line about the Russian president who, by some accounts, is modeled on Vladimir Putin.[85] At the end of the first season of *The Blacklist* (2014–present), it is revealed that Agent Keen is the daughter of a Russian spy. Finally, in the season-four episode of *Scandal* (2012–present), "First Lady Sings the Blues," the lead female character, Olivia Pope, tracks down a retired Russian spy still living in the United States. Formerly known as Black Sable, the spy now goes by the Americanized name Mary Peterson and has not practiced espionage for almost 30 years, till now. When Olivia asks her how she escaped from the KGB, and, more importantly, why she thinks she is being drawn back in now, they have the following exchange:

> Olivia: Why did you quit? How did you get them to let you quit?
> Mary: I didn't. The world changed. The Soviet Union is gone. No more KGB. The people telling me who to kill stopped telling me who to kill. Not to say that I wasn't glad. I had a husband. I got to have a baby, a family. I made friends. I let all of it go . . . I'm American now. Until yesterday morning, I thought my past was behind me.
> Olivia: What happened yesterday morning?
> Mary: I found this under my windshield wiper. It's a dead drop for later today.
> Olivia: And you don't know who wrote this?
> Mary: I haven't had a handler in 27 years.
> Olivia: What if you just ignored it?
> Mary: You ignore a job, try to run, try to get out, they kill you. Everyone was always very clear on that. Putin's hit the restart button.

Although Clinton's "reset button" was meant to keep the U.S.–Russian relations on an even keel, the "restart button" referred to in this scene suggests that Putin wants to restart the Cold War. If Cold War 2.0 escalates, it is probable that Russian villains will receive a new burst of interest and relevance in 21st-century television dramas.

Side Note: Comic Book TV

In the spring of 2011, NBC elected not to pick up the show *Wonder Woman*, a series proposed by writer and producer David E. Kelley, starring Adrianne Palicki as the DC Comics heroine. According to *Entertainment Weekly*, one possible reason for the decision was that the *Wonder Woman* pilot earned mixed reviews from audiences.[86] In addition, some fans were upset about the character's initial costume, as it was seen in promotional materials, "which seemed to de-emphasize the patriotism and play up the comic's Greek mythology."[87] Other reports suggested that the script was problematic and not true to the *Wonder Woman* character.[88] Even though the costume was tweaked, the show did not take off. This is not the only 21st-century *Wonder Woman* drama to fail. In January 2014, *The Hollywood Reporter* announced that *Amazon*, an origin story of Diana of Themysciria (*Wonder Woman*), was not going to be pursued by the network despite the fact the scriptwriters had been working on it for 2 years.[89] Despite these failures, *Wonder Woman* remains a relevant text; Harvard University professor and writer Jill Lepore spends her entire book, *The Secret History of Wonder Woman* (2015), exploring the story of the iconic figure's creation. A film featuring the character is anticipated. However, given the proliferation of comic book narratives present in 21st-century television, a trend perhaps related to the post-9/11 cultural anxiety around safety and security, it is interesting that the story of the most recognizable DC female superhero is not being revisited on television.

Certain superhero narratives are iconic components of U.S. popular culture even though the initial forms of these stories—the popular culture staple comic books—are not always recognized as literary texts. The genre, however, continues to be popular and sales have increased. *Publishers Weekly* reported that the comics and graphic novels sales for the year 2013 were 870 million dollars—365 million of this share was for sales of comic periodicals, 90 million was for digital comics, and 415 million was for graphic novels.[90] Graphic novels are longer comic stories published in book form and the recent popularity of graphic novels has resulted in renewed interest in comic book narratives and an emerging celebration of pictorial storytelling.

Today, the stories graphic novels tell are diverse in nature and the audience for them is equally broad. As *Wall Street Journal* reporter Jennifer Maloney points out: "Graphic-novel sales are outpacing the overall trade-book market, and their audience has expanded to include more women and younger readers. Graphic-novel publishers are offering an increasing number of stories featuring female protagonists. At the same time, the number of female creators in the field has grown."[91] Whereas this form of storytelling was once categorized as an element of "geek" culture, it is now part of the mainstream.

The proliferation of comic book-driven television mirrors the increasingly mainstream popularity of graphic novels and their comic book counterparts. By 2015, a variety of live action comic book/graphic novel-oriented dramas have populated the programming schedule—many of them of the hero and superhero variety. Some of these programs simply represent elements of the comic book genre. The popular *Heroes* (2006–2010) tells the stories of a group of regular people who have superhuman abilities. Many of them work together to save their city from anticipated destruction. The series returns under the title *Heroes Reborn* in the fall of 2015. The short-lived *No Ordinary Family* (2010–2011) focuses on a family that is suddenly bestowed with superhuman abilities after a plane crash. More commonly, however, television programs emerge from stories previously published in comic books and graphic novels. Running just two seasons, *Human Target* (2010–2011) is a DC Comics adaptation that tells the story of how Christopher Chance and his team protect the clients who hire them. The popular horror drama *The Walking Dead* (2010–present; Image Comics) follows a group of people trying to survive in an apocalyptic world populated with people eating zombies. *iZombie* (2015–present), a program developed from the DC Comic book, features a young female zombie, played by Liv Moore, who can pass as human, provided she eats a human brain on a regular basis. Moore's character works in a morgue, eats brains, and takes on the thoughts of the deceased, which in turn allows her to help police determine how the person was murdered.

Marvel's *Agents of S.H.I.E.L.D.* (2013–present) is an ensemble action drama about uniquely talented characters associated with Marvel's Avengers. *Gotham* (2014–present; DC Comics) showcases the city before Bruce Wayne comes of age and follows Lieutenant Jim Gordon's career and interactions with Gotham's villains before Batman's arrival. Other programs in this genre focus on a single protagonist. For instance, *Marvel's*

Agent Carter (2014–present) tells the story of secret agent Peggy Carter's ability to complete her missions despite the male-dominated power structure of 1940s United States, while DC Comics' *Constantine* (2014–present) engages with the supernatural and fights demons to protect vulnerable citizens.

Another popular approach is to retell the origin story of different superheroes. *Smallville* (2001–2011; DC Comics) tells the story of Clark Kent's youth and development into Superman whereas *Arrow* (2012–present; DC Comics), *The Flash* (2014–present; DC Comics), and *Daredevil* (2014–present; Marvel Comics) tell their eponymous lead characters' stories both by showcasing the paths they have taken to become heroes and by placing them as leaders of a support team that engages in saving their respective cities from destructive villains. The shows highlight the heroes' humanity. Viewers see Clark Kent wrestle with his heritage and powers; Oliver Queen evolves into the *Arrow* after being separated from his family and losing his father; Barry Allen becomes *The Flash* and discovers the extent of his abilities with mentoring; and Matt Murdock uses his heightened senses to "see" better than anyone else after being blinded by a child. Both *Daredevil* and the *Arrow* struggle with whether or not it is okay to kill, rather than fight and apprehend, villains. Barry Allen visibly mourns his mother's death, worries about his father's false imprisonment, and longs for a romantic relationship with his best friend. Clark Kent has to gain confidence in order to embody what Superman has come to stand for. Although the shows feature a diverse cast of men and women in supporting roles, the main story belongs to the title hero.

Robin Rosenberg, author of several books that examine the psychology of superheroes, claims that, "At their best, superhero origin stories inspire us and provide models for coping with adversity, finding meaning in loss and trauma, discovering our strengths and using them for good purpose."[92] Whether for these reasons or others, television comic book hero narratives are popular with viewers, and television programming has responded. After entering into a relationship with Marvel, Netflix is producing the series *Jessica Jones*, and is also developing programs centering Iron Fist and Luke Cage, respectively. The company has also floated the possibility for producing a television miniseries on *The Defenders*. CBS has signed on for a season of DC Comics' *Supergirl*, which started in the fall of 2015.[93] Upcoming programs slated for television include DC Comics' *Preacher* and *Lucifer*.[94] Other comic book and graphic novel-based shows—a number of them superhero oriented— are rumored to be forthcoming as well.[95] It seems clear that television producers prefer content that is representative of hero- or superhero-driven story lines, and so far, television programming does not evenly depict the breadth of graphic novel content available in bookstores and libraries. In addition, many of the lead protagonists are men. The shows *Supergirl* and *Jessica Jones* may indicate that this landscape is changing, reflecting the already established shift in the graphic novel market. However, given that many of the television dramas noted emerged from two lead comic power houses, *Wonder Woman*'s absence is strangely present.

You Are Being Watched: *Person of Interest* and Citizen Monitoring

A decade after the terrorist attacks on September 11, 2001, and just before Edward Snowden's June 2013 leak of NSA documents identifying NSA information-gathering practices, *Person of Interest* debuted on CBS. Airing on September 22, 2011, the pilot sets up the show by introducing a wealthy and mysterious Mr. Finch who engages ex-government agent Mr. Reese in helping a prosecuting attorney in danger of losing her life. Finch knows about her plight because he has a "machine" that uses sophisticated computer algorithms to synthesize collected data that identifies citizens who are in danger, and predicts violent acts. The show's opening voiceover, delivered by Finch, summarizes what the Machine can do and reminds viewers, episode to episode, of the show's premise:

> You are being watched. The government has a secret system: a Machine that spies on you every hour of every day. I know, because I built it. I designed the machine to detect acts of terror, but it sees everything. Violent crimes involving ordinary people; people like you. Crimes the government considered "irrelevant." They wouldn't act, so I decided I would. But I needed a partner, someone with the skills to intervene. Hunted by the authorities, we work in secret. You'll never find us, but victim or perpetrator, if your number's up . . . we'll find you.[96]

Person of Interest reflects the 21st-century zeitgeist of living in a post-9/11 society, asking viewers to think about issues related to technological advancement, privacy rights, government surveillance, and data breaches.

Initially, *Person of Interest* operates largely as a criminal procedural. Each episode opens with a Machine-generated number associated with a person in danger. Finch and Reese work together, and later with Detectives Carter and Fusco at the NYPD, to intervene in the life-threatening danger facing the identified person. Subplots throughout the first two seasons involve the unfolding backstories of the main characters, crime associated with a prominent mob boss, a corrupt faction of the police department called HR, and, perhaps most interestingly, how the Machine was created and used. Season three focuses less on individual Machine-generated numbers and more on narratives related to the Machine's capabilities and power, as well as the implications this power has on national and international levels. For instance, Decima Technologies, a business introduced in season two, plays a more prominent role as an international group that wants access to the Machine's power. Information about a U.S. government conspiracy called "Northern Lights" also drives the narrative. Finally, a violent vigilante group named Vigilance emerges as an organization that aligns itself as protecting individual privacy and opposing the government and their antiprivacy actions.

Throughout its procedural format, *Person of Interest*'s episodes explore 21st-century questions around privacy, government surveillance, and security. The series regularly demonstrates the ease with which hypertechnology allows for citizen tracking and displays how easily digital communications can be bugged, recorded, or copied. Scenes suggest that every image taken of an individual—stored from security cameras, government records, or personal computers—is readily available to anyone who wants them. Legal protocols and investigative techniques used by police departments are depicted as less effective than the combination of the Machine's number generation and Finch's computer-hacking skills. Moreover, the potential victims who are saved by these alternative techniques seem quite comfortable with complete strangers reviewing their private information if it means they will not be killed. Finch and his growing team of helpers are portrayed as fundamentally decent and good characters—some perhaps with checkered pasts—whose priority is to assist vulnerable citizens. As a result of positioning viewers to sympathize with the "person of interest" and those who want to protect him or her, *Person of Interest* makes it seem reasonable and even preferable that confidential information can be accessed, cell phones can be cloned, and financial states can be reviewed without permission. If a life can be saved, the series seems to suggest, what does it matter if a stranger can access someone's bank account?

At the same time, however, *Person of Interest* registers the potential problems with unfettered surveillance and unmonitored access. When the camera reveals the Machine's perspective on the people and places it is collecting data on, it looks like security footage, in which ordinary citizens are being "watched" and recorded as they move through their day—at stop lights, in hallways, in stores and businesses. The concern about the Machine's use and application of these collected data comes primarily through the Machine's creator, Finch, who is secretive and silent about the Machine's existence and anxious about the amount of power access to the Machine would give a person or organization. Finch is an ideal surveillance manager—his invention can do amazing things, but the inventor himself is conflicted about the reach of its power, qualities that might be considered positive in someone with such genius and abilities. It is Finch who voices concerns about what the Machine can do. It is Finch who articulates the potentially beautiful, and potentially disastrous, nature of the Machine. It is Finch who regrets creating the Machine in the first place. In fact, as the series continues, the focus shifts from a Machine-generated number-of-the-week procedural, where Finch uses the Machine's information to save lives, to a narrative about keeping the Machine away from those who might abuse its powers. At a turning point in the series, the Machine takes on a life of its own, becoming more of an autonomous character as its artificial intelligence capabilities allow it to outperform Finch's expectations.

It is worth emphasizing that the Machine—this supercomputer capable of generating, synthesizing, and applying vast amounts of information to predict violent crimes—is not supernatural. The Machine uses existing data—from cell phones, Internet use, security cameras, digital exchanges, and so on—to make its predictions. When Edward Snowden began to leak NSA documents that demonstrated the extent of government surveillance and the PRISM program, it may have appeared to some viewers that the show writers had inside information or perceptive foresight. However, one of the series creators, Jonathan Nolan, has addressed surveillance-oriented themes previously, cowriting the last two installments of the Batman trilogy, *The Dark Knight* and *The Dark Knight Rises*. In *The Dark Knight*, Bruce Wayne develops a similarly pervasive and powerful surveillance system that relies on citizen cell phone data. Even though the invasive system is used by Batman for good and is programmed to self-destruct after the mission is accomplished, questions about such invasions of privacy are raised in the film.[97]

In discussing *Person of Interest*, Nolan acknowledges that he follows the topic of surveillance in the news media—a topic reported on before the Snowden leaks—and both Nolan and cocreator Greg Plageman profess to reading about, researching, and thinking about privacy in a connected culture.[98] In addition, Nolan and Plageman identify the impetus for the Machine as the Total Awareness Program or Total Information Awareness (TIA), an initiative directed by former U.S. National Security Advisor, John Poindexter. In his role as director of the Defense Advanced

Research Project Agency's Information Awareness Office, Poindexter oversaw the development of a project that called for a computer data-mining system that could monitor and synthesize data, but not reveal the personal identities of those being watched.[99] Created by the Department of Defense in 2002, TIA's goal was to develop "data mining and profiling technologies that could analyze commercial transactions and private communications" to locate terrorists.[100] The program, however, collects data from citizens and noncitizens alike, raising numerous civil liberty-oriented issues.[101]

Although *Person of Interest*'s Machine may have been informed by Nolan's and Plageman's research about TIA, the Machine's characteristics are also strikingly similar to other surveillance and data-mining initiatives used by the U.S. government. The 2014 PBS *Frontline* documentary, *United States of Secrets*, provides an overview of the NSA surveillance policies as well as the players leading up to and following the Snowden leaks. *Frontline* reports that the National Security Administration's 1990s program called "Thin Thread" was a computerized system that could collect and mine large amounts of data. Built into the system were privacy protections, and any information gathered on U.S. citizens would be encrypted and thus anonymous unless one obtained a court order. On October 4, 2001, President Bush authorized an NSA surveillance operation dubbed "The Program" as a means of preventing further terrorist attacks. "The Program" uses "Thin Thread" technology stripped of the privacy protections that were in place for U.S. citizens.[102]

Even though the Machine mirrors "The Program's" capabilities, *Person of Interest* is not just about the Machine and its potential existence. It is also about the potential control that sophisticated technology has on 21st-century life. At the beginning of the series, the Machine's presence is somewhat neutral. In season two, the Machine has a more defined presence as a character of sorts, as it communicates more aggressively with the humans. In the third season, the Machine has more power than those connected to it, setting up a way of operating for these characters that may at first glance seem fantastic, but on further examination make some sense. In fact, through each episode of *Person of Interest*, the Machine directs the characters in some way. Finch "trusts" the Machine. The Machine instructs characters who to look for and how to get out of dangerous situations. The Machine directly communicates through a muse, or interface, with a woman named Root. In several interviews about the series, Nolan and Plageman have discussed the idea of a shift in power from personal agency to data dictums. They point out that, as people move through their day, it is common practice to generate data that are collected and analyzed to the point where, Nolan argues, we are living in a time when "the data starts to direct us."[103] Indeed, by the end of the third season, the Machine on *Person of Interest* is a force so independent that it "collaborates" with Finch to provide the team with new identities so they will not be as easily tracked by the pervasive and ubiquitous surveillance they use to track others. In season four, the Machine fights to survive as organized groups try to gain access to its program and power.

Person of Interest is not alone in its focus on life in a post-9/11 surveillance society. On the popular procedurals *NCIS* (2003–present) and *NCIS: Los Angeles* (2009–present), the immediate access to personal exchanges and actions allows for relatively swift success in preventing terrorism or other violent crimes. The series *24* (2001–2010) depicts the use of such technology by the government and its advisories. The counterterrorism program *Intelligence* (2014–2015) features an operative who has a computer chip in his brain that enables him to search digital files of records, security cameras, and cell phone activity, on command. Specific episodes of some series use aspects of this landscape as plot points. For example, on HBO's *Newsroom* (2012–2014), one story line is about an NSA analyst sharing information about an extensive government surveillance program titled Global Clarity.[104] On Showtime's *Homeland* (2011–present), a Foreign Intelligence Surveillance Act (FISA) court judge is manipulated into approving tremendous access to a suspected terrorist's every move.[105] And on *The Good Wife* (2009–present), the NSA listens in on conversations between the governor and his wife, lead character Alicia Florrick. Here, the listening is depicted as a means of gathering information, but *The Good Wife* also portrays the act of listening as entertainment for the NSA employees who, somewhat ironically, discuss what they are hearing as if they were discussing a television series.[106] Although these, and other, television dramas reflect aspects of 21st-century monitoring, *Person of Interest*'s approach is a bit different. By ultimately positioning the Machine as autonomous, the series poses questions about the present and future implications of citizen monitoring, data mining, and artificial intelligence.

CHAPTER 3

Women and Men

Empirical work, critical analysis, and cultural critics have examined elements of how TV "does gender"—how it presents the roles women and men embody within television narratives. Some of this work has focused on how television representations match, or fail to match, reality, whereas other analyses explore ways television narratives offer new configurations of how we see our world and the place of men and women in it. TV portrayals of gender can be progressive or traditional, stereotypical or nuanced. They can challenge the status quo or reinforce conventional ways of thinking. Whatever the depiction, images of men and women on television offer viewers unique insight into contemporary cultural changes, concerns, and practices around gender.

These portrayals are especially interesting in the early 21st century, a time of rapid changes in how U.S. culture defines and understands men and women, professionally, personally, sexually, and romantically. For example, although historically more men have pursued and achieved a college education than women, as the 21st century unfolds this trend has changed. According to The Pew Research Center, during the first decades of the 21st century, U.S. census data show that more young women went to college than men. From 1994 to 2012, the percentage of young women attending college the fall after graduating high school rose from 63 percent to 71 percent, whereas the figure for young men stayed the same at 61 percent.[1] Other studies demonstrate that in the early 21st century, women were more likely to earn a four-year degree than men and that it takes men longer to earn a bachelor's degree than women.[2] A *New York*

Times article reported that while women are in college, they earn higher grades than men and are more focused and directed in their studies. Women make up the majority of students enrolled in graduate and professional school programs as well.[3] In contrast to these successes, the plight of young men, especially men of color, has become of such concern that, in February 2014, President Obama launched a program titled "My Brother's Keeper," an initiative to help boys of color succeed.[4] The initiative was likely also informed by research showing that, in areas where family incomes are lower, the gap between young women and young men entering college is further widened.[5]

Television dramas reflect the increased educational and professional attainment of women through a wide array of popular and successful series featuring lead female characters whose intelligence, knowledge, and educational training are crucial to their professional success. For example, on *The Closer* (2005–2012), Detective Brenda Johnson's ability to piece together evidence to solicit confessions drives the award-winning procedural. On *Bones* (2005–present), anthropologist Dr. Temperance Brennan uses her breadth of knowledge to fuel her team's inquiry into each weekly mystery. Olivia Denham is a heroic FBI agent on *Fringe* (2008–2013), and Jackie Peyton (*Nurse Jackie*, 2009–present), despite her drug addiction, is a talented and caring nurse. Women of different ethnicities have also seen an increase in television representations, including Sandra Oh's long run as Dr. Cristina Yang on *Grey's Anatomy* (2005–present), Kerry Washington's role as talented crisis manager Olivia Pope on *Scandal* (2012–present), and Viola Davis as lawyer and law professor on *How to Get Away with Murder* (2014–present). This sampling of professional television women, all of whom need at least a college degree, and in most instances more specialized, advanced training, to do their job, reflects the changing demographics around women and education.

As women in television become more educated and professional, there is also a noteworthy change in how they are depicted in other traditionally female roles, including motherhood. Andrea Press points out that televised images of women in the workplace during the 1990s "were undercut by a sense of nostalgic yearning for the love and family life that they were seen to have displaced" by the time and energy demands of work.[6] There is evidence that this dynamics is changing too, as contemporary representations of women do not always follow, and sometimes outright reject, behavior typically associated with women. For instance, on *The Good Wife* (2009–present), Alicia Florrick's career becomes central to her identity after she is divorced from her husband and needs to return to her training as a lawyer. Her new focus is acknowledged, even accepted, by her children. In *The Killing* (2011–2014), determined Seattle detective Sarah Linden neglects her son, who eventually moves in with his father in another state, because she becomes so focused on solving the season's murder that she fails to meet his most basic needs. In other examples, *Damages'* (2007–2012) Patty Hewes has a fraught relationship with her son because of her career choices, and both *Mad Men's* (2007–2015) Peggy Olsen and *Homeland's* (2011–present) Carrie Mathison reject or resist motherhood to pursue their careers. Interestingly, these women are not explicitly condemned for their poor parenting choices. Although there is typically a character in each drama who tries to remind the women that they have parental responsibilities (Sarah Linden's former foster mother, Carrie Mathison's sister), the narratives seem more intent on suggesting that there are just as many ways to be a mother as there are to be a professional, reflecting in some ways the manner in which fathers have been depicted on television since *Father Knows Best*.

For their part, portrayals of men in 21st-century television have also shifted, registering a complex tension between traditional and contemporary ideas about what it means to be a man. For example, in *The Sopranos* (1999–2007), tough mob boss Tony Soprano shows his emotional side in scenes with his psychiatrist, whereas in *Breaking Bad*, the head of the family Walter White is disempowered by loss of his job. In *Friday Night Lights* (2006–2011), coach Eric Taylor is depicted as both a dedicated father and professional, and it turns out that of the two Russian spies featured in *The Americans* (2013–present), the husband, Philip, is less strident and duplicitous than his wife, Elizabeth. Other television programs point toward a past in which male and female roles were more clearly defined. *Mad Men* (2007–2015) features a male-dominated workplace where overt sexism is not just tolerated but also sometimes encouraged, whereas other period dramas like *Deadwood* (2004–2006) and *Boardwalk Empire* (2010–2014) register clear male dominance over women. These and other shows, including *Dexter* (2006–2013) and *Sons of Anarchy* (2008–2014), reflect the pervasive presence of the 21st-century antihero and perhaps best register the complex male characters of this time period. Some diverse male characters have also been featured, including multiple characters on *The Wire* (2002–2008), *The Bridge* (2013–2014), and *American Crime* (2015–present), each which engages with contemporary questions around gender in unique ways.

Although the depiction of gender roles on television is changing, so are the ways in which gender is defined. Some long-running television dramas, for instance *Nip/Tuck* (2003–2010), *Lost* (2004–2010), *Friday Night Lights* (2006–2011), and *Grey's Anatomy*, feature racially diverse ensemble casts whose characters are gay, trans, or bisexual, conveying to audiences the vast possibilities of the male and female experience. Other shows situate their characters in unique settings where gender is expressed outside of familiar tropes. *The Walking Dead* (2010–present) showcases how men and women deal with the challenges of survival in a post-apocalyptic world; the reactions and actions taken by the characters do not always fall along stereotypical gender lines. Set in space, *Battlestar Galactica* (2004–2009) conveys fear, bravery, leadership, and commitment outside of traditional gender binaries. The period drama *Mad Men* explicitly highlights sexism in the workplace and the confining gender roles of the 1960s in a way that evokes the popular 1970s advertising slogan, "You've Come a Long Way Baby."

The 21st century has also witnessed significant shifts in cultural understandings of sexual and gender identities. Although there is ongoing discussion around LGBT rights, marriage equality is a practice supported by the Obama administration, and in 2015, the Supreme Court ruled gay marriage legal in all 52 states. In addition, the LGBT community—and by extension, news organizations and talk shows—has educated Americans on the difference between one's sex (the biological determination of whether one is male or female), one's sexual preference (whether one is attracted to men, women, or men and women), and one's gender identification (how one describes his or her own gender). In the United States, many schools have adopted measures for gender-inclusive language and practices to help "transgender and gender nonconforming children" feel welcome and accepted.[7] Seeing gender as a continuum, rather than an opposition between male and female, recognizes the importance of not "enforcing fixed ideas of what it means to be a boy or a girl on children, especially in learning environments."[8] Broadening understandings of gender identity have shown up in U.S. legislation as well. For example, in 2010 the U.S. State Department created a "new policy that no longer requires passport applicants seeking a gender change to have undergone sexual reassignment surgery" to have their passport reflect their chosen gender identity.[9] Instead, U.S. citizens can change their gender category on their passport with a doctor's certification that they have "undergone treatment for gender transition."[10] In 2015, this shift was no more apparent than when Bruce Jenner, former Olympic athlete, announced in a televised interview with Diane Sawyer that he was transitioning from male to female. Soon after, Jenner revealed her new name, Caitlyn, and female self in a *Vanity Fair* cover and photo spread by Annie Leibovitz.[11]

There is other evidence of cultural changes in traditional definitions of gender. In 2013, the *Diagnostic and Statistical Manual of Mental Disor-*

ders, the most widely used reference guide for identifying and classifying mental illness, renamed its previous diagnosis "gender identity disorder" (GID) as "gender dysphoria." Both "GID and gender dysphoria describe a condition in which someone is intensely uncomfortable with their biological gender and strongly identifies with, and wants to be, the opposite gender."[12] In some cases, people suffering from this disconnect may feel so strongly about living their lives as the gender they identify with that they undergo surgery to physically change from male to female or vice versa. The change in the DMS-5 "reflects recognition that the disagreement between birth gender and identity may not necessarily be pathological if it does not cause the individual stress."[13] In other words, the change normalizes the experience of gender disagreement unless the person who experiences it feels distressed; a person can feel that the gender he or she is born with differs from the gender he or she identifies with and still be psychologically healthy. In addition, in 2014, the U.S. Department of Education "reaffirmed a 2010 declaration that 'Title IX's Sex discrimination prohibition extends to claims of discrimination based on gender identity or failure to confirm to stereotypical notion of masculinity or femininity'."[14]

Relationships on 21st-century dramas mirror these evolving cultural discussions about LGBT rights, gay marriage, and new understandings of sex and gender. Showtime's *Queer as Folk* (2000–2005) and *The L-word* (2004–2009) were the first dramas to focus on LGBT groups. *Queer as Folk* told the story of gay friends in Pittsburgh, PA, whereas the *L-word* focused on a group of lesbian and bisexual characters in a slice of California queer culture. Given the increasing visibility of queer characters, 21st-century television both acknowledges and accepts sexual diversity as part of the cultural landscape. *The Wire* (2002–2007), *True Blood* (2008–2014), *Shameless* (2011–present), *Nip/Tuck* (2003–2010), *The Bridge* (2013–2014), *Orphan Black* (2013–present), *Brothers and Sisters* (2006–2011), *Empire* (2014–present), and *How to Get Away with Murder* (2014–present) are just some of the programs featuring central characters who are gay, bisexual, or transgendered. In addition, programs set in the past position gay characters sympathetically. On *Mad Men* (2007–2015), it is made clear that gay men cannot openly engage in romantic relationships with other men, and on *Game of Thrones* (2011–present), gay men are seen engaging in intimate same-sex exchanges but must marry women.

The essays in this chapter examine some of television's specific engagement with gender in the 21st century. "Black Women on Network Television Dramas" explores three female black leads on mainstream, primetime shows, a new and notable presence. A short analysis of *Orange Is the New Black* provides further commentary on socioeconomic, as well as racial, female diversity in the series. "Walter White and the Great Recession" discusses how the award-winning show represents its male protagonist's struggle with economic hardship. "Patriarchy and the Past" examines the popularity of television dramas set in male-dominated settings at a time when there are high-profile discussions of how to end gender inequality in the culture. These programs, along with those discussed in "Side Note: Antiheroes," privilege men and male behavior in ways that speak more of the U.S. past than the present. "*Masters of Sex* and Gender" explores how today's more tolerant approach to same-sex attraction is positively reinforced when contrasted to the past and, finally, "*Transparent* Lessons" suggests that Amazon's *Transparent* is a form of instructional television. At a time of new transgender visibility and understanding, the program gives viewers information about how to understand and negotiate the new language of gender.

Black Female Leads on Network Television

In 2012, *Scandal* debuted as the "first network TV drama with a black female lead since 1974."[15] By 2014, three primetime network dramas featured sole black female leads. In addition to *Scandal*, starring Kerry Washington, which began its fourth season on ABC, the miniseries *Extant* (2014–present) debuted on CBS starring the biracial movie star Halle Berry. ABC also released *How to Get Away with Murder*, starring Viola Davis, the same year. Based on Nielsen ratings, at the end of 2014, *The Hollywood Reporter* deemed ABC's *How to Get Away with Murder* and *Scandal* the two highest rated television dramas of the fall season.[16] A look at what these three female characters and the female actors who portray them bring to the small screen, especially in the context of how race has been represented in U.S. television, reveals a shift in network program approvals and casting decisions that acknowledge the economic success of inclusive programming and the growing opportunities for female actors.

U.S. television has not always been inclusive in its representations of race, especially racially diverse women. In his historical summary titled "Racism, Ethnicity and Television," written for the Museum of Broadcast Communications, John Downing points out that in television's first decades, programs perpetuated a "mythology of whiteness that framed and sustained a racist self-understanding."[17] Shows centered primarily on white characters, whereas minority characters were marginalized. In their overview of black characters on primetime television, Holtzman and Sharpe emphasize that television programming choices represent aspects of contemporary culture as well as the economic reality that networks need to attract enough viewers to sell commercials during the programming time spot. They report that black characters' presence on television can be seen as "insignificant" or "stereotypical" in the 1950s; present but with a noted absence of racial tensions in the 1960s; and present in the form of the "happy but poor black family" in the 1970s.[18] Later, the miniseries *Roots* (1977) and situation comedies with prominent black cast members like as *The Cosby Show* (1984–1992) suggested a shift where black and white audiences watched the same programs in large numbers. This collective viewing did not last, however. By the end of the 1990s, white viewers were watching shows with predominantly white casts, whereas black viewers were watching shows with mainly black casts.[19]

Over time, critically acclaimed and popular television dramas with multiracial casts emerged, including *Law and Order* (1991–2010), *Homicide: Life on the Street* (1993–1999), and *ER* (1994–2009). The diversity in casting on these series was noteworthy because it showcased a variety of black women as main characters on primetime, network shows, serving as precursors to today's leading ladies. Since then, network television drama showrunners have continued to cast talented black women in starring and costarring roles. By the beginning of the 21st century, a number of multiracial-casted television dramas were enjoyed by black and white audiences. This is significant because, whereas cable and premium channels cater to niche markets, network television aims for a more mainstream viewing demographic, trying to recruit and retain as many viewers as possible. Programs viewed by varied demographics not only contribute to the success of the show but also reflect an understanding that mainstream audiences are diverse and do not consist of only white viewers.

Many prominent black characters on TV dramas are seen in professional positions that require at least a college degree, reflecting the larger trend in lead female characters. Some examples include the following: S. Epatha Merkerson as Lt. Anita Van Buren on *Law & Order* (1991–2010), Khandi Alexander as Dr. Alexx Woods on *CSI: Miami* (2002–2009), Marianne Jean-Baptiste as Vivian Johnson on *Without a Trace* (2002–2009), Chandra Wilson as Dr. Bailey on *Grey's Anatomy* (2005–present), Audra McDonald as Dr. Naomi Bennett on *Private Practice* (2007–2013), Nicole Beharie as Abbie Mills on *Sleepy Hollow* (2013–present), and Taraji Henson for two years as Joss Carter *on Person of Interest* (2011–present) and as Cookie Lyon on *Empire* (2015–present). These actors portray characters who are central to the ensemble casts of their respective shows, the exception being Beharie who plays one of the two lead characters on *Sleepy Hollow*.

The 2014 lineup of *Scandal, Extant,* and *How to Get Away with Murder* marked a watershed moment by showcasing three smart, powerful women of color on network television. On *Scandal*, Kerry Washington plays a Washington D.C. crisis manager or "fixer," someone who is hired to manage and diffuse a variety of crises. Loosely based on real-life fixer Judy Davis, some of the show's story lines allude to current events. The show also relies on heightened personal drama. The first two seasons of *Scandal* explore Pope's current affair with the president of the United States—a married white man with three children—while using flashback sequences to inform viewers about the couple's history. Along the way, episode-by-episode, Pope and her team of so-called gladiators help clients manage, solve, and diffuse a variety of volatile situations, both personal and professional. Eventually, Pope becomes involved with another man, who is also white, but her feelings for the president remain.

On *Extant*, Halle Berry's character Molly Woods is an astronaut who has just returned from a long solo mission in space. The series is set in the future and Woods is established as a smart, capable, and insightful scientist. She is married to a scientist, John Woods, who specializes in artificial intelligence and they have a "son," an android robot her husband and his team created, named Ethan. Over several episodes, viewers learn that, while she was in space, Molly was impregnated by an alien being. The offspring was removed from Molly, grown in a laboratory, and ultimately escapes. The creature causes chaos, inspires hallucinations in those near it, and attempts to connect its "mother," who feels a connection to the child as well. Viewers realize that Molly and her husband had trouble conceiving a child, but she is now the mother of two "sons"— android Ethan and the alien being.

On *How to Get Away with Murder*, Viola Davis portrays a powerful lawyer and law professor Annalise Keating who recruits a small team of her top students to work on her cases. Each week the show operates primarily as a procedural where Keating, her two employees, and her hired students work to defend a client. Threaded through the series are two additional ongoing story lines. The first is a mystery about a missing coed. The other is a flashback narrative about a murder in which the team of students is involved. Viewers do not learn until midseason that the murder the team of students is trying to cover up is that of Davis's husband, Sam.

There are important similarities and differences among these three lead female characters. All are educated, professionally successful, financially well-situated, and commanding leaders. They are positioned as top performers in their respective professions. As a former White House Communications Director and current crisis manager, a lawyer and an astronaut, Pope, Woods, and Keating, respectively, are capable and smart, portraying positive images of black women in professional positions. In addition, Pope and Keating are their own bosses who oversee a team of men and women. They are driven to get the job done quickly, confident in their decision-making abilities, and sympathetic to their clients. Finally, all three women are romantically involved with white men, collectively showcasing biracial romantic partnerships.

Scandal's Olivia Pope is compelling and complicated. She is smart, confident, stylish, and projects a sense of righteousness. Over the show's run, discourse about wearing "the white hat"—a metaphor for doing the right thing—and "standing in the sun"—a phrase that evokes the goal of distancing one's self from Washington, D.C., corruption—is pervasive and positions her as a hero whose actions are always done in the name of what is right. However, Pope's actions do not always merit her wearing the metaphorical white hat and she is a central participant in, or contributor to, much of the corruption and crime she professes to want to prevent, correct, or escape. She is shown engaging in legally dubious actions that benefit her clients and, viewers ultimately learn, she helped fix the election that resulted in her lover's presidential win.

Scandal's creator Shonda Rhimes discusses the fact that no one on the show is "good" and reflects on how interesting it is that, regardless of what choice Pope makes, audiences root for her anyway. Rhimes says: "I think that people are really determined that these people be good. People seem very shocked that these people are not good or that they would do something bad. To me that's very interesting because in the very first episode of the show, Olivia is purchasing a baby and she's having an affair with the president. I'm not sure why people felt like she was the queen of all goodness. I feel like it's (a) awesome, frankly revolutionary to have a black female character on television who is the lead of the show who is not a saint. Because, frankly, that's what happens, they always make them a saint and it's really boring and nobody cares. But (b) there is something about these characters that none of them can be good. The whole point of the show is that everybody has dirty little secrets."[20]

Molly Woods and Annalise Keating are not saints either, and their complicated characters become clear in the intersections between the characters' professional lives and domestic situations. In many ways, *Extant*, within its scientific premise, is a show that explicitly highlights the many roles women can assume in their lives. Motherhood is a theme in this show and it comes out in several forms. First, Molly leaves her family for a 13-month job in space and her return requires an adjustment as she tries to reconnect with her family while also remaining committed to her work. However, Woods is not simply a character caught in the familiar female struggle to find a balance between her work and family life. As the AV Club's Sonia Saraiya points out in her review of episode six, "Nightmares," "Particularly what I like about her character is that the show is unafraid of having her be many things at once—'Nightmares' alone engages with her as a friend, an employee, a wife, a mother (in two different ways), a scientist, and a rogue agent."[21]

Similar to Molly Woods, Keating on *How to Get Away with Murder* has many roles to play at once—she is a courtroom lawyer, law professor, and owns a law office; she is a mentor, mistress, and wife. She is also a master manipulator. In using her own cases as examples and case studies in her law classroom, Keating demonstrates her fierce smarts and ability to intimidate. She also toughly mentors a select group of students and gives orders to her law associates. She fights with her husband who reveals he had been sleeping with a coed, the young woman who has disappeared and is later found dead. The difficulties in this marriage are revealed in small segments over several episodes, including the fact that Keating herself has in an extramarital affair.

All three women are often depicted as emotional, an oft-noted feminist criticism of female characters on television and in film. However, the emotion here is situated in complex story lines and the characters are not defined by it. Olivia Pope may rage at her lover or cry silently when she is upset, but she works hard, motivates her staff, and challenges people in high positions of authority. Annalise Keating's emotional displays serve as a mechanism that balances out her aggressive courtroom conversation and case investigations. Molly Woods is able to overcome her horror at what has been done to her to pursue corruption in her organization.

There are few acknowledgments of the lead characters' race within their fictional environments, but the ones that exist are telling. During an argument between Pope and her lover, President Grant, Pope refers to herself as "Sally Hemings" alluding to another president, Thomas Jefferson, who is alleged to have owned a slave by the same name who was also his lover and mother of his children. Pope's father frequently tells her she has to be "twice as good." *Salon*'s Neil Drumming comments on this phrase by saying: "More than simply a family motto, the sentiment is one with which almost every African-American of my generation and before is all too familiar. Notice the *them* and the *they*—that's white folks. The *you* is every black kid who has ever brought home a bad grade or failed to study hard enough for a test being told by their concerned parents that they might never succeed if they don't work harder and smarter than their white peers."[22] During a powerful episode ending of *How to Get Away with Murder*, race is present through an action rather than words. Keating removes her hairpiece and makeup, further emphasizing what is already a vulnerable moment. *Wall Street Journal* writer John Jurgenson notes the significance of this scene: "But there was deeper symbolism in the fact that we were watching an African-American woman peel back her layers, performing an everyday ritual that's utterly invisible in the overwhelmingly white world portrayed on television. After her jewelry, Annalise removed her copper-hued wig (a hair piece that, for some fans, has come to seem like a supporting character) exposing her natural curls for the first time on the show. She peeled off her eyelashes, wiped off her makeup, and rubbed her bleary eyes. Even her eyebrows disappeared."[23]

Given the historic lack of black female lead characters on television dramas, it is not surprising that several contemporary television writers have taken note of these women. In her discussion of *Scandal, The New Yorker's* Emily Nussbaum points out that creator Shonda Rhimes is still the only black female showrunner in television, a fact that exists in contrast to how Nussbaum describes *Scandal's* setting as a "post-racial fantasy" where Olivia Pope's presence "both overrides and renders invisible any racial tensions."[24] At the same time, however, Nussbaum highlights the diverse casts on all of Rhimes's shows, noting: "it's a regrettably big deal that a black woman plays the heroine of *Scandal*, and not the heroine's best friend—and for that reason alone, I'd wish for the show to succeed."[25] *Extant* premiered during the summer of 2014 as a miniseries and was successful enough to be renewed for a summer 2015 run. A number of reviewers have discussed the show's reliance on Berry, a movie star who is credited with being the first woman of African American descent to win an Academy Award, for *Monster's Ball* (2001). *The Daily Beast's* Jason Lynch points out that "Berry utilizes her star quality to keep us riveted and awaiting whatever twist comes next. And she makes the most of her standout scene in the premiere, in which she silently and captivatingly unpacks several years of emotional baggage."[26]

The New York Times' Alessandra Stanley's review of *How to Get Away with Murder* was particularly controversial. Although the review suggests that Stanley likes the show, she uses language that invokes racial stereotypes, stating, for instance: "When Shonda Rhimes writes her autobiography, it should be called 'How to Get Away with Being an Angry Black Woman'."[27] In her essay, she suggests that Rhimes—whose production company Shondaland produces *Grey's Anatomy*, *Scandal*, and *How to Get Away with Murder*—creates "authority figures with sharp minds and potent libidos who are respected, even haughty members of the ruling elite, not maids or nurses or office workers" who "can and do get angry."[28] In discussing the casting choice for *How to Get Away with Murder*, Stanley writes: "As Annalise, Ms. Davis, 49, is sexual and even sexy, in a slightly menacing way, but the actress doesn't look at all like the typical star of a network drama. Ignoring the narrow beauty standards some African American women are held to, Ms. Rhimes chose a performer who is older, darker-skinned and less classically beautiful than Ms. Washington, or for that matter, Halle Berry, who played an astronaut on the summer mini-series Extant."[29]

In addition to correcting Stanley's discussion of Rhimes's involvement in *How to Get Away with Murder*—the show is supported by her production company, but the creator is Peter Nowalk—television critics responded to the tone and characterizations used in the article. TV critic Margaret Lyons angrily addressed Stanley's essay section-by-section, challenging the assumptions made about Rhimes and her characters' anger, as well as Davis's beauty.[30] Kara Brown took a similar stance in a *Jezebel* piece that discusses the angry black woman stereotype.[31] For her part, Rhimes took to Twitter commenting: "Wait. I'm 'angry' AND a ROMANCE WRITER?!! I'm going to need to put down the internet and go dance this one out. Because ish is getting real."[32] In response to a question tweeted about whether she had seen the article, Rhimes answered: "No. I've been too busy being angry and black. Also a woman. Takes up a lot of time."[33] *Vulture* writer Jada Yuan elicited this response to the article from Viola Davis: "My feeling about the article is it's a reflection of how we view women of color, what adjectives we use to describe them- as scary, as angry, as unattractive. I think that people are tired of it." Davis also noted "there is no one would compare Glenn Close to Julianna Margulies, Zooey Deschanel to Lena Dunham. They just wouldn't. They do that with me and Kerry because we're both African-American and we are both on Shonda Rhimes shows."[34]

Calling attention to these three black actors may suggest that black actors are different than white actors. As Davis points out, critics would not compare her to *Grey's Anatomy*'s Ellen Pompeo because she is white.[35] And indeed, it makes more sense to analyze Davis's Keating alongside Julianna Margulies's Alicia Florrick on *The Good Wife*. After all, Keating and Florrick are both successful attorneys with cheating husbands. At the same time, given that the presence of strong female black leads on network television dramas is new to the landscape, it is important to recognize and discuss the shift.

Side Note: Diversity in *Orange Is the New Black*

Critics have challenged the Netflix award-winning series *Orange Is the New Black* (2013–present) for telling its story of incarceration through the eyes of a white, middle-class woman.[36] Yet, as series creator Jenji Kohan states: "it's very hard to sell a show about women of different colors and different ages and different socioeconomic backgrounds. This way, we almost get to sneak in these amazing characters and amazing story through this white girl going to prison."[37]

The series does not shy away from the fact that the main character is white and that her position gives her a certain amount of privilege in the fictional prison of Litchfield. In the second season, when Piper gets a furlough to visit her grandmother, the other women accuse her of using her whiteness to obtain the extremely rare leave. Knowing this, and knowing that it is probably true, Piper shouts in the middle of the cafeteria:

> Yes, I am white! We have established that. And I got furlough, too. I guess white privilege wins again. And as a speaker for the entire white race, I would like to say I am sorry that you guys got the raw deal, but I love my fucking grandmother. And, yeah yeah, she may be a whitey, too but she's a fucking person and she's sick and she needs me! So shut the fuck up! It's not my problem.[38]

The fictional Piper Chapman is referred to by various nicknames that point out her difference from others incarcerated alongside her, including "College," "Princess," and "First Class." Interestingly, these names refer less to Piper's race than to her socioeconomic status, and, even though the inmates organize themselves by race, those alliances break down along class lines as well. For example, in the story of Piper's relationship with Pensatucky, it is not race that creates tension between the two women, but their access to financial resources. What Pensatucky wants more than anything else is a new set of teeth: hers have rotted away due to lack of dental care and poor diet over the course of her life. The show's depiction of whiteness complicates the intersection between race and class. As one critic writes: "I love that there is a place in this show where whiteness isn't a free pass to friendship and loyalty. . . .

What is it like to talk about 'white privilege' when you're living below the poverty lines and addicted to meth/heroin etc?"[39]

Although *Orange Is the New Black* takes on the concept of white privilege, it also has been recognized for "bringing to life a diverse group of women, representing backgrounds, body types and sexualities rarely seen on television."[40] Such depictions have been recognized for bringing new roles to female actors and representing women in ways previously unseen on television. Hailed for the images of lesbian relationships, "*Orange Is the New Black* focuses on the stories of all of those who live at the margins, whether by dint of their sexual orientation, gender identity, or cultural dislocation."[41]

Aura Bogado of *The Nation* has expressed concern about the representations of race on the series, arguing that the show uses "wildly racist tropes: black women who, aside from fantasizing about fried chicken, are called monkeys and Crazy Eyes; a Boricua mother who connives with her daughter for the sexual attentions of a white prison guard; an Asian woman who never speaks."[42] Although such commentary is important to consider, the show's depiction of diverse women, including a transgender actress who plays a transgender character, breaks new ground in 21st-century television drama. Bogado goes on to write: "I will acknowledge that *Orange Is the New Black* has created a credible role for a trans black woman, played by Laverne Cox, an actual trans black woman. And I can't deny that the series has created a payroll for many actors of color."[43] The debate often returns, however, to the fact that the main character is a white woman. Bogado states: "But again, just like the practice 150 years ago during the height of the slave narrative era, those experiences are first authenticated by a white person—in this case, a white woman whose prison stint can never be a substitute for the violence institutionally carried out against women of color in the criminal justice system."[44]

Walter White and the Great Recession

In the acclaimed series finale of AMC's successful television drama *Breaking Bad* (2008–2013), Walter White breaks into the expensive home of his former friends and business partners, Gretchen and Elliott Schwartz, and forces them, under what they think is a threat to their lives, to do a favor for him when he dies. Reluctantly, they agree, fearful of the hit men they think Walter has paid to keep them under surveillance until they follow through on their promise. "Cheer up, beautiful people," Walt tells the wealthy couple before he departs, "This is where you get to make it right."[45] This scene, and Walt's farewell line in particular, captures one of the major themes in *Breaking Bad,* evoking the period of the Great Recession during which the series ran, as well as some of the reasons the controversial protagonist became one of the great 21st-century television antiheroes.

Breaking Bad ran for five seasons during which it was nominated for 189, and won 110, awards, including multiple Golden Globes and Emmys.[46] The story of a high school chemistry teacher with a wife, disabled son, and new baby on the way, *Breaking Bad*'s Walter White is already struggling to pay the bills when he is diagnosed with incurable lung cancer. Through his brother-in-law who is a DEA officer, Walt, as he is called by his family, sees how much money can be made by cooking and selling crystal meth, a job he is uniquely qualified for with his background in chemistry. Working with his former student, Jesse, Walt gradually, and with increasing violence, builds a drug empire over which he rules, ultimately losing his job, his family, and his life as a result of his choices and actions.

Critics flocked to *Breaking Bad* claiming it to be one of the best television dramas of all time.[47] In 2014, it won a Guinness World Record for the "Highest Rated TV Series."[48] The show inspired fan-based blogs, clubs, and wikis, as well as old-fashioned fan letters from the likes of actor Anthony Hopkins and writer Stephen King.[49] Since the last episode in 2013, a Spanish version of the series, titled *Metastasis*, was released for Spanish-speaking audiences; an opera, *Breaking Bad—Ozymandias,* appeared in January 2014; and a pre-quel to the series based on the lawyer Saul Goodman, *Better Call Saul*, was released in 2015. The series was quickly renewed for a second season.

Breaking Bad follows the 21st-century trend of such dramas as *The Sopranos* (1999–2007), *The Wire* (2002–2008), and *Dexter* (2006–2013) that feature complex male antiheroes. Walter White's transformation from "Mr. Chips to Scarface," as creator Vince Gilligan puts it, is one "in which a previously good man, through sheer force of will, decides to become a bad man."[50] The moral ambiguity of Walt's actions, along with viewers' ambivalent rallying behind his success, aligns him with other antiheroes of the era. Yet, the series' release in 2008 sets *Breaking Bad* apart because of the historical moment in which the program was viewed and the themes that resonated with that time period.

Breaking Bad's pilot episode aired on January 20th, 2008, just as the U.S. public was informed that the economy had sunk to an historic low. Over the next two years, "the U.S. labor market lost 8.4 million jobs, or 6.1% of all payroll employment. This was the most dramatic employment contraction (by far) of any recession since the Great Depression."[51] The recession officially lasted from December 2007 until June 2009, but the impact on ordinary Americans was significantly longer. The wealth of middle-class families fell 35 percent between 2005 and 2011, whereas those in the upper-income bracket, frequently called the 1 percent, recovered more quickly than any other income group.[52] The mood of the nation was glum. Americans were less able to afford homes, consumer goods, or health care during the period.[53] The widespread impact of the recession created a timely backdrop for *Breaking Bad*.

The first season of *Breaking Bad* revolves around money and how to make ends meet, especially in the traditional male role of primary breadwinner. As his wife feeds him a breakfast of eggs and veggie bacon, it becomes clear that the first day of the series is also Walt's 50th birthday. His son arrives at the breakfast table complaining about the family's malfunctioning hot water heater and asking why his parents do not just buy a new one. Walt is shown teaching his high school chemistry class—a job known to have low pay—in which the students have little interest and are outright rude to him. From there, Walt goes to a second job working at a car wash where some of those same students, seeing him scrub the tires on their expensive car, arrogantly laugh at him.

Within the first 10 minutes of *Breaking Bad*, it becomes clear that Walter White's life is financially stressed. In addition to working two jobs, Walt's son, Walter junior, has cerebral palsy, a physical disability that carries its own costs, and his wife is pregnant with their second child. Throughout the first season, and the first episodes in particular, there is regular reference to using and paying off credit cards, delaying the cashing of checks, and most crucially, paying for Walt's cancer treatment. When his wife, Skyler, urges him to see a well-known specialist not covered by their insurance, she tells her husband: "I don't want us thinking about money. Money is not the issue here." Walt replies, "I'll take it out of my pension."[54] Such hardships, along with his desire to provide for his family when he is gone, serve as Walt's motive to begin cooking and selling meth: he wants to support his family. Given the economic hardships facing viewers, Walt's fierce commitment to earning money to support his family would have struck some chord of understanding. As one commentator wrote, when *Breaking Bad* "aired in January 2008, right on the eve of the Great Recession . . . [it was] a story rooted in economic anxiety and the panic of potential financial ruin. Take a man who can't support his family on a teacher's salary, who washes the cars of his wealthy students for extra money, whose cancer will rob him of life and his children of an earner. Offer this man financial security for his children at no cost to his own morality and see what happens."[55]

Other critics drew comparisons between the recession and the precarious financial situation that sets Walt's life of drug cooking into motion. Matthew Gilbert commented in 2009 that TV programs like *Breaking Bad* reflected contemporary life, claiming that the "brutal drama is acutely relevant to a moment of domestic crisis . . . a timely dark fable [in which] Rather than fight for financial security within a system that has already failed him, Walter White has taken to the street in a last-ditch effort for a rescue package."[56] Similarly, Michael Paarlberg called the series "a middle class horror show" that resonates with the times, suggesting that the "idea that a high school teacher might resort to cooking meth to provide for his family is presented as a given: extreme, perhaps, but not incredible."[57] The very fact that viewers can identify with Walt, Paarlberg states, despite his "selling poison and murdering people reflects our understanding of what would happen if he accepted the fate handed to him by the present-day market economy."[58]

It is not just the recession and its financial impact on ordinary Americans that connected the series with recession era viewer, however. Allen St. John writes one reason that *Breaking Bad* was so popular is because the series depicts "a world in which free will reigns. But so does retribution. . . . That's what school teachers and bookkeepers, cops and x-ray technicians love about *Breaking Bad*. Comeuppance. They saw their nest eggs disappear in the Great Recession while the bankers who gambled and lost got off scot free. Now they find some satisfaction in watching crime that's followed by punishment."[59] Not only were the financial institutions responsible for the recession bailed out, while individual Americans were left to fend for themselves, but the executives in charge of those institutions were not held accountable. As Matt Taibbi wrote in *Rolling Stone*: "*Nobody goes to jail.* This is the mantra of the financial-crisis era, one that saw virtually every major bank and financial company on Wall Street embroiled in obscene criminal scandals that impoverished millions and collectively destroyed hundred of billions, in fact, trillions of dollars of the world's wealth—and nobody went to jail."[60]

Ultimately, of course, Walt himself is punished for his actions when he dies on the floor of the meth lab, surrounded only by the machinery that allowed him to cook his popular version of the drug. Yet, another subplot of retribution underpins the series, specifically the story line of Gray Matter Technologies. According to Walt, Gray Matter was cofounded by himself, his friend, Elliott Schwartz, and his former girlfriend, Gretchen, who is now Elliott's wife. After a falling-out between the three of them, Walt left the company, taking a buyout of $5000 for a company that became worth billions. It becomes clear that Walt could have been wealthy, could have used his scientific knowledge to make more than a teacher's salary, if he remained in the partnership or been fairly compensated for his contributions once the company made its fortune. Walt's partnership with Elliott and Gretchen is referred to in the first two seasons, where the backstory is partially revealed to viewers when the couple offers to pay for Walt's chemotherapy after his insurance turns down his claim. "That money, as far as we're both concerned, that belongs to you," Gretchen tells Walt. "Even the name of our company, it's half yours." Walt's perspective is different, however, when he angrily asks Gretchen: "What would your presumption about me be, exactly? That I should go begging for your charity? And you waving your checkbook around, like some magic wand, is going to make me forget how you and Elliott cut me out? .... It was my hard work, my research, and you and Elliott make millions off it."[61] Like viewers across the country, who were literally cut out of jobs, retirement funds, and savings, Walt's anger targets those who are untouched by economic hardship, paralleling a big business that was bailed out by the government, and the individuals responsible for the recession who were allowed to continue making huge salaries and even bonuses.[62]

The series comes full circle in the final episode, where Walt shows up in Elliott and Gretchen's expensive home where he forces them to promise to give what money he has left to his children when he dies. The scene opens with Elliott and Gretchen arriving home to their large house late at night, talking about eating out, traveling to Napa, and wondering whether their housekeeper has stocked the refrigerator. When Walt appears before them in the living room, having followed them in when they turned off the alarm system, he asks them to give his son the 10 million dollars in cash Walt has saved from his drug empire. Knowing that his cancer has returned and that he will not be alive for another year, he says: "On my son's 18th birthday, which is ten months and two days from today, you will give him this money in the form of an irrevocable trust. You will tell him that it is his to do with as he sees fit, but with the hope that he uses it for his college education. And for the betterment of his family." Elliott protests, "It wouldn't make any sense coming from us," to which Walt responds: "It certainly would. My children are blameless victims of their monstrous father. A man who you once knew quite well." Unstated is that his children are also blameless victims of the money Walt never got from his work in Gray Matter, work that has benefitted his former friends exceptionally well. In this light, his statement "Cheer up, beautiful people. This is where you get to make it right" resonates even more deeply with viewers who, even in 2013 when the series ended, may have still felt the sting of the Great Recession and anger at the lack of accountability on Wall Street.

The series finale continues with dramatic moments and, ultimately, Walt's death. This scene, however, returns viewers to the first episode where Walt stares at the plaque on his wall that reads "Contributor to Research Awarded the Nobel Prize" in science. Had his work been fairly compensated, had the "beautiful people" not done wrong by him, perhaps his entire life would have been different. *Breaking Bad* never fully reveals exactly what happened between Walt and his Gray Matter partners, whether he was cheated out of money and recognition that was rightly his, or whether his choices were solely to blame. In the economic climate in which the entire series was viewed, however, by Americans who felt financially insecure, taken advantage of by big business, and living in a society with great economic inequities, the Gray Matter narrative thread of *Breaking Bad* provides a sense of resolution and "comeuppance" that helped ensure the series' success.

Patriarchy and the Past

At a time in which women are achieving at higher levels than ever, some of the most popular television dramas of the 21st century take place in the past, in historical moments defined by the dominance of men. These staunchly patriarchal time periods, where women have limited access to education and work, where men have more social, economic, and political power, where violence—sometimes against women—is often celebrated, and where gender roles fall along a strict male female divide, stand in contrast to the way gender is discussed, practiced, and experienced in the 21st century. A number of TV dramas suggest a cultural tension between promoting gender equality and nostalgia for more traditional gender roles.

Twenty-first-century concerns about gender equality are complex. Despite the gains young women make over men before and during college, gender differences shift after college graduation. A 2012 *Bloomberg Businessweek* article discusses the reasons behind an American Association of University Women report showing that, a year out of college, women earn less than their male counterparts in the same jobs.[63] Other notable publications point to gender gaps in higher level jobs. For example, Ann Marie Slaughter's *Atlantic Monthly* article titled "Why Women Still Can't Have It All" discusses the complicated aspects of women who work high-level jobs and while parenting.[64] The online magazine *Salon* poses suggestions for how the trend of women leaving high-powered jobs can be altered.[65] Popular Facebook COO Sheryl Sandberg's TED talks, speeches, and best-selling book *Lean In: Women, Work and the Will to Lead* encourage women to take a more active role in achieving their goals.[66] Finally, in their book *The Confidence Code*, journalists Katty Kay and Claire Shipman look at how successful women experience lower levels of confidence than men.[67] Despite lower wages, there is significant encouragement for women who seek to balance work and family, make a fair living, and influence their own as well as wide cultural goals. As more women have become primary wage earners, childcare responsibilities have shifted to depend more on men.[68] Despite the cultural practices and policies indicating changing, and complex, conceptualizations of gender roles, some 21st-century TV dramas have a distinctly nostalgic theme of the patriarchal past.

The period drama is not a new television genre, but it is interesting that, in a time when sex and gender roles are shifting dramatically, many contemporary shows depict historically male-dominated patriarchal cultures. The series *Spartacus* (2010–2013), for instance, takes place in 73 BCE and dramatizes the historic figure's life. *Rome* (2005–2007) begins in 52 BCE and uses the events leading to Rome's rise in power as a backdrop for the drama. Although some critics suggest that *Game of Thrones* (2011–present) takes place in a far-off future, the show's visuals read as fantasy genre from a medieval past.[69] Based on the novels by George R. R. Martin, *Game of Thrones* tells the stories of various characters and family structures engaged in a complicated battle for control of the fictional land Westeros. Set in Italy during the late 1400s, *The Borgias* (2011–2013) is a historical crime drama that emphasizes the connections between religion and power, whereas *The Tudors* (2007–2010) explores the reign of King Henry VIII— husband of six wives—in the 1500s, and the spy drama *Turn* (2014–present) takes place in the prerevolutionary time period of the mid-1700s. The American western *Deadwood* (2004–2006) includes such historical characters from 1870s U.S. history as Wild Bill Hickok, Wyatt Earp, and Calamity Jane. *Boardwalk Empire* (2010–2014), set in Atlantic City during the 1920s, tells the story of gangster politician Nucky Thompson, whereas the imported *Downton Abbey* (2010–present) begins in the year 1912 and follows its characters through the 1920s as they deal with the progressive dissolution of a class-oriented society in England. The character-driven advertising agency drama *Mad Men* (2007–2015) starts its story in 1960. Although set in the present day, also worth mentioning because of the patriarchal structure at the center of the narratives are *The Sopranos* (1999–2007), a mafia story based in New Jersey, and *Sons of Anarchy* (2008–2014), a Californian biker culture drama.

Understanding why these patriarchal narratives appear in TV dramas at a time when there is explicit cultural discussion about gender inequity in the broader culture must begin with a look at the disconnect between gender ideals in 21st-century life and gender portrayal in 21st-century entertainment. In her review of *Game of Thrones*, Emily Nussbaum points to a new category of television dramas:

> . . . *Game of Thrones* is the latest entry in television's most esteemed category: the sophisticated cable drama about a patriarchal subculture. This phenomenon launched with *The Sopranos* but it now includes shows such as *Deadwood, Mad Men, Downton Abbey* and *Big Love*. Each of these acclaimed series is a sprawling, multi-character exploration of closed, often violent hierarchical system. These worlds are picturesque, elegantly filmed, and ruled by rigid etiquette—lit up, for viewers, by the thrill of seeing brutality enforced (or in the case of *Downton Abbey*, a really nice house kept in the family). And yet the undergirding strength of each series is its insight into what it means to be excluded from power: to be a woman, or a bastard, or a "half man."[70]

Despite their depiction of power inequity, these shows have male and female fans, perhaps because the stories are compelling and the female lead characters are often portrayed as smart, powerful, and determined despite their position in the patriarchy. At the same time, such premium cable shows as *Game of Thrones* depict explicit sex, female nudity, and extreme brutality, often in combination with one another. In contrast, the characters in *Downton Abbey* tend to be clothed, but the women are subject to story lines that are detrimental to women, including one female lead who dies after giving birth to her son, a second who loses her husband, and a third who is raped. The Revolutionary War drama, *Turn*, features a main female character, Anna, who assists her former suitor, lead character Abe, in spying, but her participation is clearly limited by her gender. In addition, the illicit relationship between Anna and Abe ultimately positions Abe's wife as disposable; she is not nearly as developed as a character as Anna. Although *Deadwood* displays how frontier women could establish their own independent identities and *Mad Men* demonstrates the struggles career-oriented women faced in the 1960s, both programs prioritize men's perceptions of women while affirming men's superior place in the cultural hierarchy.

To complicate things, by situating these dramas in "the past," the subordinate nature of the female characters seems necessary, because it is historically accurate, and therefore acceptable to watch. After all, not to display the patriarchal system would be to misrepresent the historical time period in which the series are set. Furthermore, because many of the female characters embody skills and talents worthy of admiration, it may appear to matter less that they do not have the agency and freedoms granted to their male counterparts. Yet, as smart, willful, and spunky as many of the female characters are, most pose no real threat to their male counterparts; the patriarchal system does not allow for it. This means that, on one hand, viewers can admire and celebrate the strength of the oppressed female characters, reflecting on and discussing the failings of patriarchy and indicting dramas that depict a system that, as 21st-century viewers, they would not endorse. On the other hand, the historically situated patriarchal story lines and character traits give viewers permission to enjoy programs that clearly reinforce and celebrate male power at the expense of women or other oppressed groups. In doing so, the period genre permits viewers who support contemporary ideas of equality to enjoy programs where equality is absent or minimal. This is a curious trend given current conversations around how to diversify leadership and power, not to mention the gains women have made compared to men in recent decades.

As noted earlier, however, women's gains in education do not always lead to shifts in the gender composition of leaders in the political and corporate landscape. This trend is also present in the television industry; in fact, male show creators still outnumber women in television. HBO, the company behind the period pieces *Game of Thrones, The Sopranos, Deadwood, Boardwalk Empire*, and *Rome*, has only aired one original drama series created by a woman in 40 years.[71] In addition, when examining the gender breakdown of U.S. television drama showrunners from HBO, Showtime, AMC, FX, and Netflix, data show a total of 97 creators, 12 of them women.[72] In his book *Difficult Men*, Brett Martin discusses the writer-producers behind some of the popular television shows featuring male antihero protagonists, specifically *The Sopranos, Mad Men*, and *Deadwood*. According to Martin, the difficult men are not only Tony Soprano, Don Draper, and Al Swearengen but also the corresponding show creators David Chase, Matthew Weiner, and David Milch—men who are described by Martin as creative and passionate men who have menacing, egotistical, and ruthless qualities.[73] These shows made it to production, in part, because the industry still favors male creators. This is not to suggest that the series should not have been made, and they are certainly popular within the landscape of television dramas. Yet, there is room for other types of storytellers.

It is often mentioned that popular television shows reflect a particular understanding of the time period in which they are made. In this light, dramas that focus on the patriarchal past reflect a 21st-century understanding of periods in history as envisioned by their creators. So although these period dramas are well written, beautifully acted, and entertaining, they also reflect a contemporary patriarchy of their own—a system where male storytelling, as engaging as might be, is privileged. Collectively, these period pieces register a male-dominated television industry that favors historical dramas that depict the male-dominated period of history. It is unfortunate that these shows do not exist alongside other historical narratives penned by women. Despite women's educational successes, the demographic of television creator and showrunner reflects the challenges faced by women in other high-powered positions.

Side Note: Antiheroes

If any single character type captures early 21st-century television dramas, it is the male antihero, beginning with mobster Tony Soprano, the main character of HBO's award-winning series *The Sopranos* (1999–2007). Defined by his unsympathetic nature and morally questionable behavior, Tony Soprano became "a prototype for a wave of provocative antiheroes who . . . would place cable television at the vanguard of a creative revolution, one that would make open-ended serialized drama 'the signature American art form of the first decade of the 21st century.'"[74]

Other male antiheroes quickly appeared on the small screen. In Showtime's *Dexter* (2006–2013), lead character Dexter Morgan works by day in the Miami Police Department as a blood splatter analyst, while working at night at his real job, which is to kill serial killers in accordance with a "code" instilled in him by his adopted father. AMC's *Breaking Bad* (2008–2013) antihero, Walter White, starts cooking and selling crystal meth to support his family, a journey that leads him to lie, steal, and kill with little guilt or anxiety. *Mad Men*'s (2007–2015) Don Draper repeatedly gives in to his philandering tendencies regardless of the people, including two wives and three children, he hurts along the way. The first scene of FXs *House of Cards* (2013–present) introduces its own version of the antihero, Francis Underwood, to viewers by having him kill a dog with his bare hands, a metaphor for the lengths he goes to throughout the series to attain his political goals.[75] These antihero plots are "a real upending of TV shows' unwritten moral social contract: that the good guys kill only when forced into a corner and then have nightmares about it later. That makes for sometimes uncomfortable viewing for TV audiences"

because to enjoy them you have to, for instance, root for Francis Underwood who is the kind of man who pushes a reporter to her death in front
of a subway train because he sees her as a threat.[76] The antiheroes at the
center of other dramas, including *24*, *The Shield*, *House*, *Justified*, and
Boardwalk Empire, have their own context for similarly bad behavior.

These characters engage viewers with their complex, moral ambiguity.
For example, Dexter's methodical approach to murder, including his tro-
phy collection—drops of his victims' blood—is deplorable. Yet, as with
most 21st-century television antiheroes, viewers feel a strange allegiance
to the character, in part, because his actions reflect a twisted but somehow logical desire to do good—killing serial killers so they stop killing
innocent people—and, in part, because Dexter has moments of self-doubt
of which viewers are aware. As Murray Smith puts it, the "possibility of
redemption, no matter how slight or remote, is thus an essential ingredi-
ent in these shows: even Dexter experiences a kind of unease with himself. And self-deception is a key to the possibility of redemption: White,
Draper, and company strive to dupe themselves because at some level
they understand, but can't stand, what they are or have become."[77]

The rise of the television antihero has been explored in articles and
books on the subject, many asking what audiences find so engaging about
those characters.[78] *New York Times* writer Michiko Kakutani puts it best,
saying:

> These shows delved into their heroes' conflicted psyches and their
> strained relationships with family and colleagues, and they opened
> big new windows on the state of millennial America. Tony Sopra-
> no's worry that he "came in at the end," that the best was over for
> his profession, echoed viewers' worries about American decline and
> their own uncertain prospects, even as Walter White's metamor-
> phosis from high school science teacher to killer meth dealer raised
> questions . . . about "the American ethos of self-actualization" and
> the dark side of success. . . . "The Wire" looked at the infighting and
> rot within a big American city, while the Los Angeles police drama
> "The Shield" (which had its debut six months after Sept. 11) became
> an examination of the costs of maintaining security and the equation
> between means and ends.[79]

The television antihero, in other words, reflects larger cultural concerns
facing viewers.

The antihero era was not without controversy, and as more dramas
featured dislikeable characters, viewers registered a fatigue with such

ambiguous individuals. Articles like "How the Anti-Hero is Ruining Television," "Can We Make Walter White Our Last Antihero, Please?" and "Against Antiheroes: It's Time to Retire Television's Most Overused Buzzword" record a weariness with the antihero trope.[80] At the same time, female antiheroes—or antiheroines—in contemporary dramas started to be noticed. For example, in 2013, *New Republic* writer Lauren Bennett recognized the crucial role of "the bad wife," a term deliberately in contrast to the popular drama "The Good Wife," claiming that Walter White's wife, Skyler, is the true antihero of the series who is "just as capable as deadpan and deception as Walt."[81] Other female antiheroes might include *Damages'* (2007–2012) Patty Hewes, *The Bridge's* (2013–2014) Sonya Cross, or even *Mad Men's* Betty Draper.[82] Antihero marriages can also be observed in such dramas as *House of Cards*, where Claire Underwood is just as ruthless as her husband in her pursuit of what she wants, and *The Americans* (2013–present), which chronicles the plotting of Elizabeth and Philip Jennings, Soviet-born spies intent on serving their home country at any cost as undercover agents raising a family in the U.S. suburbs.[83]

The signature characteristic of early 21st-century television dramas is the male antihero who, beginning with Tony Soprano, asked viewers to witness bad behavior while still rooting for, even sometimes empathizing with, the character. The rise of the TV antihero reflected the cultural zeitgeist of the time. As the century unfolded, not only did antihero fatigue become evident but also other types of antiheroes, including women and married couples, took the stage.

Masters of Sex and Gender

Based on the personal and professional lives of U.S. sex researchers, Drs. William Masters and Virginia Johnson, Showtime's period drama *Masters of Sex* (2013–present) earned critical acclaim for its depiction of the couple who revolutionized how Americans thought about and practiced sex. Authors of *Human Sexual Response* (1966) and *Human Sexual Inadequacy* (1970), among other books, Masters and Johnson studied the anatomy and physiology of sexual arousal and response in human subjects for close to four decades. Unlike earlier researchers who based their conclusions on interviews, Masters and Johnson observed and recorded their subjects in a laboratory setting, collecting data on the physical changes and stages of sexual arousal. Their findings transformed the field, even as their method was controversial in its explicit, scientific approach to such a personal topic. Masters and Johnson were not without controversy themselves, participating as subjects in their own research, having an affair while Masters was still married and then, later, marrying each other and ultimately divorcing. Their work, some of which has since been debunked, remains foundational in the diagnosis, understanding, and treatment of sexual response and dysfunction.[84]

Although *Masters of Sex* depicts the relationship between the two main characters and their efforts to document sexual practices in a scientific way, the most provocative episodes focus on sexual practices and attitudes thought to be abnormal in the mid-20th century. Two story lines in particular, season one's "Love and Marriage,"[85] and season two's "Fight,"[86] depict cultural attitudes toward sex and gender that are depicted as harmful and outdated, in part, because of contemporary changes in American attitudes, legal standards, and medical practices.

In "Love and Marriage," the plight of homosexuals in the 1950s unfolds as Dr. Barton Scully, provost of the university where Masters and Johnson conducted their early research, struggles to deny his sexual attraction to men. In the episode, Scully's wife asks for a divorce, no longer able to live with their sexless marriage despite the fact that the couple cares about each other. Scully's response is to try to "cure" himself, asking his physician colleague, William Masters, whether he has any advice on treatments:

> Scully: Have you come across any information about people's abilities to change their sexual habits?—I-I only ask—
> Masters: I know why you're asking.
> Scully: Uh, I've run across a few treatments. Uh, I can't verify they work. I've also been doing some reading. Apparently, there's, uh Aversion therapy—And electroshock.
> Masters: Jesus, Barton. I do know a psychologist in New York, Dr. Sandor Rado. He's been touting something he calls "Adaptational Psychodynamics."
> Scully: Sounds like something Pavlov did to dogs.
> Masters: It's a form of aversion therapy. Patient's given a drug Apomorphine.
>   It induces nausea while the patient engages in the behavior that he wishes to change. The hope is the brain rewires itself to perceive the activity it used to enjoy as, uh repulsive.[87]

At the end of the episode, Scully is shown trying the aversion therapy. In a hotel room with his male lover, Dale, Scully says he wants to take the drug. The "[p]oint is," he says: "I look at you, I get sick, and then I'm cured of this terrible habit."[88] When aversion therapy is unsuccessful, Barton decides to secretly undergo electroshock therapy.[89] When that, too, fails to change his sexual preference, he tries to take his own life, hanging himself, and nearly succeeding, when he is discovered by his daughter and wife who save his life.[90]

Barton Scully's story line is especially poignant given early 21st-century changes in the visibility and acceptance of gay relationships. In the first two decades of the new century, "American attitudes toward homosexuality and gay marriage have undergone significant and rapid changes" toward more tolerance and acceptance.[91] In a time when words like "spouse" are used in reference to same-sex as well as heterosexual couples, and the Supreme Court has recognized gay marriage as legal in every state in the country, a historical moment in which aversion or shock therapy would be considered an exciting new option for treating a "terrible habit" reminds viewers of how times have changed.[92] When Scully tells his male partner "there is no universe where you and I are anything other than a business transaction,"[93] it is easy to look back with regret and sympathy to an earlier time when homosexuality was considered an illness. Although Masters is represented in this episode and others as having empathy toward Scully, he and Virginia Johnson actually ran a program in the 1980s that tried to help convert homosexuals to heterosexuality through the use of sexual surrogates.[94] Eventually the research was challenged as possibly falsified; however, the idea of converting homosexuals to heterosexuality remains in the popular imagination.[95] The Barton Scully story line emphasizes the cultural shifts that have unfolded since the time of Masters and Johnson's groundbreaking research as well as the lingering prejudices facing gay individuals even today.

In season two, episode three, "Fight," another subplot reminds viewers of changes in attitudes toward sex and gender since the mid-1900s. In an episode filled with references to male female gender roles, Masters delivers a baby who is diagnosed with "adrenogenital hyperplasia," born with a penis and a vagina, a fact that makes it difficult to tell if the baby is a boy or a girl.[96] The baby's father is repulsed by his child's physical difference. "I'm not holding it," he says and urges Dr. Masters to use surgical means to make the child look like a boy.[97] When Masters is unable to promise that surgery alone will make the child appear and function sexually as a male, the father lashes out saying: "I want you to cut it off. . . . You can sew a prick on him the size of the Empire State building, and it still won't make him a man. He'll never be a man, so cut it off."[98] Masters sternly responds that the decision to surgically turn the baby into a girl is not one to be rushed, especially because blood tests determine that the baby's sex is male. He tells the father: "[Y]ou will come to accept that your son—your son—has a condition that can and will be corrected. And when you come back here for the surgery that's gonna ensure that his outsides match who he is inside, you're gonna thank me for protecting your child from your own poor judgment. . . . Let him be what he is. A boy."[99]

Despite Masters's efforts, the father has his way: the child is operated on and his male genitalia are surgically removed. "We're naming her Sarah," the father tells Masters at the end of the episode, "Better a tomboy than a sissy."[100] The "Fight" episode examines the relationship between biological sex—the physical attributes with which a person is born and the male or female sex assigned as a result—and the expression of gender—the range of behaviors that are culturally recognized as male and female. As Kate Phillips writes in the *New York Times*, the episode registers that, since the 1950s "much research has been conducted amid calls for more enlightened treatment" of babies born with ambiguous genders. "Too often," she writes, "doctors chose the sex of the baby without further study of the child's own development and, of course, did so without the child's consent."[101]

The idea that a child can and even should choose his or her own gender has received attention in a parenting trend focused on raising gender-neutral children, a relatively new 21st-century cultural practice. Instead of declaring "It's a boy" or "It's a girl," parents withhold the information about the child's biological sex, allowing the child to "develop [his or her] own identity, regardless of what [his or her] gender is."[102] In 2011, for example, a Canadian family decided to raise their child, Storm, gender neutral so that the child could be free of the cultural expectations and stereotypes surrounding what it means to be a boy or a girl. The choice, and publicity around it, harbored attention from psychologists to parents whose positions on whether or not gender identity is or should be determined by biological sex were mixed.[103] Since then, such books as *Gender Neutral Parenting* (2013) and *Chasing Rainbows: Exploring Gender Fluid Parenting Practices* (2013) and articles about assigning a child a gender at birth, rather than "letting a child wait to declare for themselves what they are" register an expanding tolerance for ambiguity and choice.[104]

Such trends stand in contrast to mid-20th-century attitudes as reflected on *Masters of Sex*. Although the drama documents the 1950s revolution ushered in by Masters and Johnson's scientific approach to talking about sexual practices, the story lines remind contemporary viewers about the progress that has been made, as well as the changes still to come, in the ways Americans think about sex and gender.

Words Matter in Amazon's *Transparent*

In 2013, when online storefront Amazon.com decided to create original TV programming, it posted pilot episodes of potential shows on its web site. The retailer then asked viewers to vote on their favorite pilots, essentially participating in the decision about which would be developed into a full series.[105] The first season of Amazon Original Series yielded five new programs streamed online through Amazon Instant Video. The second pilot season, released in early 2014, included the award-winning dramedy *Transparent*, hailed by critics as "transcendent,"[106] "brilliant,"[107] "top-notch,"[108] and "Damn Near Perfect."[109] All 10 episodes were released on September 26, 2014, in online streaming format amenable to binge-watching.

Although *Transparent* is noteworthy because it puts Amazon on the map, along with Netflix and Hulu, for creating critically acclaimed streaming programming, the content of the show was just as groundbreaking. The story of the Pfeffermans, including retired professor and father, Mort, his ex-wife, Shelley, and their three adult children, Sarah, Josh, and Ali, *Transparent* is a family drama with a unique and timely twist. The pilot episode follows Mort's attempt to tell his children that he is transitioning from being a man to being a woman, from Mort to Maura. Although transgender and transitioning characters have been depicted in such movies as *Boys Don't Cry*, and trans actor Laverne Cox has drawn positive attention for her transgender character on Netflix's *Orange Is the New Black*, "Maura is the first transitioning transgender character to anchor a television series"[110] making *Transparent* the "first small-screen effort to seriously consider the process of a transgender father coming out to his loved ones."[111] In the words of creator Jill Soloway, reflecting on the heightened cultural visibility of transgender people and issues in 2014, "'Trans-ness' is in the zeitgeist."[112]

The Pilot episode centers around Mort's intention to come out to his children during a dinner he invites them to at the family home. Halfway through the meal, however, he decides not to tell them because they are so focused on themselves and unable to listen to him. Later, in his transgender support group, Mort says: "I made a commitment here last week that I was gonna come out to my kids, and I didn't do it. Because it just wasn't time, you know? But I will,—and it will be soon—Yeah. I promise you. I promise you. I promise you. They are so selfish. I don't know how it is I raised three people who cannot see beyond themselves."[113] The idea of seeing another person, as the title of the series suggests, is a recurrent theme of *Transparent* and each character begins to see and be seen more truthfully as the episodes unfold. For instance, when Mort, dressed as Maura, arrives home to find his oldest daughter Sarah kissing her former female lover, Tammy Cashman, he seizes the moment of vulnerability to tell Sarah about his change. "Are are you saying that you're going to start dressing up like a lady all the time?" Sarah asks. "No, honey, all my life my whole life I've been dressing up like a man. This is me."[114]

Mort's—now Maura's—revelation sets into motion a string of other changes in the Pfefferman household. As *New Yorker* writer Emily Nussbaum writes: "By forcing her family to see her as she sees herself, Maura also acts as a mirror, reflecting back the 'queerness' in everyone around her: Sarah, who jumps into bed with an ex-girlfriend; Ali, who abuses her body in ways both playful and hostile with drugs and sex; and Josh, whose boyishness hints at some refusal to grow into traditional manhood, a refusal possibly bound up in the secrets his family has agreed to bury."[115] The changes among Maura's children even the playing field in the sense that each member of the family—not just Maura—is forced to reflect on his or her identity. In fact, in the midst of "all this change, Maura, despite instigating so much turmoil, becomes a kind of beacon of calm,"[116] making the transition she is facing in some ways the least dramatic of any depicted on the show. As one critic writes: "Maura's the Pfefferman making the most massive, seemingly drastic change. But there are lots of ways that her transition is the most simple, too, because at least she's sure."[117] The other characters respond with their own personal, somewhat messy, transformations. Sarah leaves her husband, Leonard, to be with her former lover, setting up a female–female partnership that includes children and ex-step-children. Ali "becomes intensely interested in gender, both as a subject of study and as something to play out on a more personal level, whether by dating a female-to-male trans or dressing in everything from cleavage-baring gingham to suits and ties."[118] Josh is perhaps the character most bothered by his father's revelation, in part, because of the father–son relationship on which he formed his own identity but also because his sexuality is in some ways the most murky, making his response the most difficult to witness. In each instance, however, the characters' choices help them become more authentic individuals. As the series' creator, Jill Soloway, states the "ideas about gender freedom that the show promotes are really sort of about freedom and transitioning and transcendence and becoming whoever you want to be outside of the idea of sexuality."[119]

Soloway's choice of the word "sexuality" is deliberate here, because Maura's change is not about her sexual preference—she is still attracted to women—but about gender, and *Transparent* wants to make the distinction clear. Soloway states:

> I do think that the way the gender binary has been expressed in the past can be troubling. Light vs. Dark. Brain vs. Body. Love vs. Sex. These kinds of binaries have, for eons, informed the Male vs. Female dynamic. *Transparent* stands for gender freedom for all, and within that freedom we can find grays and muddled purples and pinks, chakras that bridge the heart and mind, sexiness that depends on a masochistic love or a sweeping soul dominancy. In particular, *Transparent* wants to invent words that bridge the binary: Genderqueer, Boygirl, Girlboy, Macho Princess, and Officer Sweet Slutty Neat Captain are just a few incredibly confusing, gender-fucking concepts that come to mind. The rest should roll [off] of our tongues and [out of our] computers and into your T.V.s as the rest of the season writing unfolds.[120]

The show registers changes in language in various ways. In season one's episode, "Rollin'," Maura and Sarah clean out the family house so it can transition from Maura's home to the home of her children and grandchildren. In the process, she and Sarah come across a set of hardcover Encyclopedias. "Which one of you are gonna take the encyclopedias?" Maura asks. "None of us, dad," Sarah responds. "Nobody in the world wants those." Maura sighs, "These are the bicentennial encyclopedias," pointing out their age and, therefore, their irrelevance, not only because of the electronic resources that have replaced them but also because the world of 1976 has so little to do with the world of 2014, especially in terms of the changes facing the Pfeffermans, not to mention the words to describe those changes. As the family adjusts to their father's transition, there are recurrent comments about what the proper words are to describe him or her. Ali says "Dad is a woman, thinks he's a woman, wants to be a woman, something like that," to which Sarah clarifies, "He's trans."[121] In another scene, Josh says, "All I'm trying to say is dad is a fucking transvestite." Sarah again corrects the language: "That is not the word, okay?—He's trans."[122] The youngest Pfefferman, Ali, no longer able to call her father "Dad" not able to call her "Mom," tells Sarah she has invented a new name altogether: "Oh, my God, and I renamed him her. Her? Him? What do I call him or her? I renamed him last night. . . . I started calling her "Moppa. . . . like momma and poppa. Moppa."[123]

Soloway, herself, seems intent on educating viewers about the new language available to identify one's gender. Interviews with her about

Transparent repeatedly return to this theme. In one interview she states: "You know, under the so-called transbrella, a lot of people in America don't even know the difference between trans women, cross-dressers and drag queens. But those are three distinctly different ways of expressing femininity. Cross-dressers and drag queens share the notion that they do it part time, and trans women are amidst a civil rights struggle to be accepted for having their gender not conform to the gender they were assigned at birth."[124] In another interview, when asked to explain why she used the plural pronoun "them" to describe Maura, Soloway answered:

> Right. Well, it's not always plural. Them or they is used for the singular when you don't know the person who's coming. Like my friend is coming from the airport. What time are they going to get here? That would be singular. And then they would refer to the fact that you don't know the gender of the friend who's coming from the airport. Similarly, there are some people who identify as male. There are some people who identify as female. And there are some people who don't want to identify and want to still be able to be spoken about in a sentence. And they and them is perfect for that. It sounds plural to people immediately, but I think as this country begins to get used to the sound of they and them—which I have, you know, it took me a while—it took me probably a year to have they or them role off the tongue. But it's just the way to speak about somebody where you don't want to gender them.[125]

This tendency to explain the meaning of words used to describe gender is a theme not only of Soloway's but also of the show itself. When Ali meets a trans woman, working as a teaching assistant in a gender studies class, they have the following exchange:

> Ali: Oh, I have so many questions. I'm afraid of being offensive.
> Dale: Let me guess, uh, the first question. All right, so I'm a man with a vag.
> Ali: Awesome. I mean, that's awesome. You have basically experienced the world as two genders. That's incredible. You're like gender enlightened.
> Dale: You know, you wouldn't believe the shit that dudes say when they think a woman isn't around. I'm like a double-agent.
> Ali: Oh, my God. I don't know, and I want to know.
> Dale: You don't really want to know.

Ali: Where do you live? Can I come over? Can I just interview you
    for a week?

Dale: Okay, I'm I'm confused. I just want to clarify. I just you're
    you're a dyke, right?

Ali: No, I'm not a dyke. God! This whole time you thought you were
    talking to a boring lesbian? Excuse me.

Dale: Well, yeah. I mean I I You kind of give off those vibes, you
    know?

Ali: No, no, I mean, politically, I'm basically a lesbian. Yeah, I see
    male privilege everywhere. And, I mean, I would totally love to be
    a lesbian, but I'm not a dyke, I'm, like, really into dudes, you
    know? Like, dude, dudely-dude, dude.

Dale: Dudely-dude.

Ali: Yeah. Dudely dudes.

Dale: Yeah.

Ali: Yeah. The dudlier the better.

Dale: Manly, you like—Manly.

Ali: Yeah. What about you?—Do you like—Dudes?

Dale: No.

Ali: No.

Dale: No, no. Well, I like women.

Ali: Yeah, right.

Dale: Yeah, let's go.

Ali: Okay.

Dale: I mean, generally I usually go for, like, really, you know, like,
    really fem women, like, really, like, lipstick and heels and—oh,
    yeah. That kind of you know, like, high fem. Not just fem, but
    high fem. You know what I mean.

Ali: Right. Cool.[126]

This extended discussion is as much about Ali and Dale's budding court-
ship as it is about creating a common language they can both understand.
The conversation about how Dale sees his gender, his preference for "high
fem" women, and even Ali's made-up word "dudey-dudes" fits into a
larger cultural broadening of terms used to talk about gender. As early as
2004, reports found that "[w]ith the universe of gender and sexual identities expanding, a gay youth culture emerging, acceptance of gays rising
and label loyalty falling, the gay lexicon has exploded with scores of
new words and blended phrases that delineate every conceivable stop on
the identity spectrum."[127] *Transparent* does not assume that viewers

understand this new language, however. Following Ali's discussion with Dale, she tries to figure out what "high fem" is. In a discussion with her friend Syd, she tries to choose a "high fem" outfit for a date with Dale:

> Ali: Is this high fem? Is this good?
> Syd: No, that's Holly Hobby.
> Ali: I don't get it the high fem thing.
> Syd: Okay, I'm low fem. Me. Low fem. Right?
> Ali: Okay, so what am I?
> Syd: You're, like, Middle Earth fem.
> Ali: Like, The hobbit?
> Syd: No, like people that live under the subway. Like mole people fem.[128]

The accompanying visuals, of Syd and Ali in pants and button up shirts, are immediately contrasted, in the next scene, with Syd helping Ali into a red, sleeveless halter dress that reveals significant cleavage. As Ali applies a smear of bright red lipstick, viewers know she has achieved the "high fem" look for which she was searching. In the process, viewers have been given a primer on some gender identifiers they might not have known at the start of the episode.

Some of the minor characters also challenge the traditional gender binary, refusing to be categorized as male or female. When Shelley's second husband, Ed, goes missing, for instance, Ali enlists the help of the condominium manager. When the two of them encounter another employee, who does not look clearly male or female, *Transparent* refuses to meet the viewer's expectation that his or her gender will be revealed. In fact, when the manager addresses his coworker he says: "Oh, here comes my man Tiffany,"[129] deliberately resisting the cultural expectation of a clear male or female distinction.

The conversation around gender terms has expanded beyond the series to actors, viewers, and even organizations that are recognizing the changing vocabulary. Articles have been published on how to talk accurately about the series, for instance, "A Guide To Not Being Ignorant When Talking about Amazon's 'Transparent'" and "We Need To Talk about Transparent"[130] try to help readers understand the gender terms used by the show. GLAAD's "Media Reference Guide—Transgender Issues" offers "Transgender-specific terminology," "Transgender Names, Pronoun Usage & Descriptions," as well as "Terms to Avoid" and why they are problematic in the 21st-century culture.[131] Judith Light, who plays Maura's ex-wife, Shelley, said in an interview: "What we found in the gay community is that they were teaching the world about sexuality. The transgender community is teaching people about gender presentation and gender fluidity." [132] Facebook's shift from offering users two gender options (male or female) to more than 50 possible identifiers further reflects the fact that cultural ideas about gender are in flux. The change also created more public conversation and media coverage of what the different terms—for instance, "cisgender," "neutrois," and "nonbinary"— actually mean. [133] This "precision about language, politics and etiquette is ever-present in the cultural milieu that Soloway entered when she sat down to create 'Transparent', . . . In an already pivotal moment for transgender people, who are emerging from culture's margins, Soloway's show tries to fast-forward past the incremental water-testing that network TV has historically applied to shifts like this, to skip the eggshell-walking and the audience-coddling. She wants to give her viewers a fully realized trans character." [134]

In one of the tensest scenes of the first season, the only scene with even a threat of violence, Sarah's ex-husband arrives in the middle of a Pfefferman family dinner to pick up his kids. Frustrated by the loss of his wife to her female lover, and confused by Mort's transition to Maura, he picks up a knife from the table and holds it in the air. Mort interrupts him, apologizing for the way things have unfolded. "Leonard, I am so sorry," Maura says. "This is my fault. I should have called you. Honey, I should have taken you out to lunch, and we should have talked. But I didn't do that. And I'm sorry about the Mort and the Maura and the he and the she. I'm just a person, and you're just a person, and here we are. And, baby, you need to get in this whirlpool or you need to get out of it." [135] Her words speak of the larger cultural landscape that *Transparent* brings to viewers, heightening awareness of the many ways gender can be expressed and the ways such expression is unfolding in the media and everyday life.

CHAPTER 4

Home and Work

Stories about the way we live and work are among the most compelling themes of television dramas, giving viewers an inside look into fictional homes where people live and love, as well as fictionalized workplaces, police stations, law offices, and hospitals. Historically, dramas that take place in the home focus on families and the dynamics among them. Sometimes, families are seen in the "everyday world, exploring the internal and external forces they face." Other times, families are depicted in difficult situations "showing how love and togetherness help them face tough times." Finally, home life television shows feature family structures where one parent or other adults must care for children.[1] Work-oriented dramas, in contrast, have focused on issues connected to the workplace itself. This storytelling technique became solidified as a genre in the 1980s with the success of *Hill Street Blues* (1981–1987) and *St. Elsewhere* (1982–1988), programs that "shifted the dramatic focus from the all-too-familiar heroics of a series star to an ensemble of coworkers and to the workplace itself—not simply as a backdrop, but as a social-service institution located in an urban-industrial war zone with its own distinctive ethos and sense of place."[2] Over time, workplace and family dramas have evolved into an integrated form of storytelling: viewers learn of characters' home and work lives even if the series takes place primarily in one setting more than the other. In addition, even if shows have a home or work focus, they may not fit neatly into the home or workplace television category; elements of home and workplace settings can inform one another or, in some cases, be one and the same.

These two locations—home and work—have distinct markers in the 21st-century television drama. Twenty-first-century homes have family structures that are more diverse than at any time in history. Nuclear and multigenerational families live side-by-side; parents are single, divorced, homosexual, heterosexual, remarried, and widowed. A 2014 Pew Research Center report states that just 46 percent of families are traditionally "nuclear"—where children live in a home with married heterosexual parents in their first marriage.[3] Other family structures include remarried parents and same-sex parent unions.[4] Single parent families are increasingly common: the U.S. Census Bureau reports that more than one quarter of all children live with just one parent, approximately 84 percent of who are mothers.[5] The Pew Report notes this trend is "one of the largest shifts in family structure" in recent history.[6] Although historically the mother has been more likely than the father to be granted custody of children, the number of households with single fathers has increased over the past 50 years.[7] Multigenerational households are also increasingly common in the United States, with about 18 percent of homes housing family members from different generations.[8]

Current home-oriented dramas reflect these shifts both in their presentation of what a family is and in how families operate in a variety of contexts. *Gilmore Girls* (2001–2007), for example, tells the story of a single mother who became pregnant as a teenager, and her academically motivated daughter. The highly regarded and award-winning drama *Six Feet Under* (2001–2005) features the Fishers, a nuclear family with three children, two grown and one teenager, and their mother, who are dealing with the family funeral home business after the sudden death of the father. With a related plot, *Brothers and Sisters* (2006–2011) follows the diverse lives of the Walker family, five grown children and their mother, after the death of the family patriarch. *Parenthood* (2010–2015) focuses on the Braverman family, a clan that includes an older couple and their four grown children's diversely structured families. *The Fosters* (2013–present), celebrated for its LGBT representation, portrays an interracial lesbian couple and their biological, adopted, and foster children. Depicting tensions that arise when family members are reunited after long periods of separation, *Rectify* (2013–present) explores what happens when a son is released from jail to his childhood home, whereas *Bloodline* (2015–present) focuses on what happens when the black sheep of the family returns to the nest.

Just as television dramas focused on the home reflect elements of 21st-century culture, so do presentations of television workplaces. Such landscapes are informed by current employee demographics, advances in technology, and contemporary social, economic, and political issues, resulting in new television constructions of familiar job-related institutions. For example, the long running hospital drama *ER* (1994–2009) incorporates current social issues and relevant health information into its storytelling, including safe sex practices, HIV, AIDS, gay rights, racism, and mental illness. *House, M.D.* (2004–2012) is a detective themed medical drama whose "Sherlock" wrestles with solving difficult medical puzzles in a managed health care setting, often breaking mandated protocols and ethical guidelines. Other medical dramas, for example *Strong Medicine* (2000–2006), *Private Practice* (2007–2013), *Grey's Anatomy* (2005–present), and *Nurse Jackie* (2009–present), feature diverse casts who engage in workplace narratives informed by social and political issues as well as medical ones. On such legal dramas as *Law and Order* (1990–2010), *The Practice* (1997–2004), *Boston Legal* (2004–2008), *The Good Wife* (2009–present), and *Suits* (2011–present), the weekly story line cases integrate current events and cultural conversations, keeping these series aligned with issues viewers may be thinking about or discussing in their own lives. Although these legal shows deal with their share of criminal activity, cases of the week also include conflicts related to privacy concerns in the age of expanding technology, corporate control at a time when Wall Street's power is being criticized, and race relations against a backdrop of contemporary racial tension. Other workplace settings may be less familiar in television programming history. Writer and producer Aaron Sorkin's interest in workplace dynamics has prompted him to explore several environments through the television medium, including the White House in the award-winning political drama *The West Wing* (1999–2006), a sports network in the situation comedy *Sports Night* (1998–2000), a behind-the-scenes look at a nighttime comedy show in the short-lived *Studio 60 on the Sunset Strip* (2007), and a cable news station in *The Newsroom* (2012–2014). As Sorkin tells *Vanity Fair*, "I really like workplace shows . . . I like creating workplace families, and writing about people who are very good at what they do, and less good at everything else."[9]

In addition to homelife structure and workplace dynamics, some dramas also rely on a specific geographic setting to inform the home and work components of the story. The privileged, hyperconnected teens on *Gossip Girl* (2007–2012) live different lives in the Upper East Side of New York City than the economically strapped teenagers in Chicago who are featured in the dramedy *Shameless* (2011–present). The characters experiencing small town Texas life on *Friday Night Lights* (2006–2011) have different concerns than the characters who live in Berkeley, CA, on

Parenthood. In *Big Love* (2006–2011), the Mormon culture in Utah informs the central plots of the entire series. Other dramas bring family and work into a single space, including the funeral business run in the lower level of the family home on *Six Feet Under,* the office located in the home of therapist Paul Weston on *In Treatment* (2008–2011), and the inn built on the family's Florida Keys compound in *Bloodline.* Occasionally, work relationships begin to seem like, and even become, family relationships. On *Boston Legal,* lawyers Alan Shore and Denny Crane often discuss their close friendship, on *The Newsroom,* colleagues Will McEvoy and Mackenzie Hale get married, and in *Downton Abbey* (2010–present), the ties between the upstairs landowners and downstairs servants are as dependent and intertwined as any family on television. Finally, dramas set in the past offer a 21st-century viewpoint on what work and family were like in earlier time periods. *Downton Abbey* follows the changing circumstances of an aristocratic British family, and their servants, in the early 1900s. *Mad Men* (2007–2015) provides insight into the 1960s culture in its ad agency drama, *Halt and Catch Fire* (2014–present) explores the origins of the personal computer revolution in the 1980s, and *The Knick* (2014–present) takes place in an early twentieth century New York hospital.

The essays in this chapter highlight several television dramas where elements of home and work inform the uniqueness of 21st-century storytelling. On the home front, "*Friday Night Lights*' Mothers and Daughters" discusses how the show endorses the nuclear family through its portrayals of four mother–daughter pairs, whereas "*Big Love*'s New Family Values" suggests that what defines a family is more complex than it may first appear. Television law offices have always engaged viewers with legal issues of the time, and "The Good 21st Century Television Drama" explores how *The Good Wife* presents legal cases in a landscape informed by current events and contemporary cultural discussions. A Side Note offers commentary on *The Good Wife*'s shooting death of the lead character Will Gardner and, finally, "*The Newsroom*'s Assessment of New Media" looks at how *The Newsroom,* set in the recent past, depicts the impact 21st-century technology has had on news gathering and reporting.

Friday Night Lights' Mothers and Daughters

Set in the fictional football-focused town of Dillon, Texas, the critically acclaimed *Friday Night Lights* (2006–2011) depicts drama on and off a high school football field in a middle-class community. This exploration comes through narratives that follow Coach Eric Taylor and his family, football team members and their families, high school students, and community members. Although there is plenty of football on *Friday Night Lights*, and interactions between Coach Taylor and his players comprise some of the show's most powerful scenes, the drama also integrates issues related to race, school funding, socioeconomics, personal agency, and parenting into its storytelling. Life in Dillon is understood through different types of character relationships, between family members, football players, peers, and the community. Relationships between mothers and daughters, however, hold a particular place in the story lines of *Friday Night Lights,* offering unique insight into some aspects of 21st-century homelife.

In U.S. culture, adolescence is a time of transition between childhood and adulthood. As such, it is marked as a period of significant change, rebellion, testing of limits, engaging in risky behaviors, and exploring one's sexuality. During this time, teens also begin to form their identities by questioning who they are, determining how they differ from their parents, and experimenting with different behaviors and appearances.[10] The relationship between mothers and teenage daughters, in particular, during this period can be trying. During adolescence, teenage girls want to maintain a close relationship with their mothers, while also breaking away to gain their own freedom. A push and pull dynamic can occur: when daughters push their mothers away in a quest for independence, hurt mothers may react by reining in their daughters too much. The result can be a tumultuous relationship comprised of both tremendous closeness and emotional conflict.[11]

Generation Me author Jean Twenge points out that today's teens, called "millennials," tend to be raised by involved parents (sometimes called helicopter parents) who try to share common interests and activities with their children.[12] As a result, this generation of mothers and teenage daughters may be characterized differently than the generations preceding them. Mothers (and fathers) are described as loving and engaged with their kids but over involved, participating in their children's lives in ways that limit the child's exposure to failure and disappointment. Millennial teenagers and young adults are described as welcoming, accepting of diversity, and engaged in community service. They are also characterized as putting themselves first and unprepared for the realities of work.[13] Some label them "the entitlement generation"—a group of young adults unprepared for the realities of life, accustomed to instant gratification, and tend to prioritize fun over work.[14]

Dramatic narratives focused on the home often explore mother and teenage daughter relationships during these periods of adolescent growth.

Such programs as *Gilmore Girls* (2001–2007), *Parenthood* (2010–2015), and *Six Feet Under* (2001–2005) contain well-developed mother and teenage daughter story lines, providing examples of how television narratives reflect those relationships in the current generation. On *Friday Night Lights*, viewers are introduced to four mother and teenage daughter pairs. The first is Pam and Lyla Garrity. Lyla is the oldest of three Garrity children, and viewers see very little of her relationship with her mother. Initially a nuclear family, the structure changes after Pam's husband, Buddy, has an affair. Pam Garrity eventually moves out and marries another man. Viewers see more of the mother–daughter dynamics between Angela and Tyra Collette. Angela is a single mother of two girls: Tyra, a Dillon high school student, and her sister Mindy, who works in a strip club. Tyra engages in a number of risky teenage behaviors, but this changes as she matures. Angela is presented as a relatively immature, fun-loving woman who makes poor choices in the men with whom she keeps company. When Angela is first introduced, she is dating an abusive man and it is Tyra who both defends her mother from his violent actions and issues an ultimatum that her mother has to stop seeing him or she will move out. Later, Angela has an affair with the married Buddy Garrity. Although she changes a bit over the show's run, Angela remains a character who is primarily concerned with having fun.

In season four, viewers meet Cheryl and Becky Sproles. Cheryl is a single mother who works in a bar and appears dissatisfied with her life. She does not have a positive relationship with Becky's father who is rarely involved in Becky's life. Viewers see her occasionally helping Becky with her beauty queen aspirations, but she does not always follow through on her commitments. As a mother, Cheryl is not depicted as nurturing and rarely displays affection, in either word or action. This is especially evident during a story line about Becky's unintended pregnancy, where her love and wishes for the future for her pregnant daughter come out in emotional, angry expressions.

The last mother–daughter pair consists of two of the show's main characters, Tami and Julie Taylor. Tami is happily married to Coach Eric Taylor and the Taylor family also has a little girl, Grace, born at the end of season one. Julie is younger than most of the teenagers featured as main characters and conflicts with her mom often have to do with the limits around what she can and cannot do. Because Tami and Julie Taylor are both main characters on *Friday Night Lights*, their individual lives and their relationship are regularly featured, and more of their conflicts are central to the show's narrative.

None of the four mother–daughter pairs mirrors the definition of the coddling parent and entitled teenager characterized in descriptions of 21st-century families. Life in small town Texas does not come with the same advantages as more affluent and college-educated communities. As a result, the mothering on the series does not suggest that these mothers want, or expect, their daughters to have a stress-free success and fun-filled teenage experience. The show implies the opposite, in fact, suggesting that the mothers expect their teenage daughters to learn that life can be challenging and unfair. Furthermore, the young women are not strangers to hard work, the realities of life, or economic hardship. Even Julie and Lyla, the girls from middle-class families, are not characteristic of the typical millennial because, even though they are not personally faced with the same type of economic challenges as Tyra and Becky, they do not present themselves as young women entitled to the best life has to offer. In many ways, *Friday Night Lights* supports the argument that discussions of the millennial teenager focus too much on the advantaged middle class, ignoring the fact that the middle class is shrinking, whereas those living at or below the poverty level are increasing.[15] Although not all families on *Friday Night Lights* live at the poverty level, the series requires viewers to consider the millennials who did not grow up with the benefit of an expendable family income and access to a variety of enrichment opportunities.

At the same time, however, the positive presentations of Tami as a mother, Julie as a daughter, and their mother–daughter relationship reflect an updated version of the nuclear, somewhat conservative, family. In fact, when looking at Tami and Julie in comparison to the other mother and daughter relationships on *Friday Night Lights*, it becomes evident that the show presents the nuclear family model as yielding the most stable mother–daughter relationship. This suggestion stands in contrast to a variety of successful family models that permeate the current cultural landscape, as well as the fact that the U.S. family is no longer predominately a nuclear one.[16]

The mother–daughter relationship between Tami and Julie stands out not only because they are main characters and more plot is dedicated to them but also because of how their relationship is portrayed. Tami is presented as a loving, engaged mother whose parenting style is to impose limits and talk through issues. The conversations the two engage in within the mother–daughter framework are perhaps the most defining feature of how their relationship is presented. In contrast to the relatively absent, immature, and aggressive conversations between Lyla and Pam, Tyra and

Angela, and Becky and Cheryl, interactions between Tami and Julie Taylor are detailed, display a range of emotional tones, and might be considered models for viewers who are also mothers of teenage girls.

In many instances, Tami and Julie are seen yelling at each other, a visual representation of the "intense" nature of the relationship between a mother and teenage daughter. Yet, conversations between Tami and Julie also model ways for a parent to approach sensitive topics with their teenager. It is clear that Tami is committed to understanding what is going on in Julie's life and is repeatedly shown asking such questions as "Is there anything you'd like to share with me?" In addition, Tami is always encouraging Julie in ways that convey her love and understanding that parts of growing up are difficult. For example, after a fight that takes place during preparations for Grace's christening, Tami tells Julie that when Grace was born she thought: "she is the luckiest girl in the world because she has Julie as her older sister" and continues by saying to Julie "You are the most special person."[17] When Tami discovers Julie and her boyfriend are having sex, she is upset but talks to her daughter. Tami begins by asking Julie whether she loves Matt and whether they are using birth control and includes advice that implies acceptance, although not endorsement, of Julie's decision. This conversation is frequently referenced as an excellent model for discussing sex with teenagers because it hits on important key points: emphasis on birth control and Julie's right to say no.[18]

Tami's conversations also extend beyond those she has with her daughter, further highlighting Tami's talents in talking with teenage girls. At different points throughout the show's run, Tami engages in conversations with Lyla, Tyra, and Becky, often providing support and guidance where the girls' mothers do not. Tami's conversations with these teenage girls who are not her daughters function in two ways: first, they highlight what a positive influence Tami is and, second, they suggest that the girls' mothers' approaches are not sufficient. It is the guidance counselor Tami, for example, who initiates the push for Lyla to consider a future that is best for her rather than one tied to her boyfriend. It is also Tami who includes Tyra in family dinners and engages her in conversations about school, her future, and social relationships in ways that her own mother does not. For example, in season two, Tyra is unsure how to act with a boy she does not really want to date, but who she does not want dating anyone else either. She asks both her mother and Tami for advice about what to do. In her response, Tami acknowledges that it feels good to have someone interested in you, but the fair thing to do is to "let him go." In comparison, Angela confesses to enjoying "the chase" and "competition" involved in competing for the affection of one guy. Whereas both

Tami and Angela provide examples from their own lives that suggest they understand what Tyra is feeling, Tami's response is clearly the more mature and offers the best guidance regarding how Tyra should proceed.[19]

A striking contrast between Tami's calm, mature, supportive style and other approaches takes place in season four when Becky finds out she is pregnant. Given Becky's distress, Tim Riggins, Becky's friend who is renting her mother's trailer, brings Becky to talk through the issue with Tami, someone Becky does not know but whom, after a minute in Tami's kitchen, feels comfortable talking to. During the conversation, Tami listens, offers to direct Becky to a number of resources, and emphasizes that Becky needs to talk to her mother. When Becky tells Cheryl, she reacts angrily and assures Becky that she will help her get an abortion. After the screening visit at the abortion clinic, Becky emotionally apologizes to her mother. Cheryl grabs Becky by her arms and yells at her that she has nothing to be sorry for and that "it's going to be okay!"[20] Although Cheryl is clearly supportive of Becky's decision, her way of displaying it is through anger. This kind of support is not the nurturing Becky needs and she ends up back in Tami's kitchen where she processes the situation, at times wondering whether she should continue the pregnancy. In this conversation, Tami is sympathetic and calm, allowing Becky to talk and cry. In part, because of her mother's urging and, in part, because of her understanding of how difficult it would be to raise a baby, Becky ends up choosing to have an abortion. Her mother takes her to the clinic.

Although both women are supportive of Becky's decision to end her pregnancy, Tami's supportive approach is depicted as preferable. Her calm nature and clear concern about Becky's well-being contrast sharply with Cheryl's loudly voiced assurances that everything will be okay. Admittedly, Tami is a counselor and such training gives her an advantage in these types of exchanges. However, such conversations also highlight the lack of support Becky and Tyra are unable to get from their own mothers and suggest that it is because of their respective homelives. In particular, as single mothers, Angela and Cheryl are depicted as not as engaged with their daughter's lives as Tami is with Julie. Angela is often seen drinking and acting irresponsibly and Cheryl repeatedly fails to be there to take Becky places after she committed to do so. In contrast, Tami's homelife is depicted as warm, welcoming, and full of conversation. The family eats dinner together and talks through their problems.

This is not to suggest that Pam, Angela, and Cheryl do not love their daughters and are "bad" mothers. The program does not resort to such simple characterizations. Yet, *Friday Night Lights* portrays their love and dedication differently. For example, in a rebellious gesture, Angela and

Tyra crash the school's daddy and daughter dance and Cheryl tries to protect Becky from getting hurt by her usually absent father by saying unkind things about him. In addition, there are moments where Pam, Angela, and Cheryl vocally encourage and support their daughters. In an emotional speech, Angela reassures Tyra that she has the ability to be who she wants to be, saying: "you are going to get everything you are reaching for."[21] And although it is overshadowed by her aggressively displayed emotion, Cheryl clearly supports Becky's choice to have an abortion because she wants her daughter to have more choices in her future than she did. These types of exchanges, however, are the exception rather than the rule, and character development around Pam, Angela, and Cheryl as mothers falls along the lines of their respective personal situations— usually connected to a romantic relationship—rather than their interactions with their daughters. For example, Cheryl's unsuccessful attempt to sleep with a recent high school graduate Tim Riggins, and his resulting eviction from her property after she mistakenly believes he is sleeping with her daughter, gets more attention than supportive interactions with her daughter during a time when she is recovering from an abortion. Although it is important for mothers to not solely be seen in parental roles, the ways *Friday Night Lights* presents Pam, Angela, and Cheryl reflect negatively on their character and draw attention to confessed instability in their personal lives. The show connects single motherhood, in particular, to instability and poor parenting choices. In comparison, when Tami is shown outside of her mother's role, she is seen as a supportive wife, an accomplished career woman, and member of a stable, loving family.

The strength of the mother–daughter relationship between Tami and Julie, Tami's awareness of what is happening in Julie's life, and Julie's respect for her parents take place in a traditional nuclear family. The other mother–daughter relationships on the show, based on what we see of them, do not suggest similar types of close relationships nor involved parenting. As single and remarried mothers, Angela, Cheryl, and Pam have relationships with their daughters that are not displayed as overly successful.* This is not a new trend. On its situation comedies and dramas, television has portrayed the family in its various forms throughout

---

*Interestingly, *Friday Night Lights* provides more positive portrayals of single mothers of sons. For example, in the first three seasons, football star Smash Williams's mother is portrayed as a medical worker who prioritizes her children and emphasizes the value of going to college. She is not depicted as unhappy, emotionally unavailable, or in search of romance. In addition, when Matt Saracen's mother reenters his life, she assists him in the care of his aging grandmother. She works as a hairdresser, and similarly is not depicted as unhappy, emotionally unavailable, or in search of romance.

the decades. Research has shown that, generally, televised family portrayals reflect real-world family trends and lifestyles but, overall, television narratives are more apt to "reinforce traditional models of family rather than to promote nonconventional configurations."[22] Research also shows that, through its narratives, television promotes traditional family models, in which the structure is nuclear (parents and dependent children living in the same household) and the father takes on a dominant, decision-making role, whereas the mother fulfills a more dependent and expressive, emotional role.[23] When parent–child conflict occurs in these traditional family models, the mothers display "expressive behaviors,"[24] talking through the conflict, being empathetic, and working to resolve the issues. In these television families, the solving of conflicts in this manner works well, thus reinforcing the preference of the traditional family model.

The portrayal of Tami and Julie Taylor reflects this television trend. In their nuclear family, the mothering role Tami embodies is one of empathy, understanding, and concern for her daughter's well-being. The same level of expressive behaviors does not take place between the other mother and daughter pairs who represent "nonconventional configurations" of families. In its adherence to the nuclear family as the best model, there are missed opportunities to engage audiences in acknowledging that other family configurations can work well, even during times of hardship. However, in its implicit dismissal of characterizations of the millennial teenager and her parents, *Friday Night Lights* provides viewers with other ways to consider the current generation of teenage daughters and their mothers.

Big Love's New Family Values

On March 12, 2006, readers of the *New York Times* may have been confused to see three side-by-side wedding announcements featuring the same man, Bill Henrickson, and three different women: Barbara Dutton, Nicolette Grant, and Margene Heffman. Each announcement, which included a short narrative about the bride and groom along with a photo of each happy couple, ended with the sentence: "The wedding will take place tonight at 10 pm, only on HBO."[25] Far from the traditional definition of marriage as between one man and one woman, the announcements evoked the Mormon practice of polygamy, or plural marriage, in which a man considers himself married to more than one woman at the same time. In fact, the HBO series being promoted by the announcements, *Big Love* (2006–2011), would turn out to depict a polygamous family. In doing so, the show engaged with early 21st-century questions about family and marriage.

The early 2000s were marked by political discourse that depended heavily on conservative ideas about social issues. As *Big Love* cocreator Will Scheffer puts it in an interview: "it was at a time at which the Republican majority was . . . really owning the idea of family values."[26] Cocreator and life partner, Mark Olsen, elaborated, explaining the origins of the idea for the series: "It was shortly after Bush's inauguration, and I became somewhat offended at some of the excesses of that dialogue, particularly notions of what is a family, what isn't a family, what is a marriage, what isn't a marriage, what society chooses to value in both arenas, and this [*Big Love*] was sort of our response to it."[27] A key topic in the family values debate of the time centered around the legality of gay marriage that, three years before *Big Love* aired, had been recognized as legal by the Massachusetts Supreme Judicial Court. Just as same-sex weddings began to be performed in Massachusetts in 2004, however, 13 states adopted constitutional amendments that banned same-sex unions. The 1996 Defense of Marriage Act—which explicitly states "the word 'marriage' means only a legal union between one man and one woman as husband and wife, and the word 'spouse' refers only to a person of the opposite sex who is a husband or a wife"—was frequently invoked by family values proponents as necessary to protect the institution of traditional marriage.[28]

Big Love premiered in the midst of this debate. The show follows the Henrickson family consisting of husband and father, Bill Henrickson, along with his first and legal wife, Barb, his second wife, Nicki, his third wife, Margene, and the combined seven children from these marriages. Viewed from the outside, Bill and Barb Henrickson look like a typical American couple—owners of a family business somewhat ironically called Home Plus, parents of three children, and residents of a Utah subdivision. This normalcy is reflected throughout the series when the camera pans the street where the Henricksons live. There are three adjacent houses connected only by the lawn and sidewalks in front of them. When the camera turns its view to the back of those same homes, however, it becomes clear that they share a fenced-in yard that joins all three houses—one for each of Bill's three wives and their respective children. The homes, in short, reflect the public and private faces of the entire Henrickson family: publicly separate and traditional, privately practicing the illegal polygamous lifestyle.

At first glance, *Big Love* seems to ask its viewers to consider whether the practice of polygamy is an acceptable, if not fully understandable, domestic arrangement. The depiction of the Henrickson's plural marriage is certainly unique and curious, and the first season takes time to help viewers understand the basic tenets of polygamy, as well as the divisions within the Mormon Church around the practice. Officially ended by the Mormon Church in 1890 as part of Utah's bid to become a state, polygamy has lived on in such fringe sects of the religion as the Fundamentalist Church of Jesus Christ of Latter-Day Saints (FLDS). These off-shoots of mainstream Mormonism are unrecognized by the main Church of Latter-Day Saints (LDS) and live in secluded communities where men can have dozens of, and in some instances more than a 100, wives. Only the first marriage is legal, the others are recognized as spiritual unions.[29] For instance, on *Big Love*, Bill and his second wife, Nicki, were raised in a polygamous FLDS-inspired compound known as Juniper Creek, under the leadership of the prophet Roman Grant. Nicki and Bill are sealed—they are not legally recognized as married and Nicki cannot say she is Bill's wife in virtually any setting outside of the home or in the company of a few close friends. In contrast, first wife, Barb, grew up in a traditional LDS Church, a religion she is now estranged from because of her polygamous lifestyle. She and Bill are legally married and she performs the functions of his wife in the public sphere.

The series does much more than portray this unique family structure and its variants, however. From the characters and story lines to the creators' clearly stated intentions, *Big Love* asks viewers to rethink conventional understandings of what makes a marriage, and what makes a family, in the 21st century. One way it does this is to align polygamy with gay marriage. The placement of the mock wedding announcement in *The New York Times*, for example, intentionally evoked the newspaper's progressive stance toward gay unions: in 2002, *The Times* began printing the announcements of gay union ceremonies, despite the fact that gay marriage was still not recognized legally in the United States. In doing so, before it was even aired, *Big Love* linked its representation of nontraditional families with the national debate over same-sex marriage, the definition of marriage, and new ideas about family.

More explicitly, in the third episode of season one, the Juniper Creek prophet, Roman Grant, argues for the legalization of polygamy by drawing a comparison to gay marriage. "Ah, the gays," he states to a reporter who is interviewing him. "If the Supreme Court says yes to the privacy rights of homosexual persons, surely, it's time to recognize our [polygamists] rights to live in peace too." Later in the episode, one of Roman's wives holds up the newspaper in which the resulting article is printed so that the camera, and therefore the viewers, can see the headline that reads: "Roman Grant, Prophet and Patriarch of Juniper Creek home to the second largest polygamous sect in Utah says, 'We're just like homosexuals'."[30]

The deliberately drawn parallel, played somewhat comically by the actors, is important for the show overall: the polygamist Henrickson family can be viewed as stand-ins for such other nontraditional, illegal relationships as those between members of the same sex.

Big Love does not simply argue for the legalization or normalization of nontraditional marriages, however. Stanley Kurtz explains: "The goal is not to adapt couples to an already existing institution but, in Scheffer's words, to 'subversively' transform the institution of marriage from within. So by highlighting the analogy between gay marriage and polygamy, *Big Love* simultaneously builds support for same-sex marriage, while also deconstructing the very notion of monogamous marriage itself."[31] Put another way, the series suggests that, in the 21st century, family is not defined by how a family is structured, but instead by the values a family practicesfor instance love, respect, and commitment, no matter what its structure might be. As series cocreators Olsen and Scheffer state, the show aims to "address our culture war over the family by trying to 'find values of family that are worth celebrating separate of who the people are and how they're doing it'."[32]

When relationships are evaluated not by their structure but by the way people in them are treated and valued, the structures become more or less irrelevant. The polygamous Henricksons, for example, are represented quite differently from the polygamous families of the Juniper Creek compound. The Henricksons "seem very normal indeed, at least in contrast to the world from which they have broken away: Juniper Creek, a grim, fundamentalist compound ruled by the messianic prophet, Roman Grant, with his fourteen wives, thirty-one children, and 187 grandchildren."[33] The Juniper Creek community, its family structure, and corrupt prophet would have been familiar to viewers who had followed the arrest of FLDS prophet Warren Jeffs in 2006 at his massive compound, the Yearning for Zion (YFZ) Ranch, near Eldorado, Texas, where he was alleged to have 78 wives.[34] In the raid that led to Jeffs arrest, more than 400 FLDS children were placed into protective custody and Jeffs was eventually sentenced to life in prison for sexually assaulting girls aged between 12 and 15, whom he considered his brides.[35] In comparison to these real stories, "the [fictional] Henricksons do look like an average suburban family, with average suburban family problems—just more of them."[36] In *Big Love*, it is not polygamy that makes a family good or bad, but the values on which that family bases its actions.

This definition of family is nowhere more apparent than in Bill and Barb's relationship. Originally married only to each other, the couple turned to polygamy at Bill's suggestion in order to bear more children after Barb fell ill with uterine cancer. At one point Barb tells Bill: "I followed you into polygamy, and let me tell you, it was pretty alien from my beliefs. But I did it out of love."[37] What she means is that the form their marriage took was less important than the fact that they love and respect each other.

The series helps viewers begin to understand the way that a family's values might take precedence over family structure in season one's episode, "Affair." Here, Bill and Barb temporarily rekindle their original "one man, one woman" relationship, meeting secretly and reminiscing about the love that originally brought them together. The poignancy of the intimacy they gave up when they entered into polygamy is palpable, yet their "affair" quickly ends when second wife Nicki announces that she feels ready to "bring another soul into the family . . . we've let wordly concerns come before what we are here for, what our purpose is."[38] Doing so is the goal of the Henrickson family unit, and Bill responds: "I am so happy. As your husband, father-to-be, and member of our holy family."[39] Nicki's announcement is a manipulative attempt to "break up" Bill and Barb, illuminating the fact that even this family is not perfect. Yet, her reason for doing so is essentially the well-being of the entire Henrickson family. When Barb responds to Nicky's news by saying "I love you Nicky," it is clear that the Henrickson family values are back in place and take priority over any one person's wish.[40]

The final season of the series confirms that the Henrickson family is successful not because of its untraditional structure but because its members have loved and supported each other over the years, in good times and bad. In the dramatic series finale, Bill is shot and killed by an anti-polygamist neighbor, leaving his three wives to create a life of their own without him. Olsen and Scheffer explain: "we wanted to find that thing which would render his life's existence the most successful. And we felt by far the greatest testimony to Bill would be that he had created a family that endured. And we felt the best way to establish that would be to remove him from the equation via Carl and find out that a year later, two years later, these women are still bound together, are bonded deeply, in something like a family."[41] That family has outlived its polygamous structure because of the family values that ultimately stood at the heart of it.

Big Love connected with early 21st-century questions about family values by suggesting that it is not the structure that defines a family, but the values within that structure. In doing so, Stanley Kurtz writes, the show participates in "the possible collapse of a social taboo—something television is ideally suited to achieve. Social taboos may erode gradually over the very long haul, but up close, and especially toward the beginning, you get little collapse—the quick and unexpected falling away of opposition. What used to be hidden emerges with startling rapidity, because much of it was there all along. Polygamy, and especially polyamory, are already widespread on the Internet. Both practices are pushing toward a major public taboo-collapsing moment . . . *Big Love* has to be getting us there a whole lot quicker then we were."[42]

Such a shift seems to have occurred in the years since *Big Love* first aired. Not only has there been federal legalization of gay marriage but also *Big Love* spawned other television shows depicting the practice of polygamy, including TLC network's reality programs *Sister Wives* (2010–present) and *My Five Wives* (2013–2014), as well as Lifetime's movie about the fundamentalist Mormon leader Warren Jeffs titled *Outlaw Prophet* (2014). Although the portrayals have not always been positive, nor positively received by practicing polygamists, the programs have further engaged viewers in thinking about the 21st-century family. Kody Brown and his four wives, featured in *Sister Wives*, even brought a suit against the state of Utah. By arguing that polygamy is simply a form of cohabitation, because the man is only legally married to one wife and spiritually married to the others, the practice was decriminalized.[43] Even the series' cocreator, Will Scheffer, admits that the series shifted his attitude toward polygamy: "I have definitely reversed some of my initial 'yuck' reaction. We don't really take a pro or con stand on polygamy, but I have to say that I have begun to imagine it as a valid lifestyle and am sympathetic to polygamists in adult relationships with each other. I think it should be decriminalized."[44] Such sentiments tend to gloss over the more complex realities of some polygamous families, including the abusive relationships engaged in by Jeffs and other FLDS leaders. The cultural dialogue that can result, however, from imagining lifestyles and family structures outside of the "norm" may continue to broaden viewers' understanding, and even acceptance, of new definitions of family.

The Good 21st-Century Television Drama

The central point of CBS's television Emmy campaign for the 2013–2014 season of *The Good Wife* was to visually demonstrate that this particular workplace drama delivers 22 episodes a year, a stark contrast to other highly regarded television dramas that do not adhere to the traditional network television production schedule. Netflix's *House of Cards*, for example, had 13 episodes in its season that year, Showtime's *Homeland* had 12, HBO's *Game of Thrones* and *True Detective* had 10 and 8, respectively, and AMC's *Mad Men* had just 7 episodes in a season.[45] Although there has been much discussion of cable, premium cable, and independent studios' ability to create award-winning television, as a network drama, *The Good Wife* competes easily in quality and excels in longevity. Even after seven seasons, *The Good Wife* remains popular among viewers and is highly regarded by television critics. In an echo of the Emmy campaign, *The New Yorker*'s Emily Nussbaum calls it "the smartest drama currently on the air" and emphasizes that showrunners Robert and Michelle King have succeeded within the parameters of network constraints: "Their series debuts every September, on schedule-no year-and-a-half-long hiatuses for them to brood about artistic aims. And on network there are ads, and pressure for product integration, and the expectations of a mass audience (must be clear, must be exciting, must be familiar, must be appealing), and the strict rules implicit in corporate culture—all of which would be difficult even if CBS didn't keep bumping *The Good Wife* back by forty minutes for football."[46] In his positive review, *Time*'s James Poniewozik describes the show as a "morally complex series, dealing with the ethical gymnastics of characters we identify with but can't always completely support."[47] *LA Times* writer Meredith Blake points out *The Good Wife*'s "reputation as the finest one hour series on broadcast television."[48]

Starring a talented ensemble cast led by Julianna Margulies, *The Good Wife* is a legal procedural. It tells the story of Alicia Florrick, an attorney who rejoins the workforce after being embarrassed by Peter, her politician husband, who engaged with a prostitute and has to serve time in jail for political corruption. Alicia is hired at the law firm of Lockhart Gardner and, over the years, advances in her work, becomes a partner, starts her own firm, wins the State's Attorney office, but withdraws and starts another law firm. Along the way, viewers are presented with stories of Alicia's personal and work lives that are intertwined with her husband's who gets out of prison, is elected State's Attorney, and eventually is elected governor. Eventually, the two live apart and pursue their own careers, although they do not divorce.

The show also has a strong and diverse slate of female characters, integrates technology seamlessly, and prompts viewers to think about a range of current events and issues. Many of the plot points reflect central aspects of 21st-century culture, referencing aspects of the contemporary social, economic, and political climate in every season. Although the concept of television narrative content being "ripped from the headlines" is not a new one, *The Good Wife*'s quick integration of news stories and cultural shifts into its layered story lines contributes to it success. A brief look at a few of these elements provides insight as to why *The Good Wife* illustrates aspects of the 21st century so vividly.

At a time when author and Facebook COO Sheryl Sandberg has encouraged women to "lean in" in her book by the same phrase, such younger actors as Emma Watson have declared their support for feminism, *The Good Wife* portrays a range of fully developed female characters of all ages who model what empowerment, and power, can look like at home and work. The oldest of these women is Jackie Florrick, Peter's mother, who has definite ideas about her son, her daughter-in-law, and her grandchildren. Although she often interferes with the family and Peter's work, she is a woman who defines herself in many ways, not just as a mother and grandmother. Diane Lockhart, one of the managing partners and founder of Lockhart Gardner, can be tough and aggressive in her work, but does not lack emotion or empathy. *The Good Wife* is chiefly Alicia's story, and viewers see her work and homelife the most. At the beginning of season one, the 40-something Alicia returns to the workforce after her husband loses his job. She stays in a complicated marriage, engages in (but ultimately ends) an office affair with another lawyer, Will Gardner, at her firm, and pursues a variety of career opportunities. The law office investigators are younger women who have strengths of their own. Kalinda Sharma uses her sexuality and street smarts and cleverness to obtain information, whereas Robyn Burdine, who viewers are introduced to later in the show's run, cleverly uses her seemingly innocent demeanor to achieve the same end. Finally, Alicia's daughter, Grace, is 14 when the show begins and, as she grows up and develops her own identity, her religious beliefs provide an interesting contrast to Alicia's atheism.

The Good Wife's lead and ensemble cast of interesting female characters suggests to viewers what they already know: women's lives involve other women and are complicated, fun, rewarding, and messy, often all at the same time. Although other 21st-century television procedural dramas showcase strong, smart female lead characters—for instance, *The Closer* (2005–2012), *In Plain Sight* (2008–2012), *Scandal* (2012–present), and *How to Get Away with Murder* (2014–present)—the strength of *The Good Wife* is that it demonstrates the diversity of the female experience within such a small sliver of U.S. culture—a wealthy part of Chicago's political and legal scene. This experience involves men as well—as colleagues, adversaries, friends, and lovers—and the men of *The Good Wife* are also complex. What emerges is collaboration between the sexes where stories of women and men working together dramatically unfold and where various elements of their political, sexual, economic, or hierarchical powers collide.

Another way *The Good Wife* represents 21st-century culture is through its pervasive use of technology. Characters rely heavily on their smart phones and tablets. At home, Alicia's children know more about social networking and the Internet than she does. At work, many characters demonstrate their knowledge of, and discuss the potential of, the viral spread of information. These characteristics essentially depict the 21st-century setting of this drama. For example, on a season-three episode titled "Bitcoin for Dummies," a case revolves around whether or not a fellow attorney should be compelled to give up the name of a client who invented Bitcoin.[49] Much of the episode dialogue functions as an instructive summary of what Bitcoin is—a controversial online currency that takes the form of computer code and allows for monetary transactions without bank fees.[50] The show also connects to on-going narratives about a Google-like company called Chum Hum. In a second season episode called "Great Firewall," the plot focuses on Chum Hum's decision to provide the Chinese government with an IP address of a Chinese dissident, nodding to contemporary concerns about Yahoo! and Google sharing similar types of information with China.[51] During the 2013–2014 season, Chum Hum is connected to an examination of National Security Agency (NSA) surveillance tactics. In "Hitting the Fan," discussions of whether or not Internet firms should be taxed, a topic of current events, influence a move Chum Hum's CEO makes to jump ship from Lockhart Gardner to the newly formed Florrick Agos. The show also incorporates an NSA subplot in season five, where the Florrick phones are tapped. The integration of technology on *The Good Wife* is not always serious, however. In her home, Alicia sometimes struggles with her technology not working, something many viewers can relate to, and in the season-five premiere, "Everything is Ending," a professional reports to work at Lockhart Gardner using an avatar robot that roams the halls somewhat comically trying to integrate into the office.

Wired's Clive Thompson argues that *The Good Wife* "offers the deftest portrayal of technology on TV."[52] He supports his argument not only by highlighting episodes that mention Anonymous, Aaron Swartz, and Twitter but also by contrasting the drama to other shows that use technology. He writes: "In most shows, technology is painted as either implausibly super powered ('Wait-enhance the image!') or alarmingly dangerous. Procedurals have been particular offenders. On *Law & Order*, the Internet is mostly just a shadowy place where teens are lured to their death. On *Person of Interest*, government agencies use pervasive surveillance technology to predict malintent [sic] with pinpoint accuracy. *The Good Wife* avoids this Manichaean trap."[53] Similarly, in *Film Quarterly*, Paul

Julian Smith points out how well *The Good Wife* infuses technology into its fictional setting. Smith argues that the "show's true political and personal concerns" are portrayed as "newly complex in a digital world."[54] He claims that the shows' characters use the technology to their benefit while at the same time are affected by others' uses—for better and for worse. Indeed, when a season-six e-mail hack exposes the firm's private e-mails to one another and the public—certainly an allusion to the Sony e-mail hack of 2014—characters are embarrassed and scramble to implement damage control.

It is in this technology-saturated world that a long list of 21st-century narratives connected to current events play out. For example, the show has honed in on aspects of the nation's immigration policy debates in several episodes. In "Mock," Alicia is assigned a case where she defends an undocumented worker who may be deported after several years in the United States. In "Silver Bullet," Peter Florrick is running for State's Attorney and Eli Gold, his manager and chief of staff, has discovered that one of Florrick's opponents employs an undocumented worker as a nanny, a woman who has been in the United States since she was two and is working with a lawyer to get citizenship. In "Next Month," the law case of the week focuses on another undocumented immigrant, a man who, if deported, would be in danger of losing his life to the hands of a Mexican cartel. These episodes give undocumented workers identities and backstories, inviting viewers to consider the complications of how immigration reform may or may not be implemented. Other episodes hone in on the military. Mirroring discussions about using drones to fight in wars, a case in "Whiskey, Tango, Foxtrot" focuses on an officer charged with 12 counts of murder because she fired a drone despite warnings that there were civilians in the vicinity. Given that the officer was under the influence of a prescription drug, that she ignored the warning, and that she never expressed remorse for the deaths of innocents, which included six children, she is found guilty. Another military themed episode, "The Art of War," focuses on a rape case, reflecting the documented systemic problem of sexual assault in the military.

The Good Wife has also used its law office setting to explore racial issues. In "Lifeguard," Alicia discovers that a judge's sentencing patterns fall along race lines, through which minorities are committed to more time in detention than white offenders. In season three, Peter Florrick is the State's Attorney and over several episodes he engages in conflicts with black employees, ultimately resulting in some losing their jobs. At the same time, Peter hires the relatively inexperienced white lawyer Cary Agos in a top position. As *The Atlantic*'s David Sims pointed out: "Peter saw Cary as a good hire, as he indisputably proved to be, but also as a peer in a way that he probably could not have with the office's more experienced black attorneys. Over the span of several episodes, the show did a nuanced job of exploring Peter's bias, which he could never really acknowledge to himself, as a way of examining ingrained white privilege."[55] *The New Yorker*'s Emily Nussbaum described this story arc as "different from other, blunter TV portraits of racism: Peter didn't think of himself as bigoted, but his enemies weren't wrong. It was smart to take on the way that organizations can harbor racism without any individual being overtly hateful."[56] More recently, in season six, *The Good Wife* referenced the police shooting death of Michael Brown in Ferguson, Ohio, which viewers may have connected to the death of Eric Garner on Staten Island, as well.[57] The episode opens with the following statement: "This episode was written and filmed prior to the grand jury decisions in Ferguson and Staten Island. All mentions of 'Ferguson' are in reference to the events in August 2014 after the shooting death of Michael Brown."[58] Titled "The Debate," the episode tracks a news story that breaks on a jury clearing two police officers who have shot and killed a black man in a shopping mall. Citizens begin protesting and the now Governor Peter Florrick connects with religious leaders and later the victim's widow to create a peaceful response. Meanwhile, Alicia and her opponent for State's Attorney, Frank Prady, engage in an unplanned debate about race. During their conversation, an observer points out that Alicia and Frank are two white people deciding what is best for minorities. The exchange is documented by a growing group of observers using cell phones, suggesting that the once private discussion will ultimately be seen by more viewers through social media than would have been watched as a scheduled debate on television.

Finally, the show does not confine itself to narratives about the United States. In addition to the aforementioned episode about Chinese protestors, episodes have connected to the current unrest in the Middle East. "Boom" alludes to reactions to images of the Islamic Prophet Mohammad through a court case involving a teenager who drew a cartoon of the Prophet and the family of an editor who died as a result of a bomb set by an extremist group in reaction to the image. In "Executive Order 13224," Alicia's legal team represented a U.S. translator who was suing the U.S. government because he was tortured after being arrested in Afghanistan. In "Live from Damascus," Lockhart Gardner takes on a class action lawsuit that claims Chum Hum sold and instructed Syria how to use data-mining software, a practice that led to the disappearance and assumed death of U.S. protesters.

The Good Wife is a 21st-century workplace drama that discusses legal issues through its courtroom narratives, while prompting viewers to consider what these cases might suggest about contemporary life. At a time when many of the complicated 21st-century concerns cannot be divorced from the technological climate they take place in, the series uses these factors to its advantage. In addition, given the show's egalitarian themes about gender and power, *The Good Wife* models power struggles, success, and disappointments in a nuanced way.

Side Note: The Death of Will Gardner

When Will Gardner, a main character on CBS's *The Good Wife*, was shot and killed in a courtroom during a season-five episode, the television world reacted with stunned surprise and grief. Much of the program's long-running narratives connected to Will, his relationship with Alicia, and his presence as the third point of the triangle between him, Alicia, and her husband, Peter. At the beginning of *The Good Wife*, Will gives former college friend Alicia—in the midst of marital strife and determined to rebuild a life for herself and her family—a second chance at a career and a job in his law firm. Over time they become lovers until Alicia breaks it off. Eventually, after making partner, Alicia leaves Lockhart Gardner to start her own firm with another colleague. Will is livid and the resulting animosity fuels their interactions as they meet in court and vie for clients. Given Will's central narrative presence on the highly regarded drama, television critics were surprised and fans were stunned at the plot twist of Will's death. What followed was a media frenzy of commentaries, as well as interviews with showrunners Robert and Michelle King, Josh Charles, and other *Good Wife* cast members. NPR's David Bianculli called the narrative turn a "shocker" and pointed out how rare it is for there to be no advance leaks of an upcoming character's demise, something *The Good Wife* was able to pull off.[59]

In *The New York Times* opinion pages, Delia Ephron mourned the loss of the now never to be reunited Will and Alicia. "Personally I think it is extremely selfish for of Josh Charles to move on," writes Ephron. "I don't understand why he doesn't care about me. About my lying in bed every Sunday evening wanting to spend time with him, wishing that one day he and Alicia would get it on one more time. That she will finally get rid of her husband. That, as imperfect as they are, she and Will finally realize they belong together. Doesn't she know that a great show isn't just something you watch? There is ritual, expectations built up over years. Love."[60] Ephron's words register that although she appears to be discussing the relationship between Will and Alicia, she is actually reflecting on her own connection with the drama, feelings to which many fans of the show could relate.

To explain the sudden tragic departure of Will Gardner, *The Good Wife* creators Robert and Michelle King posted a letter to fans on the CBS web site on March 22, 2014, shortly after the episode aired. In it, they first state that actor Josh Charles decided to leave the series and, then, explain they had him murdered because such a significant turn in a long-running show helps to keep "characters fresh."[61] They also write: "Finally, we chose the tragic route for Will's send-off for personal reasons. We've all experienced the sudden death of a loved one in our lives. It's terrifying how a perfectly normal and sunny day can suddenly explode with tragedy. Television, in our opinion, doesn't deal with this enough: the irredeemability of death. Your last time with the loved one will always remain your last time. *The Good Wife* is a show about human behavior and emotion, and death, as sad as unfair as it can be, is a part of the human experience that we want to share."[62]

Death is a staple of 21st-century television. Criminal procedurals deal with death in nearly every episode, superhero series use deaths of loved ones to motivate characters, and noncrime-oriented dramas incorporate fatal plot points because they make good narratives. Yet, on *The Good Wife*, Will died because he was shot. In the 21st century, gun violence is the topic of an ongoing national conversation, as legislators, citizens, and gun lobbyists argue about how to deal with such an emotionally charged issue. The years leading up to this specific episode were punctuated by memories of the shootings at Virginia Tech, Fort Hood, an Aurora, Colorado movie theater, and the Sandy Hook elementary school in Newtown, Connecticut. FBI reports show that there were 160 spree shooting events from 2000 to 2013, a number that has tripled in recent years.[63] Although the compound tragedies of spree shootings dominate headlines, the debate over how to best decrease gun violence in the United States is also informed by statistics that shows 100,000 people on average are shot each year in the United States.[64]

Fans' reactions to television characters' deaths can be powerful and are an explicit acknowledgment of the potential power of the art form of television. In their letter to fans, the Kings refer to the fact that tragedy can take us by surprise. In the context of the 21st century, however, is it really all that surprising that Will Gardner died because he was shot in a courtroom, in a public building? During this episode, viewers see Will's client begin to cycle out of control, then grab a gun from a court officer, and start shooting. The firearm component of the narrative is not controversial. Courtroom officers carry guns. They are licensed to carry guns. There are good reasons why they carry guns. In contrast, the fact that the narrative is not controversial highlights even more the national conversation about guns and gun violence in a different way. By presenting the shooting sequence in the way it does, *The Good Wife* asks viewers to think about the unexpected death of a loved one by a firearm in a way that is divorced from the spree shootings, multiple school shootings, and various accidental gun firings by toddlers that have become part of the fabric of our culture.

The Newsroom's Assessment of New Media

The 21st century has witnessed drastic changes in newsgathering and dissemination. The development and integration of new technologies have changed the way news is communicated. Before the Internet, news was delivered to consumers through channels now called "old media" or "traditional media"—newspapers, magazines, the radio, and television. As Internet technology developed, news production evolved from a one-way system where media gatekeepers—the professional journalists, editors, and producers—determined the news content, to a system where anyone with a computer, mobile device, and an Internet connection can contribute to the creation of news stories. Today, the so-called new media forms—webpages, wiki sites, blog posts, twitter feeds, and social media outlets—are central to the fabric of news production, distribution, and consumption. The Pew Research Center reports that 50 percent of Americans identify online outlets as a main source for news. When looking at online newsgathering by age, the Pew Report reveals that 63 percent of 30–49-year-olds and 71 percent of 18–29-year-olds cite the Internet as a main source for their news.[65] In addition, social media plays an increasingly larger role in how citizens are made aware of news stories and participate in news itself by discussing and sharing stories, images, and videos. Platforms where this is happening include Facebook, YouTube, Twitter, and reddit.[66]

This contemporary news environment challenges long-held beliefs about the division between the news producer and the news consumer. In their analysis of news and the Internet, David Tewksbury and Jason Rittenberg point out that the news consumer has more agency than ever before in terms of news choices. They write: "on the one hand, the dividing line between journalist and citizen is becoming particularly fuzzy, as more people become involved in the creation of news. On the other hand, the current technologies have facilitated a change in the meaning of an audience. . . . Today, the receivers of the news exert substantial control over their news diet. They can choose among numerous outlets, pre-select specific topics and focus their time and attention on the messages they prefer."[67] As citizen journalists become more prominent in this new news culture, traditional journalism has had to adapt. Former journalist and current professor of journalism Janet Kolodzy argues that contemporary journalists must be prepared to practice what she calls "convergence journalism—providing news to people when, where and how they want it using any and all communication tools available."[68] Kolodzy argues that journalists have to use an audience-centric approach, reporting on news stories in ways that locate the audience, accommodate audiences' tendency to multitask, and use tweets, online news summaries, and headlines to capture attention, all while adhering to ethical journalistic practice.[69]

Ethical journalistic practice has been discussed widely as news professionals and citizens witness the shifting news environment. The Society of Professional Journalists revised its code of ethics in September 2014 to better articulate ethical guidelines in today's converged journalism culture. According to one reviewer, the new code "seems to more firmly establish ethical decision-making as the responsibility of the individual journalist, recognizing the less-defined nature of employment in news media today."[70] In addition, in a fast paced, technological environment where the immediacy of reporting is privileged, new concerns about plagiarism and copyright infringement have emerged.[71]

It is against this backdrop that HBO's workplace drama *The Newsroom* debuted in 2012. Created by Aaron Sorkin, whose previous television shows *Sports Night* (1998–2000), *The West Wing* (1999–2006), and *Studio 60 on the Sunset Strip* (2006–2007), all focus on the collegial relationships, friendships, and romantic partnerships that occur in the workplace setting, *The Newsroom* takes place at a fictional cable news station named Atlantis Cable News, or ACN. The hook of *The Newsroom* is that episodes take place in the recent past, and ACN fictionally reports on real news viewers would have been familiar with from the past few years. For example, in the premiere episode, the news team reports on the April 20, 2010, Deep Horizon—better known as BP—oil spill. Other episodes cover the shooting of congress member Gabrielle Giffords, the labor protests in Madison, Wisconsin, the capture and kill of Osama bin Laden, the attack on the U.S. consulate in Benghazi, and the Boston Marathon bombing. In addition, characters on the show cover the Romney presidential campaign and the 2008 election night, discuss current national financial woes, and interact with federal whistleblowers.

Central to the way *The Newsroom* retells these stories are debates about what journalism is or should be, especially given how the landscape of journalism has changed so radically. In this context, *The Newsroom* explores the question of appropriate journalism practice at a time when ACN, like real news organizations across the country, is struggling financially and trying to maintain a viewing audience. The power players—director of the news division Charlie Skinner, lead anchor Will McAvoy, and news producer MacKenzie (Mac) McHale—constantly debate what news should ideally be in the context of station owners concerned with how they are going to pay for the news because the ratings are low. The struggle for quality journalism is also contrasted against elements of a celebrity-driven information climate. For example, the news team has to advocate for broadcasting a political debate while defending their choice not to report on a tabloid news story, a decision that results in a ratings decline. Other episodes point to the power of gossip columnists and the popular TMI (a not so subtle reference to TMZ) outlet. The tension between confirming information properly, while breaking stories quickly, is reflected in an episode titled "I'll Try to Fix You" where the team covers the serious, but ultimately nonfatal, shooting of congress member Gabrielle Giffords and refuses to announce her death because it has not been confirmed. Here, *The Newsroom*'s lesson to viewers is that when journalists do not independently confirm information, serious mistakes can be made. As many know, Gifford's death was in fact wrongly reported by prominent news media organizations at the time.

Appropriate journalism practice on *The Newsroom* is also framed against errors in reporting—most notably in season two when a narrative arc explores the possible use of sarin gas during a military operation titled Operation Genoa. Although ACN ultimately broadcasts the story, the debate over whether to air it given the limited information the reporters can confirm provides viewers with an opportunity to apply journalism ethics. Eventually, the story is revealed as false and viewers see that one of the reporters has manipulated footage to get the green light to air the story. The reporter is fired and the top newsmakers offer their resignations, modeling how important it is that the director of any news division, as well as the producer and the lead news anchor, takes responsibility for the news content no matter what the circumstances.

A good part of the series' instruction about good journalistic practices relies on descriptions of the potentially corruptive nature of new media. Although the narratives emphasize the value of responsible journalism, and what can happen when one is reckless, *The Newsroom* often functions as a chief critic of new media while modeling what it deems appropriate ways to use it. The most technologically savvy character on the show, Neil, is a staffer who maintains the ACN Wikipedia page, writes

Will's blog, and monitors the Internet. He also explains to his colleagues how components of technology work and brings the news team up to date on how new media is being used. One example takes place in a season-one episode titled "Amen" when Neil identifies an Egyptian citizen journalist, known as "Amen" on his prolific YouTube videos and tweets, who is able to report on his country's uprising with more access and detail than the dispatched ACN reporter. This episode not only refers to the well-documented use of social media by Egyptian citizens at this time but also acknowledges the potential value of citizen journalists. The ACN team, however, only agrees to use Amen's information if he agrees to state his full name in his reports. The mandate underscores what is traditionally expected to ensure credibility of reporting, but the policy causes tension in the newsroom in a later episode. Similarly, trust in citizen reports on Twitter is thin when the news of the Boston Marathon bombing begins to break in the season-three premiere. Although reporter Hallie points to multiple tweets about what is happening at the marathon finish line, news producer Mac refuses to use the information as evidence that the Boston bombing actually took place. After reading the tweets out loud, Hallie says to Mac, "This isn't speculative anymore," to which Mac replies, "We're not going based on tweets from witnesses we can't talk to. What credible news agency would do that?"[72]

The series also suggests how new media can bring stress to personal lives. In "First Thing We Do, Let's Kill All the Lawyers," a video of reporter Maggie emotionally sharing her feelings for Jim, a colleague and not the man she is romantically involved with, is posted for all to see on YouTube. In "News Night with Will McAvoy," an ex-boyfriend leaks nude photos of financial reporter Sloan Sabbath online. In "Oh Shenandoah," perhaps one of the most polarizing and controversial episodes of the series, a story line focuses on a college woman who creates a web site where other women can name men who raped them. Several critics blasted the show's implied assertion that it was more "moral" to challenge the coed's agency in launching her web site than it was to report on the web site's function of allowing women to identify their attackers. By privileging the producer's opposition to such a website because it does not jive with his belief that naming accused rapists was fair, *The Newsroom* further challenged the uses of new media.

Another way new media is contested emerges through the relationship between reporters Jim Harper and Hallie Shea. Jim first meets Hallie when he begins covering the Romney presidential campaign in season two. Eventually, the pair begins dating and simmering arguments ensue about the merits of new media reporting. This all comes to an emotional breaking point in season three when Jim is bothered by Hallie's new job at Carnivore, a thinly veiled reference to Gawker, because her contract gives her bonuses for high number of page views. Although television ratings are important in Jim's business and inform much of the tension between the ACN owners and the news director, Jim sees the emphasis on page views as unethical encouragement to write material that is deliberately provocative to cultivate readers. This detail is just one of the objections Jim has with the type of writing Hallie does and they fight over the meaning of journalism, ultimately ending their relationship after Hallie writes a blog about the struggles of being a "new media girl" who is dating an "old media guy."

In season three, the new owner of ACN, billionaire Lucas Pruit, outlines a vision for the station that infuriates the current leadership. Pruit is a quirky character who makes such observations as "Books are like the new art. We don't need them anymore but they look nice."[73] He tells Charlie Skinner that his goal is to get 18- to 25-year-olds to watch the news "so it doesn't die when you do."[74] Pruit's vision of what news can be is best illustrated by this heated exchange between him and Skinner at a social function shortly before Pruit takes over the company.

> Pruit: The news gathering on newscasts will have tentacles on every reach of the Internet—interactives, podcasts, live streams, tumblr, facebook, Twitter. We'll make our audience reporters in the field through Instagram and Vine, Snapchat and blogs. You still with me? Our users become the audience and our audience becomes contributors. That's my plan.
>
> Skinner: Needless to say I'm impressed by your indifference to talent, experience and credentials. And I assume the absence of the words truth, trust and professionalism in your mission statement was an oversight. Your contempt for the second rate seems to be a contradiction too since you believe the best reporting is done by anyone with a phone and the time it takes to write Epic Fail. And as an old guy I have a lot more respect for 18–25-year-olds than you do because I don't believe their heads will explode if you stop patronizing them for an hour a night and tell them what the fuck's going on in their lives and maybe in the lives of other people.
>
> Pruit: The air up on that pedestal must be pretty thin. 'Cause you are delusional, sir.[75]

Because Pruit is constructed as a polarizing and unlikable character, a thoughtful discussion about how ACN may need to move to a convergence journalism model is absent from the debate. Pruit does not bring to the table a considered strategy of how to use contemporary tools to engage audiences in meaningful ways, practices already implemented in many real newsrooms before 2013 when this episode takes place. Instead, Pruit's vision is positioned as extreme (and uncannily mirrors a similar change in leadership at The New Republic[76]) and furthers *The Newsroom*'s underlying theme that trustworthy journalism is at risk. This is illustrated immediately in the episode following Pruit's takeover when a stalker app is developed and used to track celebrities. After the app's creator, an ACN employee following Pruit's directives, is humiliated on the air, a series of events lead to long-time newsroom leader, Charlie, having a fatal heart attack, suggesting that perhaps new media is killing the old ways of journalism.

Discussions about how to maintain quality journalistic practice are crucial in a culture where information can be distributed incredibly quickly, across multiple platforms, with varying regard for accuracy and authenticity. In fact, global news organizations continually engage in such debates. At a November 2014 journalism conference in Dublin, Ireland, a group of news producers concluded that although social media has altered the way breaking news is disseminated, journalists are not compromising their values. The panel, which included representatives from Time, the BBC, and BuzzFeed, discussed a number of pros and cons related to social media's place in news. For example, in their commentary on authenticity, panelists not only pointed to the inherent value of a photo taken by a citizen journalist at the scene of an event but also pointed out that photographs could be easily falsely attributed to an event.[77] *The Newsroom* demonstrates the potentially problematic nature of immediate information sharing in ways that are thought provoking. However, examples of when new technology assists in journalistic practices are not spotlighted in the same way. Given that the program takes place at a time when great strides have been taken toward maintaining good journalism practices in a new media age, the ACN newsroom feels a bit dated. This is acknowledged by the two most technologysavvy characters on the show. Hallie, when frustrated that the news network will not report on the Boston Marathon bombings despite thousands of tweets on the subject, says to Neil, "Do you guys understand the explosion occurred in the 21st century?" Neil responds by tossing his arms aside and saying, "Welcome to ACN."

CHAPTER 5

Fact and Fiction

Contemporary television dramas have evolved into art forms that provide a space where factual events and real debates in the culture are transformed into narrative fiction. In doing so, these programs offer a space in which 21st-century life can be discussed, wrestled with, and reimagined. So far this book has explored several ways dramatic narratives have developed new forms of storytelling in a converged world, appropriated a post–September 11 zeitgeist, addressed representations of gender, and explored elements of televised family and workplace environments. To keep television shows timely, writers frequently integrate aspects of the changing social, economic, or political climate into their scripts. Sometimes, these choices are made with the intention of prompting viewers to think about the issue at hand. Other times, the connections are less explicit and tap into broader shifts, tensions, or ideas in the culture. Threaded throughout the programs discussed, as well as in many others, are fictionalized portrayals of many other 21st-century issues.

Since 2008, The Television Academy, sponsor of the Emmy Awards, has been bestowing "Television with a Conscience" honors to "television programming that inspires, informs, motivates and even has the power to change lives."[1] In its first year, the Academy recognized *Boston Legal* (2004–2008) for addressing "a number of issues including euthanasia, government sanctioned torture, illegal alien status, race relations, the teaching of "abstinence only" sex education and the marketing of sexually suggestive dolls to young girls among others."[2] Since then, awards have been given to several television dramas including *Transparent*

(2014–present) for increasing transgender awareness, *The Big C* (2010–2013) for its representation of a woman dealing with her terminal cancer diagnosis, *The Newsroom* (2012–2015) for its discussions of journalistic integrity, and *Friday Night Lights* (2006–2011) for its story line about unwanted pregnancy. ABC Family's *The Fosters* (2013–present) has also been recognized for its presentation of same-sex marriage, adoption, foster care, juvenile delinquency, alcoholism, and teen sex in ways that "educate viewers while entertaining them."[3]

The presentation of social issues is frequently complemented by an acknowledgment of the economic or political climate in which the drama is watched. For example, although the contexts were different, *The Wire* (2002–2008) and *Treme* (2010–2013) both weaved timely issues related to race, economics, and law enforcement into their storytelling. Whereas *The Wire* takes place in the struggling city of Baltimore at a time when law enforcement faces new budgetary pressures in the wake of the September 11 terrorist attacks, *Treme* is set in a struggling New Orleans after the devastation of Hurricane Katrina. As citizens engage in protests over such racially charged situations as the fatal police shooting of Michael Brown in Ferguson, Missouri, and others that followed, shows like *The Good Wife* (2009–present) and *Scandal* (2012–present) have included narratives that reflect aspects of these events.[4] The first season of *American Crime* (2015–present) similarly addresses contemporary issues around race, the criminal justice system, and the unforeseen impact of individual choices.

In addition to these examples, other shows reference complicated 21st-century debates. For example, the critically acclaimed, gritty police drama *The Shield* (2002–2008) highlights issues around police brutality and corruption, gang violence, and poverty in Los Angeles. Although *Jane the Virgin* (2014–present) stays away from national debates about immigration reform, the fact that Jane's grandmother is an undocumented immigrant allows the show to highlight the plight of illegal immigrants by educating viewers on medical repatriation, a practice where undocumented immigrants can be sent back to their home country after they receive care in a U.S. hospital, regardless of their living circumstances. *The Guardian*'s Alan Yuhas argues that season three of *The Walking Dead* (2010–present) incorporates issues around gun control, arguing: "*The Walking Dead*'s politics reflect those of moderate Americans: a deep respect for civil rights, coupled with anxieties about keeping the wrong guns off the market, and out of the wrong hands."[5]

Television dramas are also a vehicle for processing concerns about new directions in the culture, particularly around the future of scientific and technological innovations. In both television and film, the science fiction genre has historically envisioned fantastic worlds where humans, machines, and aliens have incredible abilities. Although such 21st-century sci-fi dramas as *Fringe* (2008–2013), *Supernatural* (2005–present), *Extant* (2014–present), and *Battlestar Galactica* (2004–2009) fall into this category, scientific and technological advances comprise the fabric of other drama genres as well. The hospital drama, *House* (2004–2012), features technology as a key component in helping the medical team make complex diagnoses. Some argue that *CSI* (2000–2015) marks a shift in television procedural storytelling because of the show's reliance on technical analysis in its crime solving, in a way that puts humans and computers on equal footing.[6] The popular BBC drama *Orphan Black* (2013–present) uses cloning technology as a narrative hook to present a series of women all cloned from the same DNA in conflict with those hoping to capitalize on this success in genetic engineering.

The essays in this chapter examine how some contemporary television dramas depict, engage with, reinforce, and even challenge issues in the current culture. "Prison Reform and *Orange Is the New Black*" connects elements of a prevailing and quickly changing social concern to the popular Netflix drama. "*Downton Abbey* Economics" examines how the economic structure in 20th-century England might be replicated by the current economic climate in the United States. "Mountaintop Removal Mining in *Justified*" looks at how Kentucky-based *Justified* presents the controversial practice of coal extraction. "Visions of AI" summarizes how several dramas choose to tell stories in a future where artificial intelligence (AI) becomes integrated into everyday life. Finally, two Side Notes, "*Orphan Black*'s Clones" and "*American Crime*," discuss how both series engage with current issues around bioengineering and race relations, respectively.

Prison Reform and *Orange Is the New Black*

In October 2004, lifestyle guru Martha Stewart reported to Federal Prison Camp (FPC) Alderson, a minimum-security prison in West Virginia, to serve a five-month sentence for insider trading. Not surprisingly, given Stewart's celebrity status in U.S. culture, there was widespread curiosity about how she would fare as a white, educated, wealthy woman during her prison term. Was she at risk of assault or violence? Would she get along with other inmates? Where would she sleep? What would she eat?[7] After her release, Stewart spoke about her time in prison stating that she missed "my animals, my homes, fresh food, travel, and the daily challenges of managing an endlessly interesting business."[8] She also spoke out on behalf of the women she met at FPC Alderson. "Ask for reforms," she wrote to her fans in a Christmas 2004 message from prison, "both in sentencing guidelines, the length of incarceration for non-violent first time offenders, and for those involved in drug-taking."[9] In addition to concerns about sentencing, Stewart also commented on how unprepared many inmates are when they get released. "There is no real help," she wrote, "no real program to rehabilitate, no programs to educate, no way to be prepared for life 'out there' where each person will ultimately find herself, many with no skills and no preparation for living."[10]

During the same months Martha Stewart was at FPC Alderson, Piper Kerman, author of *Orange Is the New Black* (2011) and inspiration for the Netflix TV series by the same name, was serving a longer 15-month sentence for money laundering and drug smuggling. Also sent to a minimum-security prison, Kerman began serving 13 of her 15 months at the Federal Correctional Institution (FCI) in Danbury, Connecticut, in 2004. Kerman mentions Stewart's trial, sentencing, and incarceration several times in her memoir, drawing a parallel between the two women who found themselves unexpectedly behind bars. Like Stewart, Kerman also called for prison reform as a result of her time served. Her memoir, which was quickly turned into an Emmy-nominated television drama, was meant to be an "exposure of that world"[11] of prison existence, including "rats in the dorms, mold in the showers, inedible food."[12] Although the television adaptation of the book does not explicitly present itself as a social commentary on prison reform, *Orange Is the New Black* (2013–present) has included plot points about mandatory sentencing, prison conditions, and the impact the War on Drugs has had on the federal prison population generally, and women and minorities specifically, in the United States. In doing so, the show has participated in a wider 21st-century cultural shift in the way Americans think about prisons and those who spend time there.

The Netflix adaptation of *Orange Is the New Black* is based on the life of Piper Kerman, a white, well-to-do young woman who, in 1998, was indicted for drug trafficking and money laundering crimes she committed in the early 1990s while involved with her female lover. Although Kerman pleaded guilty, legal issues prevented her from serving her sentence until 2004 when she reported to FCI Danbury, where she served 13 months of her 15-month sentence. The TV series follows Kerman's fictional namesake, Piper Chapman, and the diverse inmates and prison staff she encounters during her stay. Much of the series is fictionalized, departing completely from Piper Kerman's life. Yet, the depictions of the prison are intentional and realistic, based on Kerman's first-hand experience as well as research done by series creator Jenji Kohan who says she and her staff "dipped ourselves in prison culture and lore and media, and the experience and the people. We really wanted to be as informed as possible."[13] The result is a television drama that is at once entertaining and informative, shedding light on a dysfunctional criminal justice system in need of change.

The legal system that incarcerated Kerman and is depicted in *Orange Is the New Black* was shaped by the late 20th-century War on Drugs. As Kerman describes:

> Guidelines established by Congress in the 1980s required federal judges to impose set sentences for drug crimes, regardless of the specific circumstances of a case, and without discretion to evaluate the person begin sentences. The federal laws have been widely duplicated by state legislatures. The length of the sentences completely freaked me out: ten, twelve, twenty years.[14]

Since 1980, automatic sentencing for drug-related crimes, also known as mandatory minimums, has led to a nearly 900 percent surge in the federal prison population. Close to half of that change was due to individuals incarcerated on drug-related charges. The impact this growth in population has had on the nation's prisons is serious and widespread, including overcrowding, increased cost, decreased oversight of inmates, and corroding facilities.[15] Each of these issues is depicted in *Orange Is the New Black*, from food covered in mold to toilets that back up into the showers. Although the scenes are almost always laced with humor, they have been "treated as one of our only keyholes into the vast and complex workings of American's penal system"[16] and have become a frame of reference for reform. In 2014, the New York Civil Liberties Union used *Orange Is the New Black* "to call attention to conditions at Riverhead jail in Suffolk County, where parts of the second season were filmed. They describe the jail, with its 'floods of human feces' and 'brown drinking water' and 'inescapable growths of thick, black mold,' as 'too horrific for television'."[17] On the NYCLU webpage, members are pictured wearing orange prison jumpsuits and holding signs that read: "Humanity is the New Black." A statement reads: "We wear orange to demand some humanity for the people inside a jail where scenes from Netflix' Orange Is the New Black was filmed. If you thought what happened in the second season of the show was gross and inhumane, just wait until you find out about what really happens. SPOILER ALERT: It's much worse."[18]

Although prisons in general have suffered poor conditions and over-crowding as the number of Americans imprisoned has increased, *Orange Is the New Black* is about female inmates, a population especially affected by the War on Drugs and mandatory minimum sentences. According to The Sentencing Project:

> Within the prison population, women have been affected more so than men by drug law enforcement. Given that women are typically a small percentage of people who commit violent crimes, their numbers in prison historically were quite low. But as drug law enforcement accelerated rapidly beginning in the 1980s, women became much more likely to be convicted of a felony or sentenced to prison than in previous eras. By 2011, 25.1% of women in state prisons were incarcerated for a drug offense, compared to 16.2% of men.[19]

Female inmates have been additionally impacted by a corollary to the War on Drugs, late 20th-century welfare reform. In 1996, President Clinton signed the Personal Responsibility and Work Opportunity Reconciliation Act (PRWORA), the legislation that included denial of Temporary Assistance for Needy Families (TANF) and Supplemental Nutrition Assistance Program (SNAP) to anyone convicted of felony drug charges. The lifetime ban applied only to those individuals who had committed drug crimes—as opposed to other violent crimes—and especially affected women who apply for benefits in higher numbers than men and frequently need to support children through such forms of assistance.[20]

Women of color are also highly affected by the PRWORA because the majority of women imprisoned for drug-related offenses are black and Hispanic.[21] The impact on African Americans has been so extreme that author Michelle Alexander, in a 2010 *New York Times* best-selling book *The New Jim Crow: Mass Incarceration in the Age of Colorblindness*, claims that the War on Drugs and other late 20th-century legislation including PRWORA have "devastated black America" not only by the high number of blacks incarcerated but also by the high likelihood that they will fall "into permanent second-class citizenship after they get out . . . [due to] the extent of the lifelong exclusion many offenders face, including job discrimination, elimination from juries and voter rolls, and even disqualification from food stamps, public housing and student loans."[22] Alexander claims the laws have reversed strides in equality made by the Civil Rights Movement.

Orange Is the New Black incorporates such challenges into both seasons one and two of the series. In season one, episode eight, Taystee, an

African American woman who has spent most of her life in the prison system and worked for a drug dealer named Vee, is granted parole. Unable to build a life for herself outside of prison, however, by the 12th episode she has committed a crime and is rearrested, returning to Litchfield. In an exchange with her friend Pousset, she explains what happened:

> Pousset: So I know you ain't tellin' me in my face right now that you walked back in this place 'cause freedom was inconvenient for you?
>
> Taystee: It ain't like that, P. Minimum wage is some kinda joke. I got part-time workin' at Pizza Hut, and I still owe the prison $900 in fees I gotta pay back. I ain't got no place to stay. I was sleepin' on the floor in my second cousin apartment like a dog, and she still got six people in two rooms. One of the bitches stole my check. I got lice. Everyone I know is poor, in jail, or gone. Don't nobody ask about how my day went. Man, I got fucked up in the head, you know? I know how to play it here. Where to be, and what rules to follow. I got a bed. And I got you.[23]

This exchange, although dramatized, reflects a reality prisoners face on release, a reality that some critics claim the TV series has helped to expose.[24] Being released from prison is one thing, being able to navigate a world with little support, resources, and skills is another and the U.S. prison system does little to bridge this gap.

The second season of *Orange Is the New Black* depicts one approach to helping inmates prepare for life after prison. The season opens with the women of Litchfield participating in a "Mock Job Fair," in which they are told how to dress for job interviews and frame their skills in ways that may make them attractive to future employers. Yet, for many ex-prisoners, there are multiple barriers to building a new life. Most states ask job applicants to declare whether or not they have done time in jail. And although more and more states are signing on to a "Ban the Box" initiative, "which prohibits companies from asking about applicants criminal histories early in the hiring process . . . the lack of rehabilitation programs offered in prison hinders inmates' abilities to prepare for a world outside jail."[25] As one former inmate states, they "don't come out with just prison as a stigma . . . That have other barriers as well—substance abuse, childcare issues, no GED—a lot of times, they just don't have the direction."[26]

Season two draws further attention to prison issues when Piper begins to investigate the misappropriation of funds meant to build a gym for the prisoners. In addition, a new inmate, a young woman by the name of Brook Soso, initiates a hunger strike because there are no vegetarian options at the prison, a somewhat comic scene that nonetheless sets the stage for other forms of resistance among the prisoners. Just as *Orange Is the New Black* has drawn attention to early 21st-century concerns about the criminal justice system, in 2010, government officials began to make changes to sentencing laws. The Fair Sentencing Act, passed by Congress that year, "reduced the sentencing disparity between offenses for crack and powder cocaine from 100:1 to 18:1. . . . because the majority of people arrested for crack offenses are African American, the 100:1 ratio resulted in vast racial disparities in the average length of sentences for comparable offenses."[27] The new guidelines were applied retroactively to individuals already in prison giving "12,000 people—85 percent of whom are African-Americans . . . the opportunity to have their sentences for crack cocaine offenses reviewed by a federal judge and possibly reduced."[28] The bipartisan REDEEM Act, introduced in 2014, aims to help nonviolent adult offenders obtain employment by sealing criminal records and restores access to such benefits as SNAP and TANF for individuals who have served their time for use or possession of drugs.[29] The Smarter Sentencing Act of 2014, although not doing away with mandatory minimum sentences, proposes to reduce "prison costs and populations by creating fairer, less costly minimum terms for nonviolent drug offenders."[30] Season three of *Orange Is the New Black* incorporates elements of these changes into its plot. As one character states in the first episode, "Mother's Day,": "I even hear people are getting out early."[31]

Although policy makers are addressing issues in the prison system, Americans' views of the War on Drug policies have also shifted. A Pew Research Center report released in 2014 found that "67% of people said government should focus more on treating people who use illegal drugs, compared with 26% saying prosecution should be the focus. More than six-in-ten (63%) now say that state moves away from mandatory prison sentences for non-violent drug offenders is a good thing, versus 32% who called it a bad thing."[32] In 1990, by contrast, "73% of Americans favored a mandatory death penalty for 'major drug traffickers', and 57% said police should be allowed to search the houses of 'known drug dealers' without a court order."[33]

Given these figures, *Orange Is the New Black* could not have arrived on television's screens at a more timely moment. Just as Martha Stewart pleaded from prison in 2004 that Americans "ask for reforms," changes in Americans' views of the War on Drugs, along with political support for prison reform, created a receptive culture in which the Netflix series would be viewed. Even the title of the series supports the popular shifts in attitude. In a 2010 interview about *Orange Is the New Black*, Piper Kerman comments on the catchy phrase: the "real reason for the title," she states, "above and beyond being a play on the orange jumpsuit, is the fact that women are the fastest-growing segment of the U.S. prison population."[34] When Brook SoSo proclaims she is "staging a hunger strike in protest of the reprehensible conditions in this facility!"[35] as viewers we cheer on her call for change making, perhaps, prison reform "the new black" in U.S. culture.

Downton Abbey Economics

In February 2014, U.S. economist Lawrence Summers published a column in the *Financial Times* sounding the alarm about income inequality in the United States. "The share of income going to the top 1 per cent of earners has increased sharply," Summers writes. "A rising share of output is going to profits. Real wages are stagnant. Family incomes have not risen as fast as productivity."[36] As former Secretary of the Treasury, it was not surprising that Summers joined the growing conversation around economic inequities. What was unique about the article was its headline: "America Risks Becoming a Downton Abbey Economy."[37] Citing the popular TV drama *Downton Abbey* (2010–present), a series about the aristocratic Crawley family and their servants, who live and work together in the lavish English estate of the series title, Summers immediately translated complex economic ideas into terms most television viewers could understand: Americans are living more like the *Downton Abbey* help, who earn "real wages," than the landowners, who are the "one per cent." The *Downton Abbey* analogy became a new reference point in the discussion of 21st-century economic divisions in the United States.

Downton Abbey, originally produced and aired in Britain in 2010, was released in the United States on PBS in 2011. The first episode is set against the historical backdrop of the Titanic disaster of 1912 and the series follows the characters through World War I into the early 1920s. Boasting beautiful costumes, elaborate period details, and an authentic setting, *Downton Abbey* was nominated for, and won, multiple awards during its five-season run; by season three, it was recognized as the most viewed television drama in the world.[38] In the first episode, the Crawley family, consisting of Lord Grantham and his wealthy American wife, Cora, along with their three grown daughters, learn that Lord Grantham's cousin and his cousin's son—both in line to inherit Downton Abbey upon Lord Grantham's death—have drowned on the Titanic. Their deaths create a dire problem for the Crawleys because, in keeping with inheritance laws of the time, Lord Grantham can only pass Downton Abbey on to a male; his daughters are ineligible to inherit the estate. Complicating the matter, Cora's American-made wealth is what funds Downton Abbey and, should the Estate pass out of the immediate Crawley family, her fortune would also be lost because of a "deed of transference" that locks Cora's money up in the estate.[39] To keep Downton Abbey, and its financial wealth, intact, Lord and Lady Grantham had arranged for their oldest daughter, Mary, to marry the son of the heir. With the death of both the heir and his son on the Titanic, however, a distant male cousin, Matthew Crawley, is brought into the fold as the person most eligible to inherit the estate. When Matthew ultimately marries Mary, who then gives birth to a son, it appears that the Crawleys are set to retain their position in society—both economic and social—for at least the next generation. Yet, "The Inheritance Problem," as one article calls it, continues to drive the characters throughout every season as the Crawleys are faced with continual threats to their family title, estate, and fortune.[40]

Although the Crawleys strategize ways to maintain their upper-class lifestyle, the family's servants, most of who also live at Downton Abbey, are finding their own way through the changing times of the early 20th century. In keeping with the British depiction of those who live "upstairs" (the wealthy) and those who live "downstairs" (the servants), the series portrays much about the relationship between the two groups. On one hand, critics have claimed that part of the show's success comes from the positive portrayal of the relationship between those living upstairs and downstairs at Downton Abbey. "Over and over, the series emphasizes the duty felt by members of nobility to provide jobs," one critic writes. For instance, when Matthew suggests that a butler be let go, Lord Grantham asks him: "Is that quite fair? To deprive a man of his livelihood when he has done nothing wrong?"[41] In another scene, Lord Grantham's mother, the Dowager Countess, remarks that the wealthy have a responsibility to the working classes. "It's our job to provide employment," she says.[42] This apparently positive relationship between the upper and lower classes may have been part of what appealed to viewers of the show that premiered in the midst of the Great Recession. As Matthew Phillips puts it, "in an era when solid, middle-income employment seems ever more at risk, it's no wonder that such paternalistic patter can sound soothing. We can all use a bit of fantasy on a Sunday night before the workweek starts again."[43] Creator Julian Fellowes agrees. "The 'Downton' world 'seems like an ordered world at times,' he says, 'and ours feels like a rather disordered world. This is an era of insecurity, both in a very real sense for a lot of people, economically. Their jobs are either gone or insecure, and they haven't got as much money to spend, which is very tough. And a lot of people are going through that'."[44]

The paternalistic relationship portrayed in much of *Downton Abbey* becomes complicated, however, as the series unfolds. Tensions arise as changing times lead to uncertainty about the order of things at Downton. A politically active Downton chauffeur marries—against all odds and everyone's will—the youngest Crawley daughter and, when she dies, joins the family in Downton to raise their daughter, blurring the lines between upstairs and downstairs. Electricity, telephones, and war come to Downton, along with new attitudes toward those who work for a living. As one critic puts it: "Downton's soap opera characters are wrestling not only with their emotions, but also with basic Downtonomics: the threat and promise of technological change, burden of inheritance taxes, foreign investment, danger of speculation, need for retirement planning, virtue of investing for growth, and inadequacies of the social safety net."[45] Such financial concerns—which permeate the show—have different repercussions for those living upstairs and downstairs at Downton; however, it is these differences that resonate most significantly for the broader U.S. culture.

In 2011, the same year that *Downton Abbey* aired in the United States, the conversation around income inequality became especially public. The Occupy Wall Street movement, which adopted the slogan "We are the 99%" in reference to the economic inequalities between the wealthiest Americans and the rest of the country, made headlines and was reproduced in states and towns across the nation.[46] The same year, Joseph Stiglitz published an article in *Vanity Fair* titled "Of the 1%, by the 1%, for the 1%" claiming that the "top 1%" of Americans "control 40 percent" of the nation's wealth.[47] Also in 2011, President Barack Obama proposed The Buffett Rule, "a nod to billionaire investor Warren Buffett, who has criticized a system that allows the rich to pay a smaller portion of their income in taxes than middle- and working-class Americans because wages are taxed at a higher rate than investment income."[48] The law aimed to increase the tax rate on the country's millionaires. Attention to the growing income inequality was gaining strength.

In 2013, French economist Thomas Piketty's best-selling publication book *Capital in the Twenty-First Century* offered a new perspective on the topic. Referred to as the "50 Shades of Grey of economics books,"[49] *Capital* caused a sensation among economists and noneconomists alike, selling more than 1.5 million copies in a single year and noted as the all-time best-selling book of its U.S. publisher, Harvard University Press.[50]

Economist Paul Krugman summarizes Piketty's argument as follows: "The big idea of *Capital in the Twenty-First Century* is that we haven't just gone back to nineteenth-century levels of income inequality, we're also on a path back to 'patrimonial capitalism,' in which the commanding heights of the economy are controlled not by talented individuals but by family dynasties."[51] The reason for this trend is that the return on financial investments will always be greater than the growth of wages, making it impossible, in the 21st century, for people who make their money through jobs to catch up financially with those who make their money through investments. Data seem to support this claim. CBS news reported, "America is sprouting millionaires faster than any other country . . . But at the same time, the middle and lower classes are falling farther behind."[52] A 2014 Pew Research Center report found that not only was income inequality at its highest since 1928 but also that the United States had more income inequality than the majority of other developed countries and, speaking directly of Piketty's point, wealth inequality was even greater than income inequality.[53]

In other words, the world of *Downton Abbey* is not so distant as it might seem on television. In fact, some economists claim "Downton Abbey is paying homage to economic forces that transcend early 20th-century Britain and apply just as neatly to the 21st-century world."[54] Returning to Summers's warning, the United States risks becoming a "Downton Abbey Economy," in part, because "in economic terms, the United States of 2015 looks very much like Lord Grantham's Britain—except without the tuxedoes."[55] Registering the effectiveness of using *Downton Abbey* as a reference point for a discussion of economics, the series was mentioned in numerous headlines discussing postrecession economics, including "The Financial Crisis Explained, via Downton Abbey";[56] "10 ways 'Downton Abbey' servants had it better than you";[57] "Inequality Worse Now Than on 'Downton Abbey'";[58] and "Eight Things 'Downton Abbey' Can Teach Us about the Modern Economy—A Primer on Downtonomics."[59] Researchers also referred to the show, saying "that the U.S. has become just as unequal as England during the 'Downton Abbey' era a hundred years ago . . . America's richest today get a bigger chunk of the wealth than the likes of Lady Mary and the Earl of Grantham did in 1920s England. And our poor get less of the wealth than Carson the butler."[60] In fact, some economists claim that "Britain's Downton Abbey economy of the 1920s," was slightly "*less* unequal than . . . the U.S. today" (emphasis added)."[61]

Downton Abbey, then, becomes an opportunity to better understand what growing income inequalities might look like. For some, this means looking less sympathetically at the Crawleys and seeing them more akin to the wealthiest Americans who, like Lord Grantham, are "fighting hard to hold on to the 'old ways' that have brought them over 80 percent of the economic benefits generated by our economy over the past decade."[62] In his essay "America's *Downton Abbey* Economy," Terry Connelly sees in the series a more conservative story line, representing the viewpoint of the wealthiest Americans who want to maintain their positions at any cost:

> In the *Downton Abbey* world, the basic premise of the landed aris-tocracy's privileges parallels the 'trickle-down' approach to eco-nomic growth promoted by the Club for Growth, the Heritage Foundation, the Koch brothers and other propagandists for what they view as today's downtrodden rich. Lord Grantham honestly and earnestly feels a responsibility for the economic welfare of his tenants and staff, and understands his duty to carry out those respon-sibilities primarily by providing them employment . . . Forces in American society continue to fight on talk radio and other forums for a sort of Restoration of Downton values.[63]

The 1 percent, in other words, like the Crawleys, will continue to use whatever tools are available to maintain their economic position, and their ability to do so is impressive. The voices that stand in the show for the other 99 percent are carefully managed. The servants, of course, are relatively resigned to their roles in the economic system, although some imagine a better life for themselves. The chauffeur son-in-law is some-thing of a voicepiece for the working class, his socialist-informed ideas are occasionally welcomed but only when they appear to ensure that the Crawleys can maintain their place in a shifting economic culture. The one character on the series who might interest Tom romantically is a local teacher, Sarah Bunting, who resists the status quo by stressing the value of education as a way to advance economically, is rejected from the family, and eventually moves on from her friendship with Tom. Ironically, Tom makes plans to leave for the United States, where he can practice his ideology of economic equality.

Interestingly, although *Downton Abbey* viewers may be experiencing economic lives similar to those depicted on the series—a world in which they may be more and more like those who live downstairs, rather than those who live upstairs—there is a cultural fascination with everything Downton. Information about how to throw a genuine Downton party is available on web sites from *The New York Times* to the *Huffington Post*. Epicurious.com offers a "*Downton Abbey* menu" that includes

"Mrs. Patmore's London Particular," "Nan's Shepherd's Pie," and "English Eccles Cake." Pinterest has organized its *Downton Abbey* boards into categories ranging from fashion, home decoration, favorite quotes, parlor games, and how to create a Downton-inspired Christmas. Discount retailer Kohl's sold a line of "Kohl's Offers Downton Abbey Inspired Jewelry" listed between $20 and $38 with an offer of getting the second piece for half price if you buy two pieces.[64] Other evidence of *Downton* fever includes tourism at Highclere Castle, the British house depicted in the series, and walking tours of Bampton in Oxfordshire, the village where scenes from the show are set.[65] Even public television stations, for example Boston's WGBH, have taken advantage of the avid fan culture, hosting such fundraisers as "An Evening Inspired by Downton Abbey," in which guests "came in costume and enjoyed food, fashion, and music from the Edwardian Era."[66]

The disconnect between the reality of income inequality and the fan culture around life in *Downton Abbey*—in particular the life of the upstairs Crawley family—may not be that surprising given that "Americans are relatively unconcerned about the wide income gap between rich and poor."[67] As series creator Julian Fellows puts it during a 2013 interview: "I think, the—well, not even the subtext, but the supertext—of 'Downton' is that it is possible for us all to get on, that we don't have to be ranged in class warfare permanently—that for the general public, the fact that people are leading different lives with different economic realities and different expectations is perfectly cope-able with."[68] The fact that *Downton Abbey* is set in a country that prides itself on class difference, to the point of remarking on the fact that the future king, "Prince William," would choose to marry a "commoner" named Katherine Middleton seems somewhat lost in the discussion.

Mountaintop Removal Mining in *Justified*

One way 21st-century television dramas examine social, political, and economic issues is through series that are set in parts of the country not usually featured prominently in television fiction. *Friday Night Lights* (2006–2011), *Breaking Bad* (2008–2013), *True Blood* (2008–2014), *Sons of Anarchy* (2008–2014), *The Walking Dead* (2010–present), and *True Detective* (2014–present), to name a few, take place outside of large, recognizable cities. Even though the increasingly diverse and rich settings of contemporary dramas broaden the television geographic aesthetic, such locations' regional identity and cultural climate do not always inform the program's narrative. In FX's *Justified* (2010–present), however, regional characteristics are central to the program's story lines.

Justified provides a national viewing audience with insight into some of the economic issues facing citizens who live in poor, rural, mountainous regions of the country. Created by Graham Yost and derived from a short story by Elmore Leonard titled "Fire in the Hole," *Justified* takes place in Harlan, Kentucky, and tells the story of U.S. Marshal Raylan Givens who, in the program's pilot episode, is reassigned to work in his hometown after publicly killing a mob boss in broad daylight at a hotel in Miami. Leaving his life in the city of Miami, Givens adjusts to his reassignment and is surprised to find himself engaged in his role as a rural law enforcement officer who encounters local clans and their hierarchies, illegal activities that make up an underground economy, and the region's characters, many of whom he has known since childhood.

Oxford American writer Jake Blumgart points out that *Justified* offers viewers a clear and detailed sense of place by depicting its setting in ways that are not condescending to its inhabitants. The poverty of the region is conveyed through images of homes, material goods, and cars that suggest making do with what one has is the way of life. The underground economy of drug sales and theft helps define the culture of Harlan, but these elements of the town are not glamorized or celebrated. Finally, the continual references to coal mining throughout the series legitimize the setting's culture as one historically associated with the practice. There are depictions of mineshafts, comments about the mining industry, and plot points in the narrative that identify Harlan as a mining town. In addition, it is emphasized that the show's main character, Raylan Givens, once worked in a mine alongside lead adversary Boyd Crowder.[69] Although such references pervade all of *Justified*'s seasons, three episodes in season two explicitly focus on mountaintop removal mining as an aspect of the mining industry.

Mountaintop removal is a method used to extract coal by blasting off top portions of the mountain so that the layers of coal underneath can be scraped off or mined. This practice is less expensive than traditional mining and is an effective way of retrieving coal in the Appalachian region of the United States where coal is layered horizontally in the mountains.[70] Historically, mining coal has been central to the economies of Appalachia, and mountaintop mining is also considered to be safer than traditional mining, an important consideration for the labor force.[71] The practice is controversial, however, because of the ecological impact of deforestation, failed attempts to rebuild the mountaintop after mining, the residential struggles inherent in living near the mining sites (dealing with noise, pollution, flooding, etc.), and the potential health problems experienced by those in the community. In addition, many opponents of mountaintop top removal mining mourn the loss of the mountains themselves.

Although the method was developed in the 1960s, mountaintop removal has been reported on more frequently in the contemporary media.[72] Numerous documentaries produced since the year 2000 have discussed the topic, and a number of celebrity activists have raised awareness of this issue.[73] However, mainstream fictional television has rarely featured this aspect of coal mining, and Americans living in areas not impacted by mountaintop removal may not be aware of the complexities surrounding the practice. Therefore, when the popular, nationally viewed television program *Justified* features mountaintop removal as part of its narrative, the way the issue is portrayed is worth examining.

In season two of *Justified*, part of the plot focuses on a federal hearing about a coal case.[74] The controversy and fall out around the case set up an episode titled "The Spoil" where Raylan Givens is charged with protecting the coal company Black Pike's Vice President Carol Johnson who is in Harlan County trying to buy land from residents for the company's Green Mountain Project. Issues around mining practices primarily emerge in the narrative during a heated town meeting scene, although discussions about coal are present throughout the episode. The town meeting begins with Givens and Boyd Crowder describing aspects of mining in Harlan. When Johnson tries to point out to the community that miners get paid about the same amount per week as a U.S. Marshal, Givens, refusing to appear in support of her agenda, points out that law enforcement officers get paid year round and have sick and vacation time. His comments remind the townspeople that miners do not get these benefits, and as the crowd murmurs in support of Givens's argument, Crowder reminds the townspeople that the coal company provides jobs and honest work, something needed in the area. Although this debate engages some of the issues facing mining communities, the debate between Carol Johnson and Harlan resident Mags Bennett most succinctly highlights the complicated nature of coal mining in Appalachia.[75]

> Johnson: Now I come into this county and look around and I see empty businesses. I see houses in shambles. I see families struggling to make ends meet. We can bring prosperity back to this land. God put coal in these hills for just that purpose. I believe that deep down in my heart, and I think, I think you all do too.

Bennett: Apparently, Black Pike is here to help us realize God's great plan and all they're asking us to let em do is cut the top off our mountain. Well my people pioneered this valley when George Washington was the president of the United States. And as long as we've been here, story's always been the same. Big money men come in, take the timber and the coal and the strength of our people. And what do they leave behind? Poundments full of poison slurry and valleys full of toxic trash. You know what happens when 500 million gallons of slurry breaks through? The gates of hell open.

Johnson: Those poundments are built strong to keep the slurry back.

Bennett: The gates of hell open. And all that waste rolls down through the hollers and poisons the water and the land and everything it touches. Mining company has a, has a word for those leavings, didn't it? The spoil. The spoil! And that is what our lives will be if Black Pike has their way with our mountain.

Johnson: With all due respect, Mrs. Bennett, Black Pike will replace the mountain tops and leave money. A lot of money in the pockets of the working people of Bennett and Harlan counties.[76]

This fictional exchange covers the main points often used in the real media to characterize opposing sides of the debate over mountaintop removal mining. As attorney Evan Smith writes, supporters of mountaintop removal mining claim that miners can earn $50,000 a year or more in areas where 20 to 40 percent of the population lives below the poverty line. Smith also points out that, in an area where land is not naturally flat and therefore difficult to build on, supporters of mountaintop mining look to reclaim now flattened mining areas as places to develop shopping centers, golf courses, housing, and prisons.[77] Johnson, as the coal company representative, appeals to the economic struggles of the region, but she does not mention this long-term, potentially positive impact on the community. Given that her goal is to buy up land in Harlan, her point is framed very simply: selling to Black Pike gives workers money and provides the community with jobs. Doing so positions the debate as being only about a big corporation that provides jobs and buys property; there is no mention that the Green Mountain Project might represent a clear and long-term vision for Harlan's future. However, the real debate around mountaintop removal and the future of Appalachia is more nuanced. Supporters may see this practice as a safer, next stage in mining development that will ultimately lead to better economic development that is tied to industries other than mining. Opponents hope for a different future for Appalachia.[78]

According to Smith, opponents of mountaintop removal mining envision a future where the Appalachian economy thrives on traditional, underground mining, ecotourism, and the development of small businesses. They point out that flattened land is rarely redeveloped and mountaintop removal costs communities more than it provides in economic benefits. Their opposition also comes in the form of a passionate concern about losing elements of Appalachian communities and culture, as citizens must often relocate when coal companies move in to complete the work of mining. Finally, opponents cite numerous ecological, environmental, and health and safety concerns.[79] In *Justified*'s town meeting exchange, Bennett points to some of these issues, but frames them primarily as a story of a corporate entity taking what it wants from a poor community that it leaves polluted. The most passionate part of her speech is about the dangerous possibility that toxic slurry is not contained. Although this is a realistic concern—there have been slurry spills as recently as February 2014[80]—Bennett's town hall commentary focuses on the negative environmental impact if there is a spill; it does not highlight environmental concerns associated with mountaintop removal in general or health issues that arise even when mining operates as anticipated. The depiction of the debate around mountaintop removal on *Justified*, in other words, is incomplete, focusing viewers on the "what if" scenario of a toxic spill rather than the impact of mountaintop removal mining over traditional mining or the larger debate around the United States' reliance on coal as an energy form.

The two women at the heart of *Justified*'s mountaintop mining debate are worth discussing as well. Carol Johnson is an outsider, passing through Harlan to complete her company's business and be on her way. She is confident, not particularly likeable, and manipulative. As the coal mining narrative unfolds over the episodes, it comes to light that she hired someone to set off firecrackers to sound like gun shots at a time in the town hall meeting when heated discussion was elevating. For her part, Mags Bennett is a Harlan insider and a powerful one at that. She murders people who get in her way, runs a monopoly on drug running, and exerts her power over the community through violence, threats, and intimidation. Although her town meeting discourse may educate the novice viewer on some reasons why mountaintop removal should be opposed, the viewer also has to wonder about Bennett's motivations, given her role in the larger *Justified* narrative.

Ultimately, Black Pike's attempt to buy land from Harlan citizens is framed as a power struggle between Johnson and Bennett, one that reaches its conclusion in episode nine where the two women enter into a negotiation. Bennett tells Johnson that she will agree to a large payout from Black Pike, in addition to a stake in the company that owns the coal company. Johnson responds in disbelief.

> Johnson: Oh, Mags you haven't done your homework. The proper-ties you're holdin' out on are worthless for coal. Parking lots and hillsides. What in God's name would my company agree to that deal?
> Crowder: It's not about the coal, Miss Johnson. It never was.
> Johnson: Then what?
> Bennett: Look at a map honey. State roads can't carry coal trucks up that mountain. No way to get em there. You want the richest top of this piece of Appalachia you gonna have to build your own road. And the road you need to build runs through the properties I hold. So. Boyd here sussed it out. Look at the pinch points for gradin' a lane wide enough for your trucks. He come to me and we worked out a little deal of our own.
> Crowder: The Indian line property owned by Helen and Arlo Giv-ens is the last parcel. I was able to convince them to put their trust in me.
> Bennett: Without that property, without them, without me, there is no Green Mountain Project, nor will there ever be. Black Pike will cut its losses and move on to the next hill with empty hands. <pause> <laughs> Oh, sugar they didn't tell you that, did they? Sent you in blind to close the deal without ever cluing you in on the particulars. Funny way to run a business. But then . . . you pick the devil you run with.
> Johnson: I have to make a call.[81]

At the end of the three-episode story arc, Bennett gets her deal and the coal company's willingness to comply surprises Johnson. Although such a power move is true to Bennett's character, the knowledge of corporate structure that Bennett demonstrates in her negotiation challenges stereo-types of Appalachian citizens as being unintelligent, racist, and unaware of corporate economies.[82] Of course, Bennett and her clan also reinforce a stereotype of Appalachian communities as sites of violent activity, but in this instance, Crowder's and her knowledge of the land, and their ability to figure out what Black Pike is really after, reveal an understanding that the coal company's VP does not possess.[83] In her somewhat suppressed anger at being humiliated, Johnson challenges Bennett at the end of the scene:

> Johnson: And all that talk at the meeting, the whole town lookin' at you as if you're the protector of all that is green and holy and Bennett . . . they're gonna blow a thousand feet off the top of that mountain, spill it into your creeks, wipe out homesteads.
> Bennett: My people have been there for 200 years, Miss Johnson, and we will be here once your people have come and taken what they've wanted and left.
> Johnson: And everyone else, you just, sell em out.
> Bennett: Nothing changes up here, not really. I've seen the story played out time and time again before and it'll happen again in times yet to come. I'll take the cash up front. Delivered tomorrow morning. First thing.[84]

Bennett's comments suggest a resignation to the fact that the mountains are going to be altered, but there is no mention of the debates taking place in contemporary culture outside of fictional Harlan. The sequence instead defers to a narrative of "big coal" versus "small town," where big coal gets what they want. The narrative does not mention the use of coal in the United States, an omission that may impact viewers' understanding of the context of the entire issue portrayed in the episodes.

Overall, *Justified* raises the issue of mountaintop removal in a simplified, apolitical way. Although television writers are not expected to educate viewers, *Justified*'s setting and the narrative associated with it present aspects of Kentucky living that may very well be unfamiliar to viewers. Some of these characterizations are stereotypical and unfair; others provide insight into an area of the country often overlooked in the television drama landscape. Perhaps a focus on issues related to this region will inspire viewers to find out more.

Visions of AI

A 2012 *Wired* article headline reads: "Better Than Human: Why Robots Will—and Must—Take Our Jobs." In this piece, complete with entertaining photographs of comedian Jimmy Fallon posing with robots, *Wired* writer Kevin Kelly argues that, by the end of the 21st century, machines will replace 70 percent of today's jobs. In an overview of what robots are currently doing, Kelly points out that manual labor is already being replaced by robots and the trend will continue as robots become integrated in warehouse work, nighttime cleaning, fruit picking, and pill dispensing. More "bots," as they are called, will write and be paperwork oriented. Kelly suggests that, because of the gains in AI, we are at an "inflection point"—a time when contemporary robots are able to do much more than their predecessors and when such gains are only going to develop further.[85] The shift to reliance on smart machines is reflected in numerous 21st-century television dramas. From the ubiquitous presence of fast search engines and data synthesis on criminal procedurals and counterterrorism shows to several series that have integrated AI into their plot lines, a new understanding of technological advancements is a recurrent theme in contemporary dramas.

Kelly is not alone in his claims about the impact AI will have on everyday life in the coming century. In 2011, *Business Insider* listed nine jobs that robots will potentially replace—jobs that include some lawyer and paralegal positions (computer software will be able to effectively review paperwork), babysitters (robots that can keep kids entertained), and drivers (Google is having success in their development of automated cars).[86] Google's director of engineering, noted computer scientist and inventor Ray Kurzweil, believes that computers will be smarter than humans by 2029 and that they "will be able to understand what we say, learn from experience, crack jokes, tell stories, flirt."[87] Kurzweil introduced the term "singularity" into popular vernacular, a word from computer scientist and science fiction writer Vernor Vinge uses to refer to the point in time when humans and machines will converge, something he believes will happen in the not too distant future.[88] Dr. Peter Diamandis, Kurzweil's cofounder of Singularity University, a corporate entity focused on new technologies, predicts that AI and robots will replace more than 50 jobs in the next decade.[89] Moreover, Kurzweil suggests that he sees a future where computers can better understand "the semantic content of a language," an understanding that extends beyond what Watson, the computer that won the popular game show *Jeopardy*'s prize in 2011, can do, which is to read millions of pages and synthesize the information.[90] Google, Amazon, Facebook, and Microsoft are all dedicating significant resources toward developing AI, and Google, in particular, made headlines when it acquired the Deep Mind in 2014, an AI British company dedicated to designing computers to "learn" the same way the human brain does.[91] Kelly points out that AI and their robotic applications are already in play and that although robots will eventually change the fabric of our culture, this shift is not something that should be feared because ultimately it will give us more freedom. Kelly further argues that it is a misplaced idea to expect or fear that robots will be human like: "To demand that artificial intelligence be humanlike is the same flawed logic as demanding that artificial flying be birdlike, with flapping wings."[92]

Although Kelly suggests that people should not expect robots to seem like humans, MIT professor, psychologist, and technology expert Sherry Turkle points out that robots can also be designed to exhibit life-like qualities. These sociable robots, or robot companions, usually creatures designed to look like cute animals, can already be found in everyday life. In her book *Alone Together: Why We Expect More from Technology and Less from Each Other*, Turkle documents and critically discusses the presence, perceptions, and use of sociable robots by children, teenagers, adults, and elderly adults. She finds that varying levels of emotional connections are easily fostered with sociable robots.[93] This emotional component of robot integration is also seen when robots are not designed with primarily social functions. As robots are increasingly present in the U.S. military, soldiers interact with these machines by talking to them, recovering their parts after they are destroyed, and holding funerals for them that include presentation of medals and gun salutes.[94] The move to develop sociable robots is continuing. In Japan, a humanoid robot named Pepper was introduced on June 5, 2014, and hailed as an "emotional robot," a machine that speaks 17 languages and learns how to behave over time by using facial recognition technology, cameras, audio recorders, and cloud storage of feedback to then determine its consequential interactions with humans.[95] This is an example of machine learning, computer algorithms that improve automatically through experience.

Depictions of AI in popular films and television began long before robots like Pepper were created. *Knight Rider* (1982–1986) featured an AI car, the *Terminator* movies and television series *Terminator: The Sarah Connor Chronicles* (2008–2009) depicted characters that looked like people, but could reveal their machine selves, and the *Star Wars* franchise introduced the now iconic R2D2 and C3PO robots in the 1970s. Other programs include the kids television show *My Life as a Teenage Robot* (2003–2007), the sci-fi drama *Battlestar Galactica* (1978–1979; 2004–2009), and the films *A.I.: Artificial Intelligence* (2001) and, more recently, *Her* (2013). Although stories of robots and AI have always populated contemporary science fiction outlets, fictional portrayals occur in mainstream 21st-century television dramas in ways that register contemporary developments in the field and use in everyday life. Popular programming that reflects specific new shifts in technology, especially technology associated with AI, exists on television networks NBC, CBS, and FOX. These advances in machine learning are depicted on contemporary mainstream network television as supercomputers, human characters who have an integrated machine component, and human-like robot characters, sometimes called androids.

Although supercomputing and data acquisition are present on many television programs, CBS's *Person of Interest* (2011–present) uses this expanding technology in the form of a supercomputer called The Machine. This Machine demonstrates an ability to generate, synthesize, and apply vast amounts of information to predict violent crimes. To do this, the Machine uses data from cell phones, Internet use, security cameras, and digital exchanges. Essentially, The Machine functions as a supercomputer character on *Person of Interest* and highlights the potentially dangerous power of having access to too much data. The presence of The Machine results in a narrative that poses questions about data mining, storage, and access to private information. Essentially, The Machine illustrates the concept of machine learning. As the show progresses, The Machine's algorithms prompt it to improve on its abilities, ultimately resulting in The Machine becoming autonomous, no longer reliant on its human creator.

NBC's *Chuck* (2007–2012) and CBS's *Intelligence* (2014) both feature characters who have computer capabilities as part of their brain. In *Chuck*'s case, the eponymous protagonist has a copy of "the Intersect," the only copy of a merged CIA and NSA database in his brain. This data became planted in *Chuck*'s brain through an e-mail sent to him from a former college roommate who became a CIA agent. The existence of this database results in *Chuck* involuntarily seeing flashes of top secret information, often prompted by such particular triggers as images, people, or text. He is recruited to secretly help the CIA and NSA track down criminals and protect citizens and the country. The accidental nature of *Chuck*'s transformation from a regular guy to agent is played up comedically and the show is witty and entertaining, suggesting that the merger of the database and *Chuck*'s brain is simply a fun, absurd narrative device. As the show continues, however, *Chuck* gains greater control over the powerful Intersect implanted in his brain to assist in the show's problem of the week. A similar concept is positioned much more seriously on *Intelligence*. In fact, one reviewer pointed out that *Intelligence* is similar to *Chuck* but with "more frowning."[96]

On *Intelligence*, the operative Gabrielle Vaughn is outfitted with a computer chip that gives him access to countless computer files, images, and videos. Gabrielle is instantly in control of this access and can actively search for what he needs. Although some critics noted that the show was reminiscent of the *Six Million Dollar Man* (1974–1978), the setting for

Intelligence is a future not so different from the early 21st century, littered with technologies to which civilians have instant access.[97] Gabrielle's ability is a unique advancement, bankrolled by the government, and he has to be protected and monitored because of his very expensive asset status. Although the program was canceled after a season given the poor ratings and a lukewarm response by critics, *Intelligence* gestured toward issues associated with the merger of human and machine. Throughout the season, Gabrielle questions his humanness and worries that the chip is somehow interfering with his humanity. Several episodes center on the remote control of the brain chip, raising issues around one human's power over another using AI. Ultimately, however, the program does not develop these themes and Gabrielle's microchip is seen more as a hook in an otherwise relatively standard counterterrorism procedural than an opportunity for television to explore aspects of technological advancement.

Chuck and *Intelligence* do, however, engage in storytelling that registers Kurzweil's singularity—the moment when humans and machines merge. A promotional video for *Intelligence,* titled "The Science of Singularity," emphasizes how timey the program is because it constructs a narrative that is based around contemporary projections of technology. Creator and executive producer Michael Seitzman discusses Gabrielle as a complicated manifestation of this possibility, pointing out that Gabrielle uses his imagination to filter and make sense of the information he retrieves from his brain chip. Seitzman goes on to say he wanted to think about what a human would do with a chip in his brain because humans are not computers.[98] Kurzweil believes that the singularity is inevitable and will make the human race smarter and healthier. Others view the concept differently. Turkle calls it a "mythic" concept, something people either believe in or not. She states: "At the singularity, everything will be technically possible, including robots that love. Indeed, at the singularity, we may merge with the robotic and achieve immortality. The singularity is technical rapture."[99] Either way, *Chuck* and *Intelligence* do not use the term singularity explicitly to viewers nor do they probe the complexities of this discussion. Introducing the concept of data connected to the brain is as far as these programs go. Instead, both series emphasize the humanity of the characters, suggesting that the technology itself is separate from its hosts rather than part of the merger the singularity suggests.

Fox's *Almost Human* (2013–2014) and CBS's *Extant* (2014–present) take a different approach to the topic by featuring human-like robots as primary characters. *Almost Human* takes place in a technologically advanced and crime-ridden 2048 where, to deal with such pervasive corruption, each police officer is partnered with an android designed to engage in combat operations, often against criminal androids. The program tells the story of Detective John Kennex and his partner DRN, or Dorian. Dorian is an older model android, whose lot was removed from police work because the robots had trouble managing their emotions. Kennex blames the newer model, more logic-oriented androids for his partner's death and effectively destroys one of them in the series pilot. Over the season, a relationship develops between Kennex and Dorian, and viewers may note the fact that the android displays more emotion than his human partner. Although the show was canceled after a year, a significant fan following continued to rally for its reinstatement or purchase by another network.

On *Extant*, the android is a child—a robot prototype named Ethan, created by scientist John Woods after his wife Molly was unable to conceive. Woods is determined to develop his "humanichs project," an enterprise that focuses on creating AI androids that look like, interact with, and emotionally connect with humans. As the show continues, Ethan's ability to learn exceeds the expectations of his creators and presents unique issues that his "parents" must address. Although *Extant*'s science fiction narrative is more about astronaut Molly Woods's return to Earth pregnant after a 13-month solo mission, the show's story line weaves together different ways of existence: human, android, and alien life.

Extant and *Almost Human* privilege the relationship between the robots and humans, emphasizing that emotional connections can be established between the human and machine characters, metaphorically reflecting a 21st-century reality where such emotional connections exist among soldiers and their robots, the elderly and their robotic pets, and children and their robotic toys. The shows do not make light of these bonds but instead portray them seriously, as real connections. Of course, the actors portraying these robots *are* human, which contributes to viewers' easy acceptance of the relationship, but the depiction in television programs and films of believable emotional connections that are between humans and machines is a familiar trope.

Extant and *Almost Human* also model machine learning in robot form. Dorian and Ethan develop as robots each time they encounter experiences. In *Alone Together*, Turkle warns of the psychological risk to children who spend too much time with robots: "Children need to be with other people to develop mutuality and empathy; interacting with a robot cannot teach these."[100] In an ironic reversal of this statement, on *Extant*'s episode three "Wish You Were Here," Josh Woods enrolls his robot son in school so that he can interact with humans his age in an educational environment experienced by most children. Although some parents express concern about Ethan attending their child's school, his first day goes well and he befriends a child of one of the concerned parents.

Lily Alexander, author of *Fictional Worlds: Traditions in Narrative and the Age of Visual Culture*, was asked about storytelling trends in the future, the narrative focus on the singularity, and her thoughts about how stories help people understand "the implications of what some are predicting will be a post human world."[101] Alexander responded that such stories provide an opportunity for exploration and identification of the traits that define our humanity in the face of developing technology. She says:

> We can't stop the march of technology. But it is the degree to which we'll be able to maintain our passions, bonds and communities that will define our survival. Concerns for the techno-future are not about researching genes or accessing phones. They are about who wants to use science, technology and the media to subdue and control others; and what we can proffer as counter measures and solutions—alternative outcomes.[102]

The presence of these technological advances and "what ifs" on mainstream network programming indicates a cultural understanding of events once considered impossible. Even if it is not possible for a computer to become autonomous, a microchip to be implanted in a brain, or robots to be indistinguishable from humans, these narratives emerge from some real developments in science and technology that noncomputer scientists are perhaps just beginning to understand.

Side Note: *Orphan Black*'s Clones

The BBC science-fiction drama *Orphan Black* premiered in 2013 and quickly became a cult hit, causing "a fervor" among audiences intrigued by the series.[103] Calling themselves the "Clone Club," fans avidly followed the story of Sarah Manning, a young woman who accidentally discovers she is one of at least nine clones engineered as part of an experiment known as the Leda project.[104] As Sarah learns more about who she is and where she comes from, she discovers that the clones, herself included, have been closely monitored by one of the experiment's original scientists, Dr. Leekie, and the powerful company, Dyad Institute, who hopes to profit from the technology that created them.[105] Leekie and the Dyad company are "Neolutionists": they believe in self-directed evolution that the clones represent. A competing group, the "Prolethians," favor creationism over evolution, seeing the clones as "abominations" and want them killed or reformed.[106]

Each episode of *Orphan Black* reveals more about the mystery behind the clones and the dangers facing them as they begin to locate each other and join forces. Forming their own "Clone Club," the primary clones— grifter and mother, Sarah; scientist Cosima; soccer mom Allison; and the troubled Russian Helena—work together to discover their origins and free themselves from the people and systems that seem intent on destroying or controlling them. The main character, Sarah, is played by actress Tatiana Maslany who won rave reviews for the fact that she plays not one, but all of the clones, each with its own unique look, accent, mannerisms, and backstory. The award-winning series has inspired publication of a comic book series and is the impetus for fan art and a growing amount of fan fiction.[107]

Orphan Black explores 21st-century issues of bioengineering, nature versus nurture, cloning, and bioethics.[108] The episodes reflect the scientific underpinning of the series. For example, during the first season, the episode titles are drawn from phrases in Charles Darwin's *On the Origin of Species*, whereas the titles in season two are taken from the writings of Sir Francis Bacon, father of the scientific method.[109] Scientists and science bloggers have weighed in on the show, claiming that it "pushes today's science far enough into the future to be fascinating while being conservative enough to be educational. In fact, you'll learn more about human genetics from the show than just about anywhere else on television."[110] Inspired by the series, The Johns Hopkins University *Gazette*'s "Ask the Expert" feature posted an article "How Close Are We to Cloning Humans?" Emory University bloggers referred to *Orphan Black* as a context to debate the ethics of cloning, and *Forbes* ran an article titled "Clone Wars: A Look at the Science of Orphan Black."[111] Interviews with the show's science consultant, the namesake for the scientist clone, Cosima, explore the history of cloning and genetic patenting. *Slate* writer Willa Paskin frames the issues more broadly, saying: "It is a show about female bodies being used as objects, products, property. All their lives, without their knowledge, these manufactured women have been closely guarded and monitored. Most of them can't procreate. Do the clones have some purpose beyond being human? Are they freaks, or are they the future? Are they, in their very genetic material, being controlled? Does someone 'own' them?"[112]

The questions the series raises are more relevant than the casual viewer might think. At the end of the first season, Cosima discovers that the clones have been patented and a statement of ownership is printed on the DNA of each one: "This organism and derivative genetic material is restricted intellectual property."[113] As Cosima explains to Sarah: "We're property. Our bodies, our biology, everything we are, everything we become, belongs to them."[114] The same month the episode aired, the Supreme Court of the United States unanimously ruled in *Association for Molecular Pathology vs. Myriad Genetics, Inc.*, "human genes cannot be patented" challenging that idea that "something that occurs naturally in the human body can be 'owned' by a company."[115] Myriad Genetics had isolated the BRCA1 and BRCA2 genes used to help predict a genetic proclivity for developing breast cancer and the ruling prevented the company from legally owning those genes. However, the Court did express support for the patenting of "a synthetic form of DNA—called cDNA . . . [that is] particularly useful in conducting experiments and tests, such as cancer screening."[116]

In the world of *Orphan Black*, the ruling helps explain what is at stake in Cosima's discovery that the clones have been patented. As commentator Kyle Hill explains it, what the court ruling "implies is that Dyad has patented a modified sequence of DNA already found in the clones' genome. If this is the case, Dyad's patent would never hold up in our courts, and the women would have real freedom. However, it could be the case that Dyad created the entire clone genome synthetically, a process which would be patentable, and really would cause ethical and existential problems for the girls. In this scenario, Cosima wouldn't even be able to study her own genome without infringing on Dyad's rights."[117] Like any good science fiction story, the issues at the heart of *Orphan Black* question what role science plays in contemporary life and the implications it might have in the future.

Side Note: *American Crime*

Even before Barack Obama was elected president in 2008, there was speculation that he "seemed to embody the hope that America could transcend its divisions."[118] The first African American to hold the highest office in the country, Obama signified to some a "post-racial" era in which the country could consider its fraught racial history a thing of the past.[119] In the final years of his presidency, however, such claims seem more difficult to make. As the ABC drama *American Crime* depicts, in 2015 when the series debuted, race in U.S. culture remains a subject fraught with dangerous tension.

Set in Modesto, California, *American Crime* follows the story of a violent home invasion that leaves a man dead and his wife permanently disabled. Both victims are white, and the alleged suspect is an African American man addicted to drugs and in love with a young white woman, similarly substance dependent. Also implicated in the crime is a young Mexican American boy, whose father runs an auto repair shop, and an illegal Mexican immigrant with a criminal history of his own. The plot focuses as much on these characters as it does on their families: the parents of both of the victims; the sister of the accused, who has converted to Islam; the single father and sister of the boy; and the girlfriend and child of the immigrant. *American Crime* explores the widening circle of impact that a single act of violence can have on individuals, families, and communities, as well as the ambiguous nature of guilt and innocence. Race also plays a crucial role in the narrative. The victims—both white—and suspect—a black male—are quickly revealed to be more complex characters whose actions and responses challenge racial stereotypes.

Series creator and executive producer John Ridley, who also won an Oscar for the film *Twelve Years a Slave,* describes how the idea for *American Crime* originated, saying: "it was really a conversation that I had with my son about the Trayvon Marin case that really struck me. It made me wonder, 'what other spaces are there to talk about these types of things and at the same time show many different perspectives about subjects like this?'"[120] Referring to the black teenager who was shot by a white man while walking through a primarily white neighborhood, Ridley points to just one of many race-related acts of violence in the United States during the Obama presidency. There are others: The 2014 riots in Ferguson, Missouri, occurred after an unarmed 18-year-old black male, Michael Brown, was shot and killed by a white police officer who was then acquitted of the crime. The same year, a black man named Eric Gardner died after being placed in a chokehold by New York City police officers. In 2015, a 25-year-old black man, Freddie Gray, died of spinal injuries after being arrested and transported in a van for 30 minutes by the Baltimore police. Another black man, Walter Scott, was shot to death in the back by a white police officer in North Charleston, South Carolina, and in June 2015, a white young man, Dylann Roof, shot and killed nine members of a historic Charleston, South Carolina, Church during a Bible study. The riots, protests, Facebook posts, and twitter feeds that broke out in response to each of these events signal that race relations remain a difficult subject in the United States.

American Crime explores the topics of race and crime in what has been called a "No-Filter," "Unapologetic," "Rare," way for network television. Unlike the familiar crime procedural format, in this series, the mystery surrounding the crime reveals not the criminal, but the array of viewpoints from which the crime can be seen. Ridley says: "This is more than just a crime show . . . it's a show about perspective. A lot of times we get caught up in our own stuff and we never consider anyone else's perspective. This is a study in how to gain insight into other people's lives."[121] Given the events that occurred during, and after, the first season aired, in Florida, Ferguson, New York, and South Carolina, gaining perspective, and potentially empathy, seems particularly relevant. The gradual revelation of each character's backstory leads to constant reconsideration of who did what and why. In this way, *American Crime* demonstrates a "remarkable ability to harness (or event subvert) a viewer's prejudices about race, ethnicity, religion, crime, evidence and justice, as well as our ambivalence about the system's efficacy."[122] As a result, "*American Crime* feels like a sociological experiment, brazenly forcing its audiences to see another point of view—even when you're dead-set that what you believe is right."[123]

The format of *American Crime* is also significant. The series aired on network TV, yet by all counts is more like a cable television drama. As one critic writes, "It's like nothing you've seen on ABC."[124] Similar to cable series, *American Crime* brings "a big, star-studded drama to its viewers—one that promises subtle commentary, complex characters, and something to talk about at the water cooler the next day."[125] Also like cable, the series was filmed with cinematic influences, including "[q]uick cuts, overlapping dialogue and long scenes where little is said."[126] Following the anthology format noted in HBO's *True Detective*, *American Crime* will begin a new story line with a new setting, characters, and actors each season. Finally, ABC agreed to let Ridley and his team write their "scripts as whole pieces," allowing the narrative to unfold, at least initially, without worrying about "act breaks," or where commercials would fit into each episode's rhythm.[127] In other words, *American Crime* broke ground not just in content but also in network television's idea of what a drama can be.

Conclusion

Throughout its history, television has held the potential to engage viewers in social issues, contemporary concerns, and cultural changes through the genre of the television drama. In the early 21st century, television has more than lived up to this potential. Often referred to as the "new golden age," the diverse slate of high-quality programming released during this time period led to renewed interest in television as an art form worthy of analysis, discussion, and critique. *21st-Century TV Dramas* shines light on some key aspects of the new golden age and its proliferation of award-winning, innovative, and often groundbreaking dramas. After the terrorist attacks of September 11, 2001, for example, television dramas explored stories of grief, racial profiling, privacy, and security that defined the post-9/11 world. During a time of industry shifts, technological advancements, and changing audience demographics, 21st-century television narratives introduced viewers to antihero protagonists, bilingual dialogue, literary stylistics, and transmedia content. Although gender, sexuality, and sexual preference were debated in the public, private, and legal spheres, television dramas offered viewers images of gender that both reinforced and challenged traditional binary understandings of what it means to be a man or a woman. As the dynamics and demographics of the home and workplace changed—before, during, and after the economic recession of 2008—dramatic content shifted as well, incorporating concerns widely reflected in American life. These diverse, well-scripted, and intelligent television dramas have offered viewers the opportunity to think about complicated social, economic, and political issues in new ways.

The significance of today's dramas has not been limited to content. The television programming industry that evolved during the early part of this century also established important milestones in television history. The rise of HBO as a television producer, for instance, contributed to industry shifts in how series are created, and by whom. Since then, highly regarded dramas have been released by network, cable, and streaming services, further expanding the landscape of television production. Such shifts are likely to continue as streaming services Netflix and Amazon, for example, gain more traction and other content providers emerge. As television critic Andy Greenwald suggests: "The streaming services are now in the same situation the upper reaches of the cable dial were a few years ago: eager to make a splash and willing to cannonball into the unknown in order to achieve it."[1] Such shifts have made television viewing immediate, convenient, and continuous, depending completely on the viewer's preference. Binge watching, the release of complete seasons on a single day, and invitations to vote for which series are produced have changed the way television dramas are thought about by ordinary viewers.

With so much change in so few years, it seems reasonable to ask where television dramas might go from here, as the century progresses. The programs that originally prompted discussions of a new golden age—such as *The Sopranos, The Wire, Lost, Dexter,* and *Six Feet Under*—have concluded. More recent popular and highly regarded dramas, including *Mad Men* and *Breaking Bad*, have also aired their final episodes. These shows provided a foundation for the new golden age. When *Breaking Bad* ended in 2013, some argued that the era of the dark, violent program with an antihero protagonist was almost over.[2] Although there are current dramas that continue to weave similar narrative arcs, "creators found that they had to find a few lighter elements and moments just to give viewers a chance to breathe."[3]

As suggested in the pages of this book, the early 21st century is rich with programs that build on, and move beyond, the familiar characteristics of these early landmark shows. More recent dramas include diverse casts, provocative story lines, and a variety of relevant cultural concerns. They have been recognized by critics and fans alike, who follow and discuss the shows not just through formal published reviews and informal water cooler conversations, but also on such a range of platforms as Twitter, wikis, and fan sites. With so much change, perhaps the 21st-century golden age of television should be defined not by specific shows but by the standard of high-quality television—particularly in the genre of drama—that engages viewers about relevant cultural issues. Benchmarked by the dramas aired in the century's early years, that standard must be sustained, or even surpassed, by future programming if television is to continue to live up to the era's potential.

Evidence suggests that there is already a commitment to maintaining the standard set by the new golden age. As this book goes to press, there is television industry buzz around new dramas that connect viewers to contemporary life through different themes and lenses. In addition to new hospital dramas like *Chicago Med* and *Code Black*, upcoming programs like *The Advocate* and *Containment* will address specific medical issues including "hazards of our health care system" and the experience of a population quarantined by an epidemic.[4] *Blood and Oil* will portray the effects of an oil boom in North Dakota, whereas the dramedy *Mix* will focus on "the realities of modern-day families—multi-cultural, multi-generational, built through divorces, affairs and adoptions—set against the backdrop of a revered family restaurant at a crossroads."[5] New series registering the ongoing popularity of crime and security narratives include *The Catch*, *Quantico*, and *L.A. Crime*. Although these shows will connect viewers with current issues of health care, reliance on fossil fuels, and changing family composition, others will bring us contemporary stories about the past. *The Bastard Executioner*, for example, is a forthcoming period drama about a warrior knight, whereas the "rock drama," *Vinyl*, which has generated press given its all-star creation team of Martin Scorsese, Mick Jagger, and Terence Winter, is set to debut on HBO in 2016.[6] As the 2015–2016 programming schedule continues to unfold, comic book-inspired shows like *Heroes Reborn, Supergirl*, and *DC's Legends of Tomorrow* will join the slate, whereas certain already popular series as *True Detective, American Crime*, and *The Good Wife* will try to provide viewers with original narratives and plot twists.[7] Some of these dramas will be successful; others will be canceled. Some will be celebrated by critics; others will be dismissed. Some will invoke legions of fans; others will inspire small, yet loyal followings. Regardless of their reception or critical success, upcoming television dramas will continue to engage viewers in exploring important aspects about life in the 21st century.

So where do we go from here? We keep watching.

Notes

Introduction

1. Anna Everett, "Golden Age of Television Drama," *The Museum of Broadcast Communications*, n.d., accessed June 26, 2015, http://www.museum.tv/eotv /goldenage.htm.

2. Ibid.

3. Ibid.

4. Newton Minow, "Television and the Public Interest," Delivered May 9, 1961, to the National Association of Broadcasters, accessed June 26, 2015, http://www.americanrhetoric.com/speeches/newtonminow.htm.

5. Robert J. Thompson, *Television's Second Golden Age: From Hill Street Blues to ER* (New York: Syracuse University Press, 1997).

6. Ibid.

7. Ibid, 98.

8. Ibid.

9. Mark Lawson, "Are We Really in a Second Golden Age for Television," *Television and Radio* (blog), *The Guardian*, May 23, 2013, accessed June 25, 2015, http://www.theguardian.com/tv-and-radio/tvandradioblog/2013/may/23 /second-golden-age-television-soderbergh.

10. Todd Leopold, "The New, New TV Golden Age," *CNN*, May 6, 2013, accessed June 28, 2015, http://www.cnn.com/2013/05/06/showbiz/golden-age -of-tv/; David Carr, "Barely Keeping Up in TV's New Golden Age, *The New York Times*, March 9, 2014, accessed June 28, 2015, http://www.nytimes.com /2014/03/10/business/media/fenced-in-by-televisions-excess-of-excellence.html? _r=1.

11. Brett Martin, *Difficult Men* (New York: Penguin Press, 2013).

12. Ibid.

13. Dean DeFino, *The HBO Effect* (New York: Bloomsbury Academic, 2014).

14. Matt Smith, "Are We on the Verge of Television's Third Golden Age?," *Lost Remote* (blog), *Adweek*, October 27, 2014, accessed June 28, 2015, http://www.adweek.com/lostremote/are-we-on-the-verge-of-televisions-third-golden-age/48194.

Chapter 1

1. Brett Martin, *Difficult Men* (New York, Penguin Press, 2013).

2. Ibid, 5.

3. Nicole Sperling and Melissa Maerz, "Film Directors Are Embracing TV," *The Los Angeles Times*, June 5, 2011, accessed June 24, 2015, http://articles.latimes.com/2011/jun/05/entertainment/la-ca-film-to-tv-20110605.

4. Brett Martin, *Difficult Men*, 11.

5. Kim Akass and Janet McCabe, "Six Feet Under," In *The Essential HBO Reader*, ed. Gary Edgerton and Jeffrey Jones (Lexington, KY: The University Press of Kentucky, 2008), 80.

6. John Hendel, "10 Years After Its Premiere, 'The Wire' Feels Dated, and That's a Good Thing," *The Atlantic*, May 31, 2012, accessed June 23, 2015, http://www.theatlantic.com/entertainment/archive/2012/05/10-years-after-its-premiere-the-wire-feels-dated-and-thats-a-good-thing/257910/.

7. Carlos A. Scolari, "Lostology: Transmedia Storytelling and Expansion/Compression Strategies," *Semiotica*, 195 (2013): 45–68, doi:10.1515/sem-2013-0038.

8. Ibid, 49.

9. "A House Is Not a Home," *Baby Vamp Jessica* (blog), June 26, 2011, accessed June 15, 2015, http://www.babyvamp-jessica.com/?offset=1310954459443.

10. "Lafayette, Lovers and Leftovers," *Baby Vamp Jessica* (blog), July 3, 2011, accessed June 15, 2015, http://www.babyvamp-jessica.com/?offset=1310954459443.

11. Ibid.

12. Aaron Delwiche and Jennifer Jacobs Henderson, "What Is Participatory Culture," In *The Participatory Culture Handbook*, ed. Aaron Delwiche and Jennifer Jacobs Henderson (New York: Routledge, 2012), 6.

13. Henry Jenkins, "Seven Myths About Transmedia Storytelling Debunked," *Fast Company*, April 18, 2011, accessed June 15, 2015, http://www.fastcompany.com/1745746/seven-myths-about-transmedia-storytelling-debunked.

14. Ibid.

15. Jonathan Hardy, "Mapping Commercial Intertextuality: HBO's True Blood," *Convergence*, 17, no. 1 (2011): 7–17, doi:10.1177/1354856510383359.

16. Jason Mittell, "Strategies of Storytelling on Transmedia Television," In *Storyworlds Across Media: Towards a Media Conscious Narratology*, ed. Jan-Noel Thon and Marie-Lauie Ryan (Lincoln: University of Nebraska Press, 2014), 263.

17. Henry Jenkins, "Transmedia Storytelling 101," *Confessions of an ACA—Fan* (blog), March 22, 2007, accessed June 15, 2015, http://henryjenkins.org/2007/03/transmedia_storytelling_101.html.

18. Carlos A. Scolari, "Lostology: Transmedia Storytelling and Expansion/Compression Strategies."

19. Jasper Hamill, "Game of Thrones Fans Spend THREE YEARS Building a Minecraft Recreation of its Fantasy World," *The Mirror*, February 4, 2015, accessed June 15, 2015, http://www.mirror.co.uk/news/technology-science/technology/game-thrones-fans-spend-three-5102814.

20. Carlos A. Scolari, "Lostology: Transmedia Storytelling and Expansion/Compression Strategies," 65.

21. "Mad Men: The Fan Cut," n.d., accessed June 10, 2015, http://www.madmenfancut.com/.

22. Aaron Smith, "The Rise of the 'Connected Viewer,'" Pew Research Internet Project, July 17, 2012, accessed June 15, 2015, http://www.pewinternet.org/2012/07/17/the-rise-of-the-connected-viewer/.

23. "What's Empowering the New Digital Consumer?" *Nielsen Newswire*, February 10, 2014, accessed June 15, 2015, http://www.nielsen.com/content/corporate/us/en/insights/news/2014/whats-empowering-the-new-digital-consumer.html.

24. "Second Screen by the Numbers, Q3, 2012," 2nd Screen Society, n.d., accessed January 9, 2015, http://www.2ndscreensociety.com/research.

25. "What's Empowering the New Digital Consumer?" *Nielsen Newswire*.

26. Mary McNamara, "Scandal Has Become Must-Tweet TV," *The Los Angeles Times*, May 11, 2013, http://articles.latimes.com/print/2013/may/11/entertainment/la-et-st-scandal-abc-social-media-20130511.

27. Willa Paskin, "Network TV is Broken. So How Does Shonda Rhimes Keep Making Hits?" *The New York Times Magazine, The New York Times*, May 9, 2013, http://www.nytimes.com/2013/05/12/magazine/shonda-rhimes.html.

28. Shelli Weinstein, "How 'Scandal' Paved the Way for ABC's Twitter-Based '#TGIT' Marketing Strategy," *Variety*, September 22, 2014, accessed January 1, 2015, http://variety.com/2014/tv/news/scandal-twitter-shonda-rhimes-tgit-abc-shondaland-1201311282/.

29. Jefferson Graham, "American Crime Cast Took Twitter Classes," *USA Today*, March 3, 2015, accessed June 15, 2015, http://www.usatoday.com/story/tech/2015/03/03/american-crime-cast-takes-twitter-classes/23959513/.

30. "Check out Breaking Bad Story Sync While Watching the Premiere This Sunday Night," *AMC*, August 8, 2013, accessed June 9, 2015, http://www.amc.com/shows/breaking-bad/talk/2013/08/check-out-breaking-bad-story-sync-while-watching-the-premiere-this-sunday-night.

31. Michael Agresta, "'Girls,' 'Mad Men,' and the Future of TV-as-Literature," *The Atlantic*, June 15, 2012, accessed June 1, 2015, http://www.theatlantic.com/entertainment/archive/2012/06/girls-mad-men-and-the-future-of-tv-as-literature/258469/; Adam Kirsch and Mohsin Hamid, "Are the New 'Golden

Age' TV Shows the New Novels?" *The New York Times*, February 25, 2014, LexisNexis Academic; Thomas Doherty, "Storied TV: Cable is the New Novel," *The Chronicle of Higher Education*, September 17, 2012, accessed June 1, 2015, http://chronicle.com/article/Cable-Is-the-New-Novel/134420/.

32. Michael Agresta, "'Girls,' 'Mad Men,' and the Future of TV-as-Literature."

33. Ibid.

34. Thomas Doherty, "Storied TV: Cable is the New Novel."

35. John Bingham, "TV Drama Is the New Literature, Says Salman Rushdie," *The Telegraph*, June 12, 2011, accessed June 28, 2015, http://www.telegraph.co.uk/culture/books/booknews/8571010/TV-drama-is-the-new-literature-says-Salman-Rushdie.html.

36. Michael Agresta, "'Girls,' 'Mad Men,' and the Future of TV-as-Literature."

37. Laura Bliss, "Previously On: In Praise of the Television Recap Sequence," *The Atlantic*, February 4, 2015, accessed June 28, 2015, http://www.theatlantic.com/entertainment/archive/2015/02/previously-on-in-praise-of-the-television-recap/385036/.

38. Mark Caro, "Television Becomes Recapper's Delight," *Chicago Tribune*, June 13, 2014, http://www.chicagotribune.com/entertainment/ct-tv-recaps-analysis-20140613-column.html#page=1.

39. Christopher Orr, "*True Detective*: The Best Show on TV," *The Atlantic*, February 11, 2014, accessed June 28, 2015, http://www.theatlantic.com/entertainment/archive/2014/02/-em-true-detective-em-the-best-show-on-tv/283727/; Doviak, Scott Von, "The best TV shows of 2014 (part 2)," *The A.V. Club*, December 11, 2014, accessed June 28, 2015, http://www.avclub.com/article/best-tv-shows-2014-part-2-212571; Andrew Romano, "'True Detective' Review: You Have to Watch HBO's Revolutionary Crime Classic," *The Daily Beast*, January 11, 2014, accessed June 28, 2015, http://www.thedailybeast.com/articles/2014/01/11/true-detective-review-you-have-to-watch-hbo-s-revolutionary-crime-classic.html.

40. Andrew Romano, "Inside the Obsessive, Strange Mind of True Detective's Nic Pizzolatto," *The Daily Beast*, February 4, 2014, accessed June 28, 2015, http://www.thedailybeast.com/articles/2014/02/04/inside-the-obsessive-strange-mind-of-true-detective-s-nic-pizzolatto.html.

41. Kim Spurr, "Fiction Writer, Poet Pizzolatto to be Visiting Writer in 2005–2006," University of North Carolina at Chapel Hill News Press Release, June 16, 2005, accessed March 2, 2015, http://www.unc.edu/news/archives/jun05/kenanwriter061605.htm.

42. Andrew Romano, "Inside the Obsessive, Strange Mind of True Detective's Nic Pizzolatto."

43. Ibid.

44. David Walker, "Nic Pizzolatto, New Orleans-Born Novelist, Discusses HBO's Upcoming 'True Detective'," *The Times-Picayune*, July 7, 2013, accessed June 28, 2105, http://www.nola.com/tv/index.ssf/2013/07/nic_pizzolatto_new_orleans-bor.html.

45. Micah Conkling, "The Literary 'True Detective'," *Deep South Magazine*, February 25, 2014, accessed June 28, 2015, http://deepsouthmag.com/tag/true -detective/.

46. Ibid.

47. Christopher Orr, *"True Detective*: The Best Show on TV'."

48. Micah Conkling, "The Literary 'True Detective'."

49. Maureen Ryan, "'True Detective,' Flat Circles and the Eternal Search for Meaning," *The Huffington Post*, February 24, 2014, accessed June 28, 2015, http://www.huffingtonpost.com/maureen-ryan/true-detective-hbo_b_4847971 .html.

50. Kate Arthur, "The 'True Detective' Creator Debunks Your Craziest Theories," *BuzzFeed*, March 6, 2014, accessed June 28, 2015, http://www.buzzfeed .com/kateaurthur/true-dectective-finale-season-1-nic-pizzolatto#.trz9z893NA.

51. Micah Conkling, "The Literary 'True Detective'."

52. Ibid.

53. Dustin Rowles, "Television's 5 Greatest Extended Literary References," *UPROXX*, March 7, 2014, accessed June 28, 2015, http://uproxx.com/tv/2014 /03/televisions-5-greatest-extended-literary-references/.

54. Liesl Bradner, " 'Lost' Reading List: The Show's Creators Discuss Literary Influences, from Stephen King to Flannery O'Connor," *What You're Watching* (blog), *The Los Angeles Times*, May 14, 2010, accessed June 28, 2015, http:// latimesblogs.latimes.com/showtracker/2010/05/lost-in-books-.html.

55. Jen Chaney, " 'Lost' Literature: Not Just For Desert Islands," *NPR Books*, January 13, 2009, accessed June 28, 2015, http://www.npr.org/templates/story /story.php?storyId=99296794.

56. Billy Parrott, "The 'Mad Men' Reading List," *Biblio File* (blog), *The New York Public Library*, February 27, 2012, accessed June 28, 2015, http://www .nypl.org/blog/2012/02/27/mad-men-reading-list.

57. Matt Zoller Seitz, "Kurt Sutter Explains His Cultural Influences," *Vulture*, September 8, 2013, accessed June 28, 2015, http://www.vulture.com/2013 /09/kurt-sutter-explains-his-cultural-influences.html.

58. "Sons of Anarchy," Season 7, Episode 13: Papa's Goods.

59. Chris E. Hayner, " 'Sons of Anarchy': What Was That Shakespeare Quote in the Series Finale?" *zap2it blogs, zap2it*, December 10, 2014, accessed June 23, 2015, http://www.zap2it.com/blogs/sons_of_anarchy_william_shakespeare_quote _hamlet_series_finale-2014-12.

60. Rich Bellis, "Which Great Literary Work Explains *Breaking Bad* Best?" *The Atlantic*, October 2, 2013, accessed June 28, 2015, http://www.theatlantic .com/entertainment/archive/2013/10/which-great-literary-work-explains-em -breaking-bad-em-best/280149/; Tom Mendelsohn, "Is Breaking Bad's Ozymandias the Greatest Episode of TV Ever Written?" *The Independent*, September 17, 2013, accessed June 28, 2015, http://www.independent.co.uk/arts-entertainment /tv/features/is-breaking-bads-ozymandias-the-greatest-episode-of-tv-ever-written -8821985.html.

61. Rich Bellis, "Which Great Literary Work Explains *Breaking Bad* Best?"

62. Tom Mendelsohn, "Is Breaking Bad's Ozymandias the Greatest Episode of TV Ever Written?"

63. Michael M. Hughes, "The One Literary Reference You Must Know to Appreciate *True Detective*," *True Detective* (blog), i09, February 14, 2014, accessed June 28, 2015, http://io9.com/the-one-literary-reference-you-must-know -to-appreciate-1523076497.

64. Alan Yuhas, "True Detective Finale: All the Clues, Patterns and Theories So Far," *TV and Radio Blog, The Guardian*, March 7, 2014, accessed June 28, 2015, http://www.theguardian.com/tv-and-radio/2014/mar/07/true-detective-finale -clues-patterns-theories.

65. Graeme Virtue, "Best TV of 2014: No 7—True Detective," *TV and Radio Blog, The Guardian*, December 15, 2014, accessed June 28, 2015, http://www .theguardian.com/tv-and-radio/tvandradioblog/2014/dec/15/best-tv-of-2014 -no-7-true-detective-hbo.

66. Russell Smith, "Decoding the Secrets of True Detective," *The Globe and Mail*, February 19, 2014, accessed June 28, 2015, http://www.theglobeandmail .com/arts/television/decoding-the-secrets-of-true-detective/article16982428/.

67. David Carr, "Barely Keeping Up in TV's New Golden Age," *The New York Times*, March 9, 2014, accessed June 28, 2015, http://www.nytimes.com /2014/03/10/business/media/fenced-in-by-televisions-excess-of-excellence.html? _r=1.

68. Ibid.

69. Chris Harvey, "True Detective, Sky Atlantic, Review: A Work of Depth and Cinematic Flair," *The Daily Telegraph*, February 22, 2014, accessed June 28, 2015, http://www.telegraph.co.uk/culture/tvandradio/tv-and-radio-reviews /10654871/True-Detective-Sky-Atlantic-review-a-work-of-depth-and-cinematic -flair.html.

70. Anne Billson, "Is True Detective Leading to an 'Undumbing of American TV'?" *Telegraph*, April 9, 2014, accessed June 28, 2015, http://www.telegraph .co.uk/culture/tvandradio/10721228/Is-True-Detective-leading-to-an-undumbing -of-American-TV.html.

71. David Hinckley, "Emmys 2014: from 'Mad Men' to 'Breaking Bad,' the Top 10 Dramas of All Time," *The New York Daily News*, August 22, 2014, accessed June 20, 2015, http://www.nydailynews.com/entertainment/tv/breaking -bad-game-thrones-rank-time-best-dramas-list-article-1.1912409.

72. "Mad Men Awards," *IMDb.com*, n.d., accessed June 29, 2015, http:// www.imdb.com/title/tt0804503/awards.

73. "About the Show," *AMCtv.com*, n.d., accessed June 29, 2015, http://www .amc.com/shows/mad-men/exclusives/about.

74. Bernie Heidkamp, "New 'Mad Men' TV Show Uses the Past to Reveal Racism and Sexism of Today," *Alternet*, August 23, 2007, accessed June 20, 2015, http://www.alternet.org/story/60278/new_%22mad_men%22_tv_show _uses_the_past_to_reveal_racism_and_sexism_of_today.

75. Ibid.

76. Ashley Shaw, "Meet the Winners of the Banana Republic *Mad Men* Casting Call," *AMC* blog, October 29, 2010, accessed June 20, 2015, http://blogs .amctv.com; Adam Tschorn, "Brooks Bros. Dapper Draper Caper: Selling Limited 'Mad Men' suits," *All the Rage* (blog), *The Los Angeles Times*, October 13, 2009, accessed June 28, 2015, http://latimesblogs.latimes.com/alltherage/2009 /10/brooks-brothers-introduces-limited-edition-mad-men-suit-don-draper-roger -sterling.html; Stuart Elliott, "'Mad Men' Dolls in a Barbie World, but the Cocktails Must Stay Behind," *The New York Times*, March 9, 2010, LexisNexis Academic; Graeme Allister, "How Mad Men Became a Style Guide," *TV and Radio Blog*, *The Guardian*, August 1, 2008, accessed June 25, 2014, http://www.theguardian .com/culture/tvandradioblog/2008/aug/01/youdonthavetowatchmadmen; Kim Cook, "'Mad Men' Inspires Midcentury Modern Décor Resurgence," *AZCentral .com*, April 27, 2012, accessed June 28, 2015, http://archive.azcentral.com/style /hfe/decor/20120427mad-men-inspires-midcentury-modern-decor-resurgence; Sharon Forrester, "Mad Men Nails," *Vogue*, August 5, 2010, accessed June 28, 2015, http://www.vogue.co.uk/beauty/2010/08/05/janie-bryant-mad-men-nail -polish-line.

77. Kona Gallagher, "Behind the Scenes of Unilever's Retro 'Mad Men' ads," *The Aol.com*, September 3, 2010, accessed June 28, 2015, http://www.aoltv.com /2010/09/03/behind-the-scenes-of-unilevers-retro-mad-men-ads/.

78. National Museum of American History, "National Museum of American History Accepts Mad Men Artifacts Against Backdrop of Real Advertising History," March 27, 2015, accessed June 29, 2015, http://americanhistory.si.edu /press/releases/mad-men.

79. Billy Parrott, "The 'Mad Men' Reading List," *Biblio File* (blog), *The New York Public Library*, February 27, 2012, accessed June 28, 2015, http://www .nypl.org/blog/2012/02/27/mad-men-reading-list.

80. Scott Meslow, "The Problem of Marketing 'Mad Men'," *The Atlantic*, June 11, 2012, accessed June 28, 2015, http://www.theatlantic.com/entertainment /archive/2012/06/the-problem-of-marketing-mad-men/258335/.

81. David W. Dunlap, "A Season Premiere, a Falling Man, and Memories of 9/11," *City Room* (blog), *The New York Times*, February 28, 2012, accessed June 28, 2015, http://cityroom.blogs.nytimes.com/2012/02/28/a-season-premiere -a-falling-man-and-memories-of-911/?_r=0.

82. Jake Coyle, "Netflix Show 'House of Cards' Is a Big Gamble," *The Huffington Post*, January 24, 2013, accessed June 28, 2015, http://www.huffingtonpost .com/2013/01/24/netflix-show-house-of-cards_n_2545332.html.

83. Ibid.

84. Ibid.

85. Eric Elia, "Binge Programming: How Netflix's 'House of Cards' Changes the Game," pbs.org, February 6, 2013, accessed June 1, 2015, http://www.pbs .org/mediashift/2013/02/binge-programming-how-netflixs-house-of-cards -changes-the-game037/.

86. Tim Wu, "Netflix's War on Mass Culture," *New Republic*, December 4, 2013, accessed June 28, 2015, http://www.newrepublic.com/article/115687/netflixs -war-mass-culture.

87. David Carr, "Giving Viewers What They Want," *The New York Times*, February 24, 2013, LexisNexis Academic.

88. Greg Satell, "What Netflix's 'House of Cards' Means for the Future of TV," *Forbes*, March 4, 2013, accessed June 28, 2015, http://www.forbes.com /sites/gregsatell/2013/03/04/what-netflixs-house-of-cards-means-for-the-future -of-tv/.

89. David Carr, "Giving Viewers What They Want."

90. Joan Solsman, "Netflix Won't Even Reveal 'House Of Cards' Audience Numbers To Show's Creator," *CNET Magazine*, April 24, 2014, accessed June 28, 2015, http://www.cnet.com/news/netflix-wont-even-reveal-house-of-cards-audience -numbers-to-shows-creator/.

91. Lucia Graves, "Frank Underwood and a Brief History of Ruthless Pragmatism," *National Journal*, February 19, 2014, accessed June 28, 2015, http:// www.nationaljournal.com/politics/frank-underwood-and-a-brief-history-of -ruthless-pragmatism-20140219.

92. "*House of Cards*, Awards," *IMDb*, n.d., accessed June 23, 2015, http:// www.imdb.com/title/tt1856010/awards; Brian Stelter, "Emmys Highlight a Changing TV Industry," *The New York Times*, September 20, 2013, LexisNexis Academic.

93. Frank Newport, "Dysfunctional Government Surpasses Economy as Top U.S. Problem," *Gallup*, October 9, 2013, accessed June 28, 2015, http:// www.gallup.com/poll/165302/dysfunctional-gov-surpasses-economy-top -problem.aspx; "Public Trust in Government 1958-2014," The Pew Research Center, November 13, 2014, accessed June 1, 2015, http://www.people-press .org/2014/11/13/public-trust-in-government/.

94. "House of Cards," Season 1, Episode 1: Chapter 1.

95. Ari Melber, "The Terrible, True Insight of 'House of Cards': Bad People Run D.C.," *The Atlantic*, February 12, 2013, accessed June 28, 2015, http:// www.theatlantic.com/entertainment/archive/2013/02/the-terrible-true-insight -of-house-of-cards-bad-people-run-dc/273063/.

96. "Public Trust in Government 1958–2014," The Pew Research Center, November 13, 2014; "Trust in Government Nears Record Low, But Most Federal Agencies Are Viewed Favorably," The Pew Research Center, October 18, 2013, accessed June 1, 2015, http://www.people-press.org/2013/10/18/trust-in -government-nears-record-low-but-most-federal-agencies-are-viewed-favorably/.

97. Maureen Ryan, "'House of Cards' Review: Kevin Spacey's Trip Through Washington's Dark Side," *The Huffington Post*, January 31, 2013, accessed June 28, 2015, http://www.huffingtonpost.com/maureen-ryan/house-of-cards -review_b_2592432.html.

98. Erin Whitney, "How Claire Underwood and 'House of Cards' Changed the TV Antihero Forever," *The Huffington Post*, March 5, 2014, accessed

June 28, 2015, http://www.huffingtonpost.com/2014/03/05/house-of-cards-tv
-antihero-archetype_n_4899440.ht.

99. "House of Cards," Season 2, Episode 14: Chapter 14.

100. Conor Friedersdorf, "Feminism, Depravity, and Power in *House of Cards*,"
The Atlantic, February 20, 2014, accessed June 28, 2015, http://www.theatlantic
.com/politics/archive/2014/02/feminism-depravity-and-power-in-em-house-of
-cards-em/283960/.

101. Erin Whitney, "How Claire Underwood and 'House of Cards' Changed
the TV Antihero Forever."

102. Conor Friedersdorf, "Feminism, Depravity, and Power in *House of Cards*."

103. Anna Brown, "U.S. Hispanic and Asian Populations Growing, But for
Different Reasons," Pew Research Center, June 16, 2014, accessed June 1, 2015,
http://www.pewresearch.org/fact-tank/2014/06/26/u-s-hispanic-and-asian
-populations-growing-but-for-different-reasons/.

104. "Between Two Worlds: How Young Latinos Come of Age in America,"
Pew Research Center, December 9, 2009, accessed June 1, 2015, http://www
.pewhispanic.org/2009/12/11/between-two-worlds-how-young-latinos-come-of
-age-in-america/.

105. Francis Negron-Muntaner, "The Latino-Media Gap: A Report on the
State of Latinos in U.S. Media," Columbia University, June 2, 2014, accessed June
1, 2015, https://pmcdeadline2.files.wordpress.com/2014/06/latino_media_gap
_report-wm.pdf.

106. Ibid.

107. Anthony LaPastina, "Telenovela," *The Museum of Broadcast Communications*, n.d., accessed June 16, 2015, http://www.museum.tv/eotv/telenovela.htm.

108. Ibid.

109. Brenda Salinas, "Is America Ready to Fall In Love With The Telenovela?"
NPR Code Switch, November 9, 2014, accessed June 1, 2015, http://www.npr
.org/sections/codeswitch/2014/11/09/362401259/is-america-ready-to-fall-in
-love-with-the-telenovela.

110. Scott Clarke, "Created in Whose Image? Religious Characters on Network Television," *Journal of Media and Religion*, 4, no. 3 (2005): 137–153, doi:
10.1207/s15328415jmr0403_2.

111. Erika Engstrom and Joseph M. Valenzano III, "Demon Hunters and
Hegemony: Portrayal of Religion on the CW's *Supernatural*," *Journal of Media
and Religion*, 9 (2010): 67–83, doi:10.1080/15348421003738785.

112. Ibid, 79.

113. "How Race and Religion Shape Millennial Attitudes on Sexuality and
Reproductive Health," *Public Religion Research Institute*, March 27, 2015,
accessed June 1, 2015, http://publicreligion.org/research/2015/03/survey-how
-race-and-religion-shape-millennial-attitudes-on-sexuality-and-reproductive
-health/#.VR11xuG5LkN; "Poll: Latino Voters Hold Compassionate Views on
Abortion," *The Latina Institute*, November 30, 2011, accessed June 1, 2015,
http://latinainstitute.org/en/latinopoll.

114. Bel Hernandez, "Bridge Across the Border," *LatinoMagazine.com*, Fall 2013, accessed June 28, 2015, http://latinomagazine.com/Fall2013/the-bridge.html.

115. Michael Schneider, "From *The Returned* to *The Bridge,* Viewers Adjust to Subtitles as TV Gets More Global," *TV Guide*, December 5, 2013, accessed June 28, 2015, http://www.tvguide.com/news/returned-bridge-viewers-1074256/.

116. Bel Hernandez, "Bridge Across the Border."

117. James Poniewozik, "Must-Read TV: *The Bridge*'s Elwood Reid on Getting America to Watch Subtitles," *Time*, July 10, 2014, accessed June 1, 2015, http://time.com/2966884/tv-subtitles-the-bridge-fx/.

118. Bel Hernandez, "Bridge Across the Border."

119. James Poniewozik, "Must-Read TV: *The Bridge*'s Elwood Reid on Getting America to Watch Subtitles."

120. "FX's 'The Bridge' Finds Authenticity In Spanish-Language Scenes," *Morning Edition*, National Public Radio (Boston, MA: WBUR, October 1, 2014).

121. Inkoo Kang, "On FX's *The Bridge,* Serial Killers Are a First-World Problem," *Village Voice*, September 25, 2013, http://www.villagevoice.com/film/on-fxs-the-bridge-serial-killers-are-a-first-world-problem-6439586.

122. "Autism Theatre Initiative," Theatre Development Fund, n.d., accessed March 12, 2015, https://www.tdf.org/nyc/40/Autism-Theatre-Initiative.

123. "Services for Guests With Cognitive Disabilities," Walt Disney World, n.d., accessed March 12, 2015, https://disneyworld.disney.go.com/guest-services/cognitive-disabilities-services/; Taylor Strickland, "Universal Orlando: Complete Guide to Attraction Assistance for Special Needs Families," *Orlando Informer*, n.d., accessed March 12, 2014, http://www.orlandoinformer.com/universal/guest-assistance-passes/.

124. "Wings for Autism," *Massport*, n.d., accessed March 12, 2014, http://www.massport.com/logan-airport/about-logan/airport-programs/wings-for-autism/.

125. Centers for Disease Control and Prevention, "Autism Spectrum Disorder," n.d., accessed March 12, 2015, http://www.cdc.gov/ncbddd/autism/index.html.

126. Centers for Disease Control and Prevention, "Facts About ASD," n.d., accessed March 12, 2015, http://www.cdc.gov/ncbddd/autism/facts.html.

127. Centers for Disease Control and Prevention, "CDC Estimates 1 in 68 Children Has Been Identified with Autism Spectrum Disorder," March 27, 2014, accessed March 12, 2015, http://www.cdc.gov.

128. Madison Park, "Medical Journal Retracts Article Linking Autism to Vaccine," CNN, February 2, 2010, accessed March 15, 2015, http://www.cnn.com/2010/HEALTH/02/02/lancet.retraction.autism/.

129. "McCarthy's Vaccination Stance Complicates Job on 'The View'," *All Things Considered*, National Public Radio (Boston, MA: WBUR, July 16, 2013).

130. Maggie Furlong, "The Latest Trend on TV: Characters With Asperger's," *The Huffington Post*, July 10, 2013, accessed March 15, 2015, http://www.huffingtonpost.com/maggie-furlong/aspergers-on-tv_b_3574336.html.

131. Brian Bethune, "Autistic Licence: Suddenly Asperger's is the New 'It' Disorder on Screen and in Fiction," *MacLeans*, July 13, 2009, accessed March 15, 2015, http://www.macleans.ca/culture/autistic-licence/.

132. Emily Shire, "Finally, a Realistic Autistic Character on Television," *Salon*, July 11, 2013, accessed March 15, 2015, http://www.salon.com/2013/07/11/finally_a_realistic_autistic_character_on_television/.

133. Alan Sepinwell, "How TV Shows Try (or Choose not) to Depict Asperger's Syndrome: Sepinwall on TV," *The Star Ledger*, February 28, 2010, accessed March 15, 2015, http://www.nj.com/entertainment/tv/index.ssf/2010/02/how_tv_shows_try_or_choose_not.html.

134. Michelle Diament, "Max from NBC's Parenthood Talks Aspergers," *Disability Scoop*, November 9, 2010, accessed March 15, 2015, http://www.disabilityscoop.com/2010/11/09/parenthood/11084/.

135. Alan Sepinwell, "How TV Shows Try (or Choose not) to Depict Asperger's Syndrome: Sepinwall on TV."

136. Jean Winegardner, "He's Not Autistic But He Plays One on TV: Ryan Cartwright on Syfy's Alphas," *Autism Unexpected* (blog), *The Washington Times*, August 2, 2011, accessed March 1, 2015, http://communities.washingtontimes.com/neighborhood/autism-unexpected/2011/aug/2/autistic-tv-ryan-cartwright-syfy-alphas/.

137. Emily Shire, "Finally a Realistic Autistic Character on Television."

138. Ibid.

139. Beth Arky, "Touch and Autism," Child Mind Institute, January 31, 2012, accessed March 1, 2015, http://www.childmind.org/en/posts/articles/2012-1-31-fox-show-touch-mixed-response-autism-advocates.

140. Lynne Soraya, "When Will ABC Get Asperger's Right?" *Asperger's Diary* (blog), *Psychology Today*, February 10, 2009, accessed March 1, 2015, https://www.psychologytoday.com/blog/aspergers-diary/200902/when-will-abc-get-aspergers-right.

141. Ibid.

142. Landon Bryce, "Awful Aspergers Parenthood," *thAutcast* (blog), March, 3, 2011, accessed March 1, 2015, http://thautcast.com/drupal5/content/awful-aspergers-parenthood.

143. Landon Bryce, "Outstanding Neurotypical Media Allies of 2011," *thAutcast* (blog), December 27, 2011, accessed March 1, 2015, http://thautcast.com/drupal5/content/outstanding-neurotypical-media-allies-2011.

144. Emily Shire, "Finally a Realistic Autistic Character on Television."

145. John Elder Robison, "The Bridge and the End of Asperger's on TV," *Vulture*, July 12, 2013, accessed March 1, 2015, http://www.vulture.com/2013/07/aspergers-tv-the-bridge-diane-kruger-sheldon-cooper.html.

146. Raul Ojeda, "Aspie World 9—The Bridge," *Alien Ghost* (blog), August 16, 2013, accessed March 1, 2015, http://www.alienghost.com/2013/08/16/the-bridge/.

Chapter 2

1. Amy Damico, "Television," in *September 11 in Popular Culture*, ed. Sara Quay and Amy Damico (Santa Barbara: ABC-CLIO, 2010), 131–172.

2. Ibid.

3. Ibid.

4. Department of Homeland Security, "About DHS," n.d., accessed June 1, 2015, http://www.dhs.gov/about-dhs.

5. George W. Bush, "Proposal to Create the Department of Homeland Security," June, 2002, assessed May 19, 2015, http://www.dhs.gov/proposal-create-department-homeland-security.

6. William Haynes, "Enemy Combatants," Council on Foreign Relations, December 12, 2002, accessed May 19, 2015, http://www.cfr.org/international-law/enemy-combatants/p5312.

7. Amy Damico, "Television."

8. Ibid.

9. Johanna Blakley and Sheena Nahm, "The Primetime War on Drugs and Terror," The Norman Lear Center at the USC Annenberg School for Communication and Journalism, September 2011, accessed May 19, 2015, http://learcenter.org/project/mcd/drugsterror/.

10. Kennedy Elliot and Terry Rupar, "Six Months of Revelations on NSA," *The Washington Post*, December 23, 2013, accessed May 19, 2015, http://www.washingtonpost.com/wp-srv/special/national/nsa-timeline/.

11. Gregg Easterbrook, "America's Creepy, Surveillance-Endorsing Love of NCIS," *The Atlantic*, March 17, 2014, accessed May 15, 2015, http://www.theatlantic.com/entertainment/archive/2014/03/americas-creepy-surveillance-endorsing-love-of-em-ncis-em/284453/.

12. Sara Quay, "Everyday Life," in *September 11 in Popular Culture: A Guide*, ed. Sara Quay and Amy Damico (Santa Barbara: ABC-CLIO, 2010), 1–50.

13. Amy Damico, "Television," in *September 11 in Popular Culture: A Guide*, ed. Sara Quay and Amy Damico (Santa Barbara: ABC-CLIO, 2010), 131–172.

14. Sean Daly, Michelle Spark, and Sharon Kennedy Wynne, "Saying Goodbye to FX's Rescue Me: TV's Only 9/11 Centered Series Departs Days before the 10th Anniversary," *The Feed, Tampa Bay Times*, September 6, 2011, accessed June 1, 2015, http://www.tampabay.com/blogs/media/content/saying-goodbye-fxs-rescue-me-tvs-only-911-centered-series-departs-days-10th-anniversary.

15. "Rescue Me," Season 7, Episode 1: Mutha.

16. Yvonne D. Sims, "Firefighters," in *September 11 in Popular Culture: A Guide*, ed. Sara Quay and Amy Damico (Santa Barbara: ABC-CLIO, 2010), 32–33.

17. Randee Dawn, "10 Years Later, TV Still Has Trouble Capturing 9/11," *Today Television*, September 6, 2011, accessed June 29, 2015.

18. Ibid.

19. Sean Daly, Michelle Spark, and Sharon Kennedy Wynne, "Saying Goodbye to FX's Rescue Me."

20. "Rescue Me," Season 1, Episode 1: Guts.

21. David Wiegand, "'Rescue Me' Helped Us Deal with Sadness of 9/11," *SFGate*, September 7, 2011, accessed June 29, 2015, http://www.sfgate.com /entertainment/article/Rescue-Me-helped-us-deal-with-sadness-of-9-11 -2310788.php.

22. Sean Daly, Michelle Spark, and Sharon Kennedy Wynne, "Saying Good-bye to FX's Rescue Me."

23. Ibid.

24. Ibid.

25. Ibid.

26. Ibid.

27. Randee Dawn, "10 Years Later."

28. Ibid.

29. "Rescue Me," Season 1 Episode 1: Guts.

30. "Rescue Me," Season 7, Episode 9: Ashes.

31. "Rescue Me," Season 1, Episode 1: Guts.

32. "Rescue Me," Season 7 Episode 9: Ashes.

33. Ibid.

34. Jeremy Egner, "A TV Series Winds Down, Portraying Characters Who Will Never Forget," *The New York Times*, July 1, 2010, LexisNexis Academic.

35. Randee Dawn, "10 Years Later."

36. The Federal Bureau of Investigation, "Decidedly Uncivil Part Two: Mus-lim Mother Target of Hate Crime," May 2, 2007, accessed May 1, 2015, http:// www.fbi.gov/news/stories/2007/may/hate050207.

37. Amy Damico, "Television."

38. Evelyn Alsultany, "24 Challenging Stereotypes," in *How to Watch Television*, ed. Ethan Thompson and James Mittell (New York and London: New York University Press, 2013), 85–93.

39. Steven Prothero, *Religious Literacy: What Every American Needs to Know—And Doesn't* (San Francisco: Harper Collins, 2007).

40. Yair Rosenberg, "'Homeland' Is Anything But Islamaphobic," *The Atlantic*, December 18, 2012, accessed June 29, 2015, http://www.theatlantic.com /entertainment/archive/2012/12/homeland-is-anything-but-islamophobic /266418/.

41. "Parents Beware of 24," *The Weekly Wrap*, Parents Television Council, November 21, 2008, accessed June 29, 2015, https://www.parentstv.org/PTC /publications/emailalerts/2008/wrapup_112108.htm#3.

42. Ibid.

43. Adam Green, "Normalizing Torture on 24," *The New York Times*, May 22, 2005, LexisNexis Academic.

44. Ibid.

45. Andrew Buncombe, "US Military Tells Jack Bauer: Cut the Torture Scenes . . . Or Else!" *The Independent*, February 13, 2007, accessed June 29,

2015, http://www.independent.co.uk/news/world/americas/us-military-tells-jack-bauer-cut-out-the-torture-scenes—or-else-436143.html.

46. Ibid.

47. Jeremey Askenas, Hannah Fairfield, Josh Keller, and Paul Volpe, "7 Key Points from the CIA Torture Report," *The New York Times*, December 9, 2014, LexisNexis Academic.

48. "BBC Show Spooks Prepares to Screen REAL Waterboarding Torture Scenes," *The Daily Mail*, October 27, 2008, accessed June 29, 2015, http://www.dailymail.co.uk/news/article-1080888/BBC-Spooks-prepares-screen-REAL-waterboarding-torture-scenes.html.

49. Emily Nussbaum, "Faint Praise," *The New Yorker*, October 28, 2013, accessed June 29, 2015, http://www.newyorker.com/magazine/2013/10/28/faint-praise-2.

50. Catherine Rampell, "Television convinces Americans That Torture is Okay," *The Washington Post*, December 11, 2014, LexisNexis Academic.

51. Bill Keveney, "2nd 'Sleeper Cell' Gets Into Torture," *USA Today*, December 7, 2006, accessed June 1, 2015, http://usatoday30.usatoday.com/life/television/news/2006-12-07-sleeper-cell_x.htm.

52. Laila Al-Arian, "TV's Most Islamophobic Show," *Salon*, December 15, 2012, accessed June 1, 2015, http://www.salon.com/2012/12/15/tvs_most_islamophobic_show/; Rachel Shabi and Alex Andreou, "Does Homeland Just Wave the American Flag?," *Take Two* (blog), *The Guardian*, October 16, 2012, accessed June 1, 2015, http://www.theguardian.com/commentisfree/2012/oct/16/homeland-american-flag-waving.

53. Rob Owen, "TV's High-Stakes Takes on a Serious Issue," *Variety*, 320 (2013), 21; Alexandra Sifferlin, "Homeland and Bipolar Disorder: How TV Characters are Changing the Way We View Mental Illness," *Time*, October 9, 2013, accessed June 1, 2015, http://healthland.time.com/2013/10/08/homeland-and-bipolar-disorder-how-tv-characters-are-changing-the-way-we-view-mental-illness/.

54. "Homeland," Opening Credits, Season 1.

55. "Homeland," Season 1, Episode 1: Pilot.

56. Ibid.

57. John Avlon, "Forty-Five Foiled Terror Plots Since 9/11," *The Daily Beast*, September 8, 2011, accessed June 1, 2015, http://www.thedailybeast.com/articles/2011/09/08/9-11-anniversary-45-terror-plots-foiled-in-last-10-years.html.

58. Matthew Gilbert, "Blurred Lines between Good, Evil in Superb 'Homeland'," *Boston.com*, September 30, 2011, accessed June 1, 2015, http://www.boston.com/ae/tv/articles/2011/09/30/blurred_lines_between_good_evil_in_showtimes_superb_homeland/.

59. "Judging the Impact: A Post 9–11 America," National Public Radio, July 16, 2004, accessed June 1, 2015, http://www.npr.org/911hearings/security_measures.html.

60. "Homeland," Season 1, Episode 1: Pilot.

61. Ibid.

62. "Bipolar Disorder," *WebMD*, n.d., accessed June 3, 2014 http://www .webmd.com/depression/guide/bipolar-disorder-manic-depression.

63. Amy Chozik, "Claire Danes on Playing a Bipolar CIA Agent on 'Homeland'," *Speakeasy* (blog), *The Wall Street Journal*, September 14, 2011, accessed June 1, 2015, http://blogs.wsj.com/speakeasy/2011/09/14/claire-danes-on-playing -a-bipolar-cia-agent-in-homeland/.

64. "Homeland," Season 1, Episode 1: Pilot.

65. "Homeland," Season 1, Episode 5: The Blind Spot.

66. Ibid.

67. "Homeland," Season 1, Episode 11: The Vest.

68. "Homeland," Season 1, Episode 12, Marine One.

69. Ibid.

70. Ibid.

71. Ibid.

72. Mark Landler, "Lost in Translation: A U.S. Gift to Russia," *The New York Times*, March 7, 2009, LexisNexis Academic.

73. Craig Whitlock, "'Reset' Sought on Relations with Russia, Biden Says," *The Washington Post*, February 8, 2009, accessed June 1, 2015, http://www .washingtonpost.com/wp-dyn/content/article/2009/02/07/AR2009020700756 .html.

74. Jerry Markon and Philip Rucker, "The Suspects in a Russian Spy Ring Lived All-American Lives," *The Washington Post*, June 30, 2010, accessed June 1, 2015, http://www.washingtonpost.com/wp-dyn/content/article/2010/06/29 /AR2010062905401.html.

75. The Federal Bureau of Investigation, "Operation Ghost Stories: Inside the Russian Spy Case," October 31, 2011, accessed June 1, 2015, https://www .fbi.gov/news/stories/2011/october/russian_103111/russian_103111.

76. Jerry Markon and Philip Rucker, "The Suspects in a Russian Spy Ring Lived All-American Lives."

77. Laura M. Holson, "The Dark Stuff, Distilled," *The New York Times*, March 29, 2013, LexisNexis Academic.

78. Steven Kurutz, "Russians: Still the Go-To Bad Guys," *The New York Times*, January 17, 2014, LexisNexis Academic.

79. Olga Khazan, "*The Americans*' Refreshingly Real Take on Russians," *The Atlantic*, May 22, 2014, accessed June 1, 2015, http://www.theatlantic.com /entertainment/archive/2014/05/the-americans-refreshingly-real-take-on -russians/371471/; Eric Kohn, "*The Americans*': Were the KGB the Good Guys?" *BBC.com*, January 28, 2015, accessed June 1, 2015, http://www.bbc.com /culture/story/20150128-were-the-kgb-the-good-guys.

80. "In 'The Americans,' Art Imitates Real Life Lies," National Public Radio, January 28, 2015, accessed June 1, 2015, http://www.npr.org/2015/01/28 /382218372/in-the-americans-art-imitates-real-life-lies.

81. Julian Borger, "US and Russia in Danger of Returning to Era of Nuclear Rivalry," *The Guardian*, January 4, 2015, accessed June 29, 2015, http://www .theguardian.com/world/2015/jan/04/us-russia-era-nuclear-rivalry; Jeffrey Tayler, "The Seething Anger of Putin's Russia," *The Atlantic*, September 22, 2014, accessed June 28, 2015, http://www.theatlantic.com/international/archive/2014 /09/russia-west-united-states-past-future-conflict/380533/.

82. Brad Plumer, "A Short Timeline of Deteriorating U.S.-Russia Relations," *Wonkblog, The Washington Post*, August 8, 2013, accessed June 29, 2015, http://www.washingtonpost.com/blogs/wonkblog/wp/2013/08/08/ten-reasons -the-u-s-and-russia-are-at-odds/.

83. Jennifer Harper, "Americans Place Russia First on the List of U.S. Enemies: Here Comes the Cold War, part II," *The Washington Times*, February 16, 2015, accessed June 29, 2015, http://www.washingtontimes.com/news/2015/feb /16/inside-the-beltway-here-come-the-cold-war-part-ii/?page=all.

84. Eve Conant, "Is the Cold War Back?" *National Geographic*, September 13, 2014, accessed June 29, 2015, http://news.nationalgeographic.com/news /2014/09/140912-cold-war-geography-russia-ukraine-sanctions/.

85. Erin Whitney, "Pussy Riot Tells Off Fictional Russian President On 'House of Cards'," *The Huffington Post*, February 27, 2015, accessed June 29, 2015, http://www.huffingtonpost.com/2015/02/27/pussy-riot-house-of-cards_n _6761956.html.

86. Lynette Rice, "NBC Rejects 'Wonder Woman'," *Entertainment Weekly*, May 12, 2011, accessed June 29, 2015, http://www.ew.com/article/2011/05/12 /nbc-rejects-wonder-woman.

87. Ibid.

88. Jace Lacob, "Wonder Woman: A Sneak Peak at David E. Kelley's Script," *The Daily Beast*, February 2, 2011, accessed June 26, 2015, http://www .thedailybeast.com/articles/2011/02/02/wonder-woman-a-sneak-peak-at-david -e-kelleys-script.html.

89. Lesley Goldberg, "Wonder Woman Prequel Amazon Dead at CW," *The Hollywood Reporter*, January 15, 2014, accessed June 29, 2015, http://www .hollywoodreporter.com/live-feed/wonder-woman-prequel-amazon-dead -671309.

90. Calvin Reed, "Comics, Graphic Novels Market Hit $870 Million in 2013," *Publishers Weekly*, July 16, 2014, accessed June 29, 2015, http://www .publishersweekly.com/pw/by-topic/industry-news/comics/article/63319-comics -graphic-novels-market-hit-870-million-in-2013.html.

91. Jennifer Maloney, "The New Wave of Graphic Novels," *The Wall Street Journal*, December 31, 2014, accessed June 29, 2015, http://www.wsj.com /articles/the-new-wave-of-graphic-novels-1420048910.

92. Robin Rosenberg, "The Psychology Behind Superhero Origin Stories," *Smithsonian Magazine*, February 2013, accessed May 1, 2015, http://www .smithsonianmag.com/ist/?next=/arts-culture/the-psychology-behind-superhero -origin-stories-4015776/.

93. Sandy Shaefer, "Supergirl TV Show Gets Official Season Order from CBS," *Screenrant*, May 7, 2015, accessed May 10, 2015, http://screenrant.com /supergirl-tv-show-season-1-cbs/.

94. Ibid.

95. Rob Leane, "23 New Comic Book TV shows Airing in 2015 and Beyond," *Den of Geek*, May 1, 2015, accessed May 20, 2015, http://www.denofgeek.com /tv/comic-book-tv-shows/33601/updated-23-new-comic-book-tv-shows-airing -in-2015-and-beyond.

96. "Person of Interest," Season 1, Episode 1: Pilot.

97. *The Dark Knight*, directed by Christopher Nolan (Burbank, CA: Warner Brothers Home Video, 2008), DVD.

98. Vicky Gan, "How TV's 'Person of Interest' Helps Us Understand The Surveillance Society," *Smithsonian Magazine*, October 24, 2013, accessed June 1, 2014, http://www.smithsonianmag.com/smithsonian-institution/how-tvs-person -of-interest-helps-us-understand-the-surveillance-society-5407171/.

99. Ibid.

100. Jeffrey Rosen, "Total Information Awareness," *The New York Times*, December 15, 2002, LexisNexis Academic.

101. Ibid.

102. Michael Kirk and Mike Wiser, "United States of Secrets (Part One)," in *Frontline*, directed by Michael Kirk (Boston, MA: WGBH, 2014).

103. Joshua Rothman, "'Person of Interest': The TV Show That Predicted Edward Snowden," *The New Yorker*, January 14, 2014, accessed June 29, 2015, http://www.newyorker.com/culture/culture-desk/person-of-interest-the-tv-show -that-predicted-edward-snowden.

104. "Newsroom," Season 1, Episode 8: The Blackout Part 1: Tragedy Porn.

105. "Homeland," Season 1, Episode 2: Grace.

106. "The Good Wife," Season 5, Episode 18: All Tapped Out.

Chapter 3

1. Mark Hugo Lopez and Anna Gonzalez-Barrera, "Women's College Enrollment Gains Leave Men Behind," Pew Research Center, March 6, 2014, accessed June 17, 2015, http://www.pewresearch.org/fact-tank/2014/03/06/womens -college-enrollment-gains-leave-men-behind/.

2. Tamar Lewin, "At Colleges, Women Are Leaving Men in the Dust," *The New York Times*, July 9, 2006, http://www.nytimes.com/2006/07/09/education /09college.html?pagewanted=all.

3. Ibid.

4. The White House, Office of the Press Secretary, "Opportunity for All: President Obama Launches My Brother's Keeper Initiative to Build Ladders of Opportunity for Boys and Young Men of Color," February 27, 2014, accessed June 17, 2015, https://www.whitehouse.gov/the-press-office/2014/02/27/fact -sheet-opportunity-all-president-obama-launches-my-brother-s-keeper-.

5. Tamar Lewin, "At Colleges, Women Are Leaving Men in the Dust."

6. Andrea Press, "Gender and Family in Television's Golden Age and Beyond," *Annals of the American Academy of Political and Social Science*, 625 (2009): 148.

7. Emanuella Grinberg, "6 Ways to Embrace Gender Differences at School," *CNN.com*, October 3, 2014, accessed June 17, 2015, http://www.cnn.com/2014 /10/03/living/children-gender-inclusive-schools/.

8. Ibid.

9. CNN Wire Staff, "Surgery No Longer a Requirement for Changing Gender on Passport," June 9, 2010, accessed June 17, 2015, http://www.cnn.com /2010/US/06/09/passports.transgender/.

10. Ibid.

11. Buzz Bizzinger, "He Says Goodbye, She Says Hello," *Vanity Fair*, Cover Story, July 2015, accessed September 30, 2015, http://www.vanityfair.com/magazine /july2015.

12. Wynne Parry, "Gender Dysphoria: DSM-5 Reflects Shift in Perspective on Gender Identity," *The Huffington Post*, June 4, 2013, accessed June 17, 2015, http://www.huffingtonpost.com/2013/06/04/gender-dysphoria-dsm-5_n _3385287.html.

13. Ibid.

14. Ibid.

15. Emily Nussbaum, "Primary Colors: Shonda Rhimes's Scandal and the Diversity Debate," *The New Yorker*, May 21, 2012, http://www.newyorker.com /magazine/2012/05/21/primary-colors.

16. Michael O'Connell, "The Highest Rated Broadcast Series of 2014—And How People Watched Them," *The Hollywood Reporter*, December 30, 2014, accessed June 15, 2015, http://www.hollywoodreporter.com/live-feed/highest -rated-broadcast-series-2014-760484.

17. John Downing, "Racism, Ethnicity and Television," *The Museum of Broadcast Communications*, n.d., accessed June 15, 2015, http://www.museum .tv/eotv/racismethni.htm.

18. Linda Holtzman and Leon Sharpe, *Media Messages, Second Edition* (New York, ME. Sharpe, Inc., 2014), 384.

19. Ibid, 384–385.

20. Willa Paskin, "Shonda Rhimes: 'Calling a Show a 'Guilty Pleasure'—It's Like Saying it's a Piece of Crap'," *Salon*, February 10, 2013, accessed June 17, 2015, http://www.salon.com/2013/02/10/shonda_rhimes_calling_a_show_a_guilty _pleasure_%E2%80%94_it%E2%80%99s_like_saying_its_a_piece_of_crap/.

21. Sonia Saraiya, "Extant: 'What in the World Is Happening'/'Nightmares'," *The AV Club*, August 14, 2014, accessed June 17, 2015, http://www.avclub.com /tvclub/extant-what-world-happeningnightmares-208140.

22. Neil Drumming, "*Scandal*'s Racially Charged Motto: You Have to Be Twice as Good as Them," *Salon*, October 4, 2013, accessed June 17, 2015, http:// www.salon.com/2013/10/04/scandals_racially_charged_motto_you_have_to _be_twice_as_good_as_them/.

23. John Jergunsen, "Viola Davis on the Shocking How to Get Away With Murder Ending," *The Wall Street Journal*, October 17, 2014, accessed June 17, 2015, http://blogs.wsj.com/speakeasy/2014/10/17/viola-davis-on-shocking-how-to-get-away-with-murder-ending/.

24. Emily Nussbaum, "Primary Colors: Shonda Rhimes's Scandal and the Diversity Debate."

25. Ibid.

26. Jason Lynch, "Surprise! Halle Berry's Career Is Extant," *The Daily Beast*, July 9, 2014, accessed June 17, 2015, http://www.thedailybeast.com/articles/2014/07/09/surprise-halle-berry-s-career-is-extant.html.

27. Alessandra Stanley, "Wrought in Rhimes's Image," *The New York Times*, September 18, 2014, http://www.nytimes.com/2014/09/21/arts/television/viola-davis-plays-shonda-rhimess-latest-tough-heroine.html.

28. Ibid.

29. Ibid.

30. Margaret Lyons, "There Are Just so Many Things Wrong With the New York Times' Shonda Rhimes Article," *Vulture*, September 19, 2014, accessed June 17, 2015, http://www.vulture.com/2014/09/shonda-rhimes-new-york-times-alessandra-stanley.html.

31. Kara Brown, "The *New York Times*, Shonda Rhimes & How to Get Away With Being Racist," *Jezebel*, September 19, 2014, accessed June 17, 2015, http://jezebel.com/the-new-york-times-shonda-rhimes-how-to-get-away-wit-16368 68442.

32. Shonda Rhimes, Twitter post, September 19, 2014, accessed June 15, 2015, 7:33 a.m., http://twitter.com/shondarhimes.

33. Ibid, 2:04 p.m.

34. Jada Yuan, "Viola Davis Finally Gets the Lead Role She's Been Waiting for in *How to Get Away With Murder*," *Vulture*, October 2, 2014, accessed June 17, 2015, http://www.vulture.com/2014/10/viola-davis-how-to-get-away-with-murder.html.

35. Ibid.

36. Aura Bogado, "White Is the New White," *The Nation*, August 16, 2013, accessed September 30, 2015, http://www.thenation.com/blog/175786/white-new-white; Matthew Gilbert, "Orange Is the New Black: Yuppie, Interrupted," *The Boston Globe*, July 10, 2013 https://www.bostonglobe.com/arts/television/2013/07/10/orange-new-black-yuppie-interrupted/sfQieZah74YFAVWZYu gu2O/story.html.

37. Maurice Chammah, "The Prison Show's Dilemma," *The Los Angeles Review of Books*, June 20, 2014, accessed June 17, 2015, http://lareviewofbooks.org/essay/prison-shows-dilemma.

38. "Orange Is the New Black," Season 2, Episode 8: Appropriately Sized Pots.

39. Gabrielle Rivera, "Orange Is the New Black: 7 Things We Should Talk About," *Autostraddle* (blog), July 21, 2013 (7:30 a.m.), accessed September 30,

2015, http://www.autostraddle.com/orange-is-the-new-black-7-things-we-should-talk-about-186228/.

40. Dave Itzkoff, "Jailhouse Blues," *The New York Times*, May 28, 2014, http://www.nytimes.com/2014/06/01/arts/television/stars-and-creators-of-orange-is-the-new-black-talk-shop.html.

41. Nico Land, "*Orange Is the New Black* Proves to be the Model of Queer TV," *Advocat*, June 20, 2104, accessed June 17, 2015, http://www.advocate.com/commentary/2014/06/30/op-ed-orange-new-black-proves-be-model-queer-tv.

42. Aura Bogado, "White Is the New White."

43. Ibid.

44. Ibid.

45. "Breaking Bad," Season 5, Episode 16: Felina.

46. "Awards," Breaking Bad (2008–2013), *IMDb.com*, n.d., accessed November 2, 2014, http://www.imdb.com/title/tt0903747/awards?ref_=tt_awd.

47. Allen St. John, "Why 'Breaking Bad' Is the Best Show Ever And Why That Matters," *Forbes*, September 16, 2013, accessed June 27, 2015, http://www.forbes.com/sites/allenstjohn/2013/09/16/why-breaking-bad-is-the-best-show-ever-and-why-that-matters/; Richard Lawson, "The Case for 'Breaking Bad' as Television's Best Show," *The Wire*, July 13, 2012, accessed June 27, 2015, http://www.thewire.com/entertainment/2012/07/case-breaking-bad-televisions-best-show/54565/; Maureen Ryan, "'Breaking Bad': Five Reasons It's One of TV's All-Time Greats," *The Huffington Post*, July 11, 2012, accessed June 27, 2015, http://www.huffingtonpost.com/maureen-ryan/breaking-bad-greatest-show_b_1665640.html.

48. Mike Janela, "Breaking Bad Cooks Up Record-breaking Formula for Guinness World Records 2014 Edition," *Guinness World Records*, September 4, 2013, accessed June 27, 2015, http://www.guinnessworldrecords.com/news/2013/9/breaking-bad-cooks-up-record-breaking-formula-for-guinness-world-records-2014-edition-51000/.

49. Anthony Hopkins, "Anthony Hopkins's Letter to Breaking Bad Star Bryan Cranston," *The Guardian*, October 17, 2013, accessed June 27, 2015, http://www.theguardian.com/film/2013/oct/17/anthony-hopkins-bryan-cranston-breaking-bad-fan-letter; Stephen King, "Stephen King: I Love 'Breaking Bad'!" *Entertainment Weekly*, March 6, 2009, accessed June 27, 2015, http://www.ew.com/article/2009/03/06/stephen-king-why-i-love-breaking-bad.

50. Paul MacInnes, "Breaking Bad creator Vince Gilligan: The Man Who Turned Walter White from Mr Chips Into Scarface," *The Guardian*, May 18, 2012, accessed June 27, 2015, http://www.theguardian.com/tv-and-radio/2012/may/19/vince-gilligan-breaking-bad.

51. "The Great Recession," *The State of Working America*, November 2012, accessed November 2, 2014, http://stateofworkingamerica.org/great-recession/.

52. Danielle Kurtzleben, "Middle Class Households' Wealth Fell 35 Percent from 2005 to 2011," *Vox*, August 23, 2014, accessed June 27, 2015, http://www.vox.com/2014/8/23/6057467/middle-class-households-wealth-fell-35-percent

-from-2005-to-2011; Binyamin Appelbaum, "Fed Says Growth Lifts the Affluent, Leaving Behind Everyone Else," September 4, 2014, *The New York Times*, LexisNexis Academic.

53. Robert Pear, "Recession Holds Down Health Spending," *The New York Times*, January 9, 2012, LexisNexis Academic.

54. "Breaking Bad." Season 1, Episode 4: Cancer Man.

55. Marshall Crook, "'Breaking Bad,' Season 5, Episode 13, 'Tp'hajiilee': TV Recap," *Speakeasy* (blog), *The Wall Street Journal*, September 8, 2013, accessed June 27, 2015, http://blogs.wsj.com/speakeasy/2013/09/08/breaking-bad-season -5-episode-13-tohajiilee-tv-recap/.

56. Matthew Gilbert, "Stretching a Dollar With Roseanne? Or Scheming With Alexis?" *The Boston Globe*, March 8, 2009, accessed June 27, 2015, http://www.boston.com/ae/tv/articles/2009/03/08/stretching_a_dollar_with _roseanne_or_scheming_with_alexis/?page=full.

57. Michael Paarlberg, "Breaking Bad Is A Middle-Class Horror Story," *The Guardian*, September 9, 2013, accessed June 27, 2015, http://www.theguardian .com/commentisfree/2013/sep/09/breaking-bad-middle-class-horror-story.

58. Ibid.

59. Allen St. John, "Episode 512: How Breaking Bad Breaks Away from the Sopranos and the Wire and Why Vince Gilligan should Run for the SEC," *Forbes*, September 1, 2013, accessed June 27, 2015, http://www.forbes.com/sites /allenstjohn/2013/09/01/walter-white-tony-soprano-and-why-breaking-bad -creator-vince-gilligan-should-run-the-sec/.

60. Matt Taibbi, "Why Isn't Wall Street in Jail?" *Rolling Stone*, February 16, 2011, EBSCO HOST (58637937).

61. "Breaking Bad," Season 2, Episode 6: Peekaboo.

62. Louise Story and Erica Dash, "Bankers Reaped Lavish Bonuses During Bailouts," *The New York Times*, July 31, 2009, LexisNexis Academic.

63. Elizabeth Dwoskin, "Why Women Earn Less Than Men a Year Out of School," *Bloomberg Businessweek*, October 25, 2012, accessed June 17, 2015, http://www.bloomberg.com/bw/articles/2012-10-25/why-women-earn-less -than-men-a-year-out-of-school.

64. Ann Marie Slaughter, "Why Women Still Can't Have it All," *The Atlantic Monthly*, June 13, 2012, accessed September 30, 2015, http://www.theatlantic .com/magazine/archive/2012/07/why-women-still-cant-have-it-all/309020/.

65. James Dasilva, "Women Leaving High Powered Jobs: Two Ways to Slow the Trend," *Salon*, October 14, 2013, accessed June 17, 2015, http://www.salon .com/2013/10/14/women_leaving_high_power_jobs_two_ways_to_slow_the _trend_newscred/.

66. Sheryl Sandberg, *Lean in: Women, Work and the Will to Lead* (New York: Knopf, 2013).

67. Katty Kay and Claire Shipman, *The Confidence Code: The Science and Art of Self Assurance—What Women Should Know* (New York: Harper Business, 2014).

68. Catherine Rampell, "U.S. Women on the Rise as Family Breadwinners," *The New York Times*, May 29, 2013, http://www.nytimes.com/2013/05/30 /business/economy/women-as-family-breadwinner-on-the-rise-study-says.html.

69. Adrian McKinty, "When and Where Are George RR Martin's Game of Thrones Novels Set?" *The Guardian* Books Blog, March 17, 2014, accessed June 17, 2015, http://www.theguardian.com/books/booksblog/2014/mar/17/game-of -thrones-george-rr-martin-song-ice-fire.

70. Emily Nussbaum, "The Aristocrats: The Graphic Arts of Game of Thrones," *The New Yorker*, May 7, 2012, accessed September 30, 2015, http:// www.newyorker.com/magazine/2012/05/07/the-aristocrats.

71. Maureen Ryan, "Who Creates Drama at HBO? Very Few Women or People of Color," *The Huffington Post*, Huff Post TV, March 6, 2014, accessed June 17, 2015, http://www.huffingtonpost.com/2014/03/06/hbo-diversity_n _4899679.html.

72. Ibid.

73. Brett Martin, *Difficult Men* (New York: Penguin Press, 2013).

74. Michiko Kakutani, "Tortured Souls, Terrific Television," *The New York Times*, June 24, 2013, http://www.nytimes.com/2013/06/25/books/brett-martins -difficult-men-sees-a-new-golden-age-for-tv.html.

75. Brett Martin, *Difficult Men* (New York: Penguin Books, 2013).

76. Randee Dawn, "As TV Antiheroes Grow Ever Darker, Viewers Deal With Empathy Conflict," *The Los Angeles Times*, May 29, 2014, http://www.latimes .com/entertainment/envelope/tv/la-et-st-en-bad-triumphs-tv-antihero-20140529 -story.html.

77. Murray Smith, "Mad, Bad and Dangerous to Know: TV's Anti-Heroes," *Times Higher Education*, July 17, 2014, accessed June 17, 2015, https://www .timeshighereducation.co.uk/features/culture/mad-bad-and-dangerous-to-know -tvs-anti-heroes/2014483.article.

78. Alan Sepinwall, *The Revolution Was Televised* (New York: Somon & Schuster, 2012).

79. Michiko Kakutani, "Tortured Souls, Terrific Television."

80. Chris Osterndorf, "How the Anti-Hero Is Ruining Television," *The Daily Dot*, April 17, 2014, accessed September 30, 2015, http://www.dailydot.com /opinion/darkness-anti-heroes-ruining-tv/; Margaret Lyons, "Can We Make Walter White Our Last Antihero, Please?" *Vulture*, October 1, 2013, accessed September 30, 2015, http://www.vulture.com/2013/10/let-antiheroes-end-with -walter-white.html; Laura Bennett, "Against Antiheroes: It's Time to Retire Tele- vision's Most Overused Buzzword," *New Republic*, August 17, 2013, accessed September 30, 2015, http://www.newrepublic.com/article/114346/anti-antihero -against-cultural-buzzwords.

81. Laura Bennett, "The True Anti-Hero of 'Breaking Bad' Isn't Walter White," *New Republic*, August 8, 2013, accessed June 17, 2015, http://www .newrepublic.com/article/114245/breaking-bad-review-walter-white-not-anti hero.

82. Tierney Sneed, "Meet Sonya Cross, the Anti-Anti-Hero," *U.S. News & World Report*, July 10, 2016, accessed September 30, 2015, http://www.usnews.com/news/articles/2013/07/10/on-fxs-the-bridge-diane-kruger-plays-an-anti—anti-hero.

83. Akash Nikolas, "Where Is the Female Tony Soprano?" *The Atlantic*, June 27, 2013, accessed September 30, 2015, http://www.theatlantic.com/entertainment/archive/2013/06/where-is-the-female-tony-soprano/277270/; Meghan Lewit, "Bad Husband, Bad Wife, Good TV: The Fascinating Rise of Antihero Marriages," *The Atlantic*, April 30, 2013, accessed September 30, 2015, http://www.theatlantic.com/entertainment/archive/2013/04/bad-husband-bad-wife-good-tv-the-fascinating-rise-of-antihero-marriages/275347/.

84. Thomas Maier, "Can Psychiatrists Really 'Cure' Homosexuality?" *Scientific American*, April 22, 2009, accessed September 30, 2015, http://www.scientificamerican.com/article/homosexuality-cure-masters-johnson/.

85. "Masters of Sex," Season 1, Episode 8: Love and Marriage.

86. "Masters of Sex," Season 2, Episode 3: Fight.

87. "Masters of Sex," Season 1, Episode 8: Love and Marriage.

88. Ibid.

89. "Masters of Sex," Season 2, Episode 1: Parallax.

90. "Masters of Sex," Season 2, Episode 2: Kyrie Eleison.

91. Karlyn Bowman, Andrew Rugg, and Jennifer K. Marsico, "Polls on Attitudes on Homosexuality & Gay Marriage, March 2013," *AEI Public Opinion Study*, March 21, 2013, accessed June 17, 2015, http://www.aei.org/publication/polls-on-attitudes-on-homosexuality-gay-marriage-march-2013/.

92. "Gay Marriage and the Evolving Language of Love," *NPR.org*, March 29, 2013, accessed September 30, 2015, http://www.npr.org/2013/03/30/175682777/gay-marriage-and-the-evolving-language-of-love; Nolan Feeney, "It Wasn't Bigotry Back Then: The Unsettling Message of *Masters of Sex*," *The Atlantic*, November 18, 2013, accessed September 30, 2015, http://www.theatlantic.com/entertainment/archive/2013/11/it-wasnt-bigotry-back-then-the-unsettling-message-of-i-masters-of-sex-i/281575/; Daniel D'Addario, "This Is the Best Gay Character on Television: How 'Masters of Sex' Gets the Tragedy of 1950s Gay Life Right," July 27, 2014, accessed July 9, 2015, http://www.salon.com/2014/07/27/this_is_the_best_gay_character_on_television_how_masters_of_sex_gets_the_tragedy_of_1950s_gay_life_right/.

93. "Masters of Sex," Season 1, Episode 8: Love and Marriage.

94. William H. Masters and Virginia E. Johnson, *Homosexuality in Perspective* (Toronto; New York: Bantam Books, 1979); Lindsay Abrams, "California's Historic Move to Ban Gay Conversion 'Therapy'," *The Atlantic*, August 31, 2012, accessed September 30, 2015, http://www.theatlantic.com/health/archive/2012/08/californias-historic-move-to-ban-gay-conversion-therapy/261755/.

95. Thomas Maier, "Can Psychiatrists Really 'Cure' Homosexuality?" *Scientific American*, April 22, 2009, accessed June 17, 2015, http://www.scientificamerican.com/article/homosexuality-cure-masters-johnson/.

96. "Masters of Sex," Season 2, Episode 3: Fight.

97. Ibid.

98. Ibid.

99. Ibid.

100. Ibid.

101. Kate Phillips, "'Masters of Sex' Recap: Of Might and Men," *The New York Times*, July 27, 2014, accessed June 17, 2015, http://artsbeat.blogs.nytimes.com/2014/07/27/masters-of-sex-recap-of-might-and-men/.

102. Linda DiProperzio, "Should You Raise a Gender-neutral Baby?" *Parents*, 2013, accessed July 9, 2015, http://www.parents.com/parenting/gender-neutral-parenting/; Lisa Eliot, "Good Luck Raising that Gender Neutral Child," *Salon*, September 26, 2014, accessed July 9, 2015, http://www.salon.com/2009/09/26/gender_difference/; Richard Alleyne, "Couple Raising Child as 'Gender Neutral' to Avoid Stereotyping, *The Telegraph*, January 20, 2012, accessed July 9, 2015, http://www.telegraph.co.uk/news/9028479/Couple-raise-child-as-gender-neutral-to-avoid-stereotyping.html.

103. Linsey Davis and Susan Donaldson James, "Canadian Mother Raising 'Genderless' Bay, Storm, Defends Her Family's Decision," *ABCNews.com*, May 30, 2011, accessed June 17, 2015, http://abcnews.go.com/Health/genderless-baby-controversy-mom-defends-choice-reveal-sex/story?id=13718047.

104. Christin Scarlett Milloy, "Don't Let the Doctor Do This to Your Newborn," *Slate*, June 26, 2014, accessed June 17, 2015, http://www.slate.com/blogs/outward/2014/06/26/infant_gender_assignment_unnecessary_and_potentially_harmful.html.

105. Bill Keveney, "Amazon: Vote for Shows You Want Us to Make," *USA Today*, April 14, 2013, http://www.usatoday.com/story/life/tv/2013/04/19/amazon-studios-releases-pilots/2095383/.

106. Willa Paskin, "Amazon Has Finally Made Its *House of Cards*," *Slate*, February 11, 2014, accessed June 17, 2005, http://www.slate.com/blogs/browbeat/2014/02/11/amazon_s_new_pilots_transparent_mozart_in_the_jungle_the_after_the_rebels.html.

107. David Wiegland, "TV: 'Transparent'—Brilliant Dark Comedy," *SF Gate*, September 21, 2014, accessed June 17, 2015, http://www.sfgate.com/tv/article/TV-Transparent-brilliant-dark-comedy-5770231.php.

108. Verne Gay, "'Transparent' Gives Amazon a Top-Notch Series," *Newsday*, September 26, 2014, accessed June 17, 2015, http://www.newsday.com/entertainment/tv/transparent-gives-amazon-a-top-notch-series-1.9417898.

109. Margaret Lyons, "Amazon's *Transparent* Is Damn Near Perfect," *Vulture*, September 26, 2014, accessed June 17, 2015, http://www.vulture.com/2014/09/tv-review-transparent-is-damn-near-perfect.html.

110. Mary McNamara, "Amazon's Transgender Transition 'Transparent' Astonishes," *The Los Angeles Times*, September 26, 2014, http://www.latimes.com/entertainment/tv/la-et-st-transparent-review-20140926-column.html.

111. Joanne Ostrow, "Jeffrey Tambor Is Brilliant in 'Transparent' Dramedy on Amazon Prime," *Denver Post*, September 25, 2014, http://www.denverpost.com /television/ci_26599614/jeffrey-tambor-is-brilliant-transparent-dramedy-amazon -prime.

112. Ibid.

113. "Transparent," Season 1, Episode 1: Pilot.

114. Ibid.

115. Emily Nussbaum, "Open Secret: Powerful Revelations on 'Happy Valley' and 'Transparent'," *The New Yorker*, September 29, 2014, accessed September 30, 2015, http://www.newyorker.com/magazine/2014/09/29/open-secret.

116. Willa Paskin, "See Me: *Transparent* Is The Fall's Only Great New Show," *Slate*, September 29, 2014, accessed June 17, 2015, http://www.slate.com/articles /arts/television/2014/09/transparent_on_amazon_prime_reviewed_it_s_the_fall _s_best_new_show.html.

117. Margaret Lyons, "Amazon's *Transparent* Is Damn Near Perfect."

118. Willa Paskin, "See Me: *Transparent* Is the Fall's Only Great New Show."

119. Joanne Ostrow, "Jeffrey Tambor Is Brilliant in 'Tansparent' Dramedy on Amazon Prime."

120. Jill Soloway, "Let's Mix Up These Rochdale Principles With a Little Matrixial Trans-Subjectivity," *Flaunt*, June 4, 2014, accessed June 17, 2015, http:// flaunt.com/art/jill-soloway/.

121. "Transparent," Season 1, Episode 5: The Wedge.

122. Ibid.

123. "Transparent," Season 1, Episode 4: Moppa.

124. James Poniewozik, "Q & A: *Transparent* Creator Jill Soloway on Transgender Stories and Indie TV," *Time*, September 25, 2014, accessed June 17, 2015, http://time.com/3422038/transparent-interview-jill-soloway/.

125. "Funny, Dirty, Sad: The 'Holy Trinity' for 'Transparent' Creator Jill Soloway," *Fresh Air*, National Public Radio (Boston, MA: WBUR, 2014).

126. "Transparent," Season 1, Episode 6: The Wilderness.

127. Rona Marech, "Nuances of Gay Identities Reflected in New Language/ 'Homosexual' Is Passé in a 'Boi's' Life," *SF Gate*, February 8, 2004, accessed June 17, 2015, http://www.sfgate.com/news/article/Nuances-of-gay-identities -reflected-in-new-2824367.php.

128. "Transparent," Season 1, Episode 7: Symbolic Exemplar.

129. "Transparent," Season 1, Episode 5: Wedge.

130. Lauren Duca and Erin Whitney, "A Guide to Not Being Ignorant When Talking about Amazon's 'Transparent'," *Huff Post TV*, September 26, 2014, accessed September 30, 2015, http://www.huffingtonpost.com/2014/09/26/amazon -transparent-glossary_n_5883992.html; Erin Whitney and Lauren Duca, "We Need to Talk about Transparent," *Huff Post TV*, October 2, 2014, accessed September 30, 2015, http://www.huffingtonpost.com/2014/10/02/transparent -amazon_n_5909474.html.

131. "GLAAD Media Reference Guide—Transgender Issues," *GLADD*, n.d., accessed January 17, 2015, http://www.glaad.org/reference/transgender.

132. Cathy Carvajal, "'Transparent' about Gender Transition Gets Golden Globe Nod," *Fox News*, December 11, 2014, accessed June 17, 2015, http://www.myfoxny.com/story/27605644/transparent-about-gender-transition-gets-golden-globe-nod.

133. Debby Herbenick and Aleta Baldwin, "What Each of Facebook's 51 New Gender Options Means," *The Daily Beast*, February 15, 2014, accessed June 17, 2015, http://www.thedailybeast.com/articles/2014/02/15/the-complete-glossary-of-facebook-s-51-gender-options.html.

134. Taffy Brodesser-Akner, "Can Jill Soloway Do Justice to the Trans Movement?" *The New York Times Magazine*, August 29, 2014, http://www.nytimes.com/2014/08/31/magazine/can-jill-soloway-do-justice-to-the-trans-movement.html?_r=0.

135. "Transparent," Season 1, Episode 6: The Wilderness.

Chapter 4

1. Michael Kassel, "Dramatic Family Genre," in *The Guide to United States Popular Culture*, ed. Ray Browne (Madison, WI: University of Wisconsin Press, 2001), 251.

2. Thomas Schatz, "Workplace Programs," The Museum of Broadcast Communication, n.d., accessed May 1, 2015, http://www.museum.tv/eotv/workplacepro.htm.

3. Gretchen Livingston, "Less Than half of U.S. Kids Today Live in a Traditional Family," Pew Research Center, December 22, 2014, accessed June 29, 2015, http://www.pewresearch.org/fact-tank/2014/12/22/less-than-half-of-u-s-kids-today-live-in-a-traditional-family/.

4. Ibid.

5. Timothy Grall, "Custodial Mothers and Fathers and Their Child Support: 2007," Current Population Reports, United States Census Department, November, 2009, accessed June 1, 2014, www.census.gov/prod/2009pubs/p60-237.pdf.

6. Gretchen Livingston, "Less Than half of U.S. Kids Today Live in a Traditional Family."

7. Gretchen Livingston, "The Rise of the Single Father," Pew Research Center, July 2, 2013, accessed July 2, 2014, http://www.pewsocialtrends.org/2013/07/02/the-rise-of-single-fathers/.

8. Richard Fry and Jeffrey Passel, "In Post-Recession Era, Young Adults Drive Continuing Rise in Multi-Generational Living," Pew Research Center, July 17, 2014, accessed July 2, 2014, http://www.pewsocialtrends.org/2014/07/17/in-post-recession-era-young-adults-drive-continuing-rise-in-multi-generational-living/.

9. James Kaplan, "The Sorkin Way," *Vanity Fair*, May 2012, accessed July 2, 2014, http://www.vanityfair.com/unchanged/2012/05/aaron-sorkin-newsroom-sneak-peek.

10. Victor C. Strasburger and Barbara J. Wilson, eds., *Children, Adolescents and the Media* (Thousand Oaks: Sage, 2002), 14.

11. Family Education Network, "Parent Teen Relationships: Mothers and Daughters," n.d., accessed June 27, 2015, http://life.familyeducation.com/parenting/teen/42917.html.

12. Jean Twenge, *Generation Me* (New York: The Free Press, 2006), 1–72.

13. Morley Safer, "The Millennials Are Coming," CBS News, May 25, 2007, accessed June 29, 2015, http://www.cbsnews.com/news/the-millennials-are-coming/.

14. Martha Irvine, "The Young Labeled Entitlement Generation," The Associated Press, June 26, 2005, accessed June 27, 2015, http://www.freerepublic.com/focus/f-news/1431497/posts.

15. Karen Sternheimer, "Millennials at Work," *Everyday Sociology* (blog), W. W. Norton & Company, December 9, 2007, accessed June 2, 2014, http://nortonbooks.typepad.com/everydaysociology/2007/12/millennials-at.html.

16. Amy Benfer, "The Nuclear Family Takes a Hit," *Salon*, June 7, 2001, accessed June 27, 2015, http://www.salon.com/2001/06/07/family_values_2/.

17. "Friday Night Lights," Season 2, Episode 9: The Confession.

18. Meredith Hoffa, "Teach Me Tami," *Open Salon Blog, Salon*, January 25, 2010, accessed June 27, 2015, http://opensalon.com/blog/momlogic/2010/01/25/teach_me_tami; Sarah Seltzer, "On Friday Night Lights, the TV Sex Talk Done Right, RHRealityCheck.org, March 27, 2009, accessed June 27, 2015, http://www.rhrealitycheck.org/print/9679.

19. "Friday Night Lights," Season 2, Episode 14: Leave No One Behind.

20. "Friday Night Lights," Season 4, Episode 10: I Can't.

21. "Friday Night Lights," Season 3, Episode 11: A Hard Rain's Gonna Fall.

22. James Robinson and Thomas Skill, "Five Decades of Families on Television: From the 1950s Through the 1990s," in *Television and the American Family, Second Edition*, ed. Jennings Bryant and Alison Bryant (Mahwah, NJ: Lawrence Erlbaum, 2001), 140.

23. William Douglas, "Subversion of the American Family," in *Television and the American Family, Second Edition*, ed. Jennings Bryant and Alison Bryant (Mahwah, NJ. Lawrence Erlbaum, 2001), 231–232.

24. Ibid, 232.

25. Brenda Cossman, "Betwixt and Between Recognition: Migrating Same-Sex Marriages and the Turn Toward the Private," *Law and Contemporary Problems* 71, no. 3 (2008), 153–168, EBSCO HOST (35709001).

26. "The Polygamous Stylings of 'Big Love'," *Fresh Air,* National Public Radio (Boston, MA: WBUR, August 1, 2007).

27. Ibid.

28. "Defense of Marriage Act," 104th Congress, 2nd Session, 1996; Associated Press, "Milestones in the Drive to Legalize Gay Marriage," *APNews.org,* May 15 2014, http://news.yahoo.com/milestones-drive-legalize-gay-marriage-172202692 .html.

29. Jim Dalrymple II, "Polygamy Is Legal in Utah, For Now," *Buzzfeed.com,* August 27, 2014, accessed June 23, 2015, http://www.buzzfeed.com/jimdalrympleii /polygamy-is-legal-in-utah-for-now#.kfErjbpYR.

30. "Big Love," Season 1, Episode 3: Home Invasion.

31. Stanley Kurtz, "*Big Love,* from the Set," *National Review Online,* March 13, 2006, accessed June 29, 2015, http://www.nationalreview.com/article /217027/big-love-set-stanley-kurtz.

32. Ibid.

33. Brenda Cossman, "Betwixt and Between Recognition: Migrating Same-Sex Marriages and the Turn Toward the Private."

34. Warren Richey, "Prophet to Pedophile: Polygamist Warren Jeffs Sentenced to Life in Prison," *CSMonitor.com*, August 9, 2011, accessed June 29, 2015, http://www.csmonitor.com/USA/Justice/2011/0809/Prophet-to-pedophile -Polygamist-Warren-Jeffs-sentenced-to-life-in-prison.

35. "Timeline of Raid on FLDS-Owned YFZ Ranch," *Deseret News,* May 23, 2008, accessed June 1, 2015, http://www.deseretnews.com/article/700228439 /Timeline-of-raid-on-FLDS-owned-YFZ-Ranch.html?pg=all; Warren Richey, "Prophet to Pedophile: Polygamist Warren Jeffs Sentenced to Life in Prison."

36. Brenda Cossman, "Betwixt and Between Recognition: Migrating Same-Sex Marriages and the Turn Toward the Private."

37. "Big Love," Season 5, Episode 11: Where Men and Mountains Meet.

38. "Big Love," Season 1, Episode 4: Affair.

39. Ibid.

40. Ibid.

41. "Big Love's Creators Deconstruct the Show's Finale," *Fresh Air,* National Public Radio (Boston, MA: WBUR, March 21, 2011).

42. Stanley Kurtz, "*Big Love,* fFom the Set."

43. Brady McCombs, "My Five Wives: Utah Polygamous Family Gets Full Reality TV Series," *MagicValley.com*, December 19, 2013, accessed June 27, 2015, http://magicvalley.com/entertainment/my-five-wives-utah-polygamous -family-gets-full-reality-tv/article_fad0077e-6906-11e3-b620-001a4bcf887a .html; Jim Dalrymple II, "Polygamy Is Legal in Utah, For Now."

44. Don Lattin, "Gay Monogamous Couple are Brains Behind Polygamy," *SFGate,* June 10, 2007, accessed June 27, 2015, http://www.sfgate.com /entertainment/article/Gay-monogamous-couple-are-brains-behind-polygamy -2573064.php.

45. Lacey Rose, "Emmys: Good Wife Campaign Attacks 'True Detective' and Cable Rivals, *The Hollywood Reporter*, April 16, 2014, accessed June 27, 2015, http://www.hollywoodreporter.com/news/emmys-good-wife-campaign-attacks -696284.

46. Emily Nussbaum, "Shedding Her Skin, *The Good Wife*'s Thrilling Transformation," *The New Yorker*, October 13, 2014, accessed June 27, 2015, http://www.newyorker.com/magazine/2014/10/13/shedding-skin.

47. James Poniewozik, "*The Good Wife* Watch: The So-Bad-She's-Good-Wife," *Time.com*, October 15, 2014, Retrieved from Business Source Complete.

48. Meredith Blake, "*The Good Wife* Cast Wraps Season Five in a Triumphant Mood," *The LA Times*, May 17, 2014, accessed June 29, 2015, http://www.latimes.com/entertainment/tv/la-et-st-good-wife-finale-20140518-story.html.

49. "The Good Wife," Season 3, Episode 13: Bitcoin for Dummies.

50. Leah McGrath Goodman, "The Face Behind Bitcoin," *Newsweek*, March 6, 2014, accessed May 1, 2015, http://www.newsweek.com/2014/03/14/face-behind-bitcoin-247957.html.

51. Verne Kopytoff, "Are Google, Yahoo and Microsoft Living Up to Their Promises in China?" Time, January 8, 2014, accessed June 29, 2015, http://business.time.com/2014/01/08/are-google-yahoo-and-microsoft-living-up-to-their-promises-in-china/.

52. Clive Thompson, "From Anonymous to Bitcoin, *The Good Wife* is the Most Tech Savvy Show on TV," *Wired*, September 27, 2013, accessed June 1, 2015, http://www.wired.com/2013/09/screen-smarts/.

53. Ibid.

54. Paul Julian Smith, "10 O'Clock Staying Power," *Film Quarterly*, 64, no. 3 (Spring 2011), 10–11, doi:10.1525/FQ.2011.64.3.10.

55. David Sims, "*The Good Wife* Takes a Weak Swipe at Racism," *The Atlantic*, January 12, 2015, accessed June 29, 2015, http://www.theatlantic.com/entertainment/archive/2015/01/the-good-wife-stumbles-trying-to-confront-institutional-racism/384448/.

56. Emily Nussbaum, "Shedding Her Skin, *The Good Wife*'s Thrilling Transformation."

57. Michael Brown Shooting, "NBC Storyline," *NBC News*, n.d., accessed June 29, 2015, http://www.nbcnews.com/storyline/michael-brown-shooting; J. David Goodman and Al Baker, "Wave of Protests After Jury Does Not Indict Officer in Eric Garner Chokehold Case," *The New York Times*, December 3, 2014, LexisNexis Academic.

58. "The Good Wife," Season 6, Episode 12: The Debate.

59. "The Good Wife Delivers a Game Changing Stunner," *Fresh Air*, National Public Radio (Boston, MA: WBUR, March 28, 2014).

60. Delia Ephron, "The Woman Who Gave Up Sex," *The New York Times*, March 25, 2014, accessed June 29, 2015, http://www.nytimes.com/2014/03/26/opinion/the-woman-who-gave-up-sex.html.

61. Robert King and Michelle King, "A Letter from Robert & Michelle King," CBS, March 22, 2014, accessed May 1, 2015, http://www.cbs.com/shows/the_good_wife/news/1002177/.

62. Ibid.

63. Richard Serrano, "Mass Shootings in U.S. Have Tripled in Recent Years, FBI says," *The LA Times*, September 24, 2014, accessed June 29, 2015, http://www.latimes.com/nation/nationnow/la-nn-na-mass-shootings-fbi-20140924-story.html.

64. Kevork Djansezian, "Just the Facts: Gun Violence in America," NBC News, January 16, 2013, accessed June 1, 2015, http://usnews.nbcnews.com/_news/2013/01/16/16547690-just-the-facts-gun-violence-in-america?lite.

65. Andrea Caumont, "12 Trends Shaping Digital News," Pew Research Center, October 16, 2013, accessed June 1, 2015, http://www.pewresearch.org/fact-tank/2013/10/16/12-trends-shaping-digital-news/.

66. Monica Anderson, "How Social Media is Reshaping News," Pew Research Center, September 14, 2015, accessed June 1, 2015, http://www.pewresearch.org/fact-tank/2014/09/24/how-social-media-is-reshaping-news/.

67. David Tewksbury and Jason Rittenberg, *News on the Internet* (New York: Oxford University Press, 2012), 4.

68. Janet Kolodzy, *Practicing Convergence Journalism* (New York: Routledge, 2013), 1.

69. Ibid.

70. Kirstie Hettinga, "Initial Reactions to the New SPJ Ethics Code," *Media Ethics Magazine* 26, no. 1 (Fall 2014), accessed June 1, 2015, http://www.mediaethicsmagazine.com/index.php/browse-back-issues/193-fall-2014-vol-26-no-1-new/3999041-initial-reactions-to-the-new-spj-ethics-code.

71. Janet Kolodzy, *Practicing Convergence Journalism*.

72. *The Newsroom*, Season 3, Episode 1: Boston.

73. *The Newsroom*, Season 3, Episode 4: Contempt.

74. Ibid.

75. Ibid.

76. Ben Terris, "Charlie Hughes: From Savior to Villain at The New Republic," *The Washington Post*, December 14, 2014, accessed June 1, 2015, http://www.washingtonpost.com/lifestyle/style/chris-hughes-from-savior-to-villain-at-the-new-republic/2014/12/12/5494ffd2-80fb-11e4-8882-03cf08410beb_story.html.

77. Stuart Dredge, "Social Media, Journalism and Wars: Authenticity Has Replaced Authority," *The Guardian*, November 5, 2014, accessed June 1, 2015, http://www.theguardian.com/technology/2014/nov/05/social-media-journalism-wars-authenticity.

Chapter 5

1. "Television Academy Honors," n.d., accessed June 22, 2015, http://www.emmys.com/awards/honors/summary.

2. "First Annual Television Academy Honors," n.d., accessed June 22, 2015, http://www.emmys.com/awards/honors/first.

3. "The Fosters," Television Academy Honorees, May 24, 2014, accessed June 22, 2015, http://www.emmys.com/awards/honors/seventh/honoree3.

4. Richard Perez-Pena, "Fatal Police Shootings: Accounts Since Ferguson," *The New York Times*, April 8, 2015, http://www.nytimes.com/interactive/2015/04/08/us/fatal-police-shooting-accounts.html?_r=0.

5. Alan Yuhas, "The Walking Dead Is All about Blood, Gore—And Gun Control," *The Guardian*, April 1, 2013, accessed June 23, 2015, http://www.theguardian.com/commentisfree/2013/apr/01/walking-dead-blood-gore-gun-control-background-checks.

6. Tally Yaacobi-Gross and Amit Pinchevski, "Body of Evidence: *CSI*, The Detective Genre, and the Post Human Condition," Conference Paper, International Communication Association 2010 Annual Meeting, Communication and Mass Media Complete Data Base, Accession Number 59227364.

7. Sandra D. Jordan and Scott Sobel, "Martha Stewart Begins Prison Sentence," *The Washington Post*, October 8, 2004, LexisNexis Academic, http://www.washingtonpost.com/wp-dyn/articles/A17324-2004Oct8.html.

8. Martha Stewart, "Making Prison Life Just That Little Bit Better," *The Guardian*, March 21, 2006, accessed June 25, 2015, http://www.theguardian.com/books/2006/mar/22/extract.features11.

9. Brooke A. Masters, "Stewart Calls for Sentencing Reform," *The Washington Post*, December 23, 2004, LexisNexis Academic.

10. Ibid.

11. Dave Itzkoff, "Jailhouse Blues," *The New York Times*, May 28, 2014, LexisNexis Academic.

12. Aimee Lee Ball, "Prison Life, Real and Onscreen," *The New York Times*, August 2, 2013, LexisNexis Academic.

13. Christina Radish, "Creator Jenji Kohan Talks Orange Is the New Black, Her Research into Prison Life, and Graphic Sex Scenes," *Collider.com*, July 9, 2013, accessed June 25, 2015, http://collider.com/jenji-kohan-orange-is-the-new-black-interview/.

14. Piper Kerman, *Orange Is the New Black* (New York: Random House, 2011).

15. Nathan James, "The Federal Prison Population Buildup: Overview, Policy Changes, Issues, and Options," *Congressional Research Service*, April 15, 2014, accessed June 25, 2015, https://www.fas.org/sgp/crs/misc/R42937.pdf.

16. Maurice Chammah, "The Prison Show's Dilemma," *The Los Angeles Review of Books*, June 20, 2014, accessed June 25, 2015, http://lareviewofbooks.org/essay/prison-shows-dilemma.

17. Ibid.

18. "Fix the Orange Is the New Black Jail," New York Civil Liberties Union, 2015, accessed July 28, 2014, http://www.nyclu.org/oitnbjail.

19. Marc Mauer and Virginia McCalmont, "A Lifetime of Punishment: The Impact of the Felony Drug Ban on Welfare Benefits," *The Sentencing Project*, 4, November 2013, accessed June 27, 2015, http://www.sentencingproject.org/detail/publication.cfm?publication_id=523.

20. Ibid.

21. Sadhbh Walshe, "Welfare Ban for Ex-Drug Offenders Hurts Minority Women," *Aljazeera America*, December 9, 2013, accessed June 25, 2015, http://america.aljazeera.com/opinions/2013/12/welfare-ban-for-exdrugoffendersdispr oportionatelyhurtsminoritywo.html; Marc Mauer and Virginia McCalmont, "A Lifetime of Punishment."

22. Jennifer Schuessler, "Drug Policy as Race Policy: Best Seller Galvanizes the Debate," *The New York Times*, March 6, 2012, LexisNexis Academic.

23. "Orange Is the New Black," Season 1, Episode 12: Fool Me Once.

24. Rachel Simon, "Has 'Orange Is the New Black' Made Post-Convict Life Easier for Prisoners?," *The Huffington Post*, July 9, 2014, accessed June 27, 2015, http://www.huffingtonpost.com/bustle/has-orange-is-the-new-oitnb_b_5509126 .html; Maurice Chammah, "The Prison Show's Dilemma,"; Ruth Margalit, "The Disgusting Jail on 'Orange Is the New Black'," *The New Yorker*, June 8, 2014, accessed September 30, 2015, http://www.newyorker.com/culture/culture-desk /the-disgusting-jail-on-orange-is-the-new-blackhttp; Nia-Malika Henderson, "Lawyers Say the Real 'Orange Is the New Black' Jail Is Worse than the Fictional One," *The Washington Post*, June 9, 2014, accessed June 25, 2015, http://www .washingtonpost.com/blogs/she-the-people/wp/2014/06/09/lawyers-say-the-real -orange-is-the-new-black-jail-is-worse-than-the-fictional-one/.

25. Rachel Simon, "Has 'Orange Is the New Black' Made Post-Convict Life Easier for Prisoners?"

26. Ibid.

27. "Fair Sentencing Act," American Civil Liberties Union (ACLA), n.d., accessed June 25, 2015, https://www.aclu.org/node/17576.

28. Ibid.

29. Ed O'Keefe, "Cory Booker, Rand Paul Team Up on Sentencing Reform Bill," *The Washington Post*, July 8, 2014, accessed June 25, 2015, http://www .washingtonpost.com/blogs/post-politics/wp/2014/07/08/cory-booker-rand-paul -team-up-on-sentencing-reform-bill/.

30. "The Smarter Sentencing Act of 2014," 100th Congress, 2013–2014.

31. "Orange Is the New Black," Season 3, Episode 1: Mother's Day.

32. Drew Desilver, "Feds May Be Rethinking the Drug War, but States Have Been Leading the Way," Pew Research Center, April 2, 2014, accessed June 25, 2015, http://www.pewresearch.org/fact-tank/2014/04/02/feds-may-be-rethinking -the-drug-war-but-states-have-been-leading-the-way/.

33. Ibid.

34. "Orange Is the New Black in Federal Women's Prison," *Talk of the Nation*, National Public Radio (Boston, MA: WBUR, 2010).

35. "Orange Is the New Black," Season 2, Episode 9: 40 Oz. of Furlough.

36. Lawrence Summers, "American Risks Becoming a Downton Abbey Economy," *Financial Times*, February 16, 2014, accessed June 25, 2015, http://www.ft.com/cms/s/2/875155ce-8f25-11e3-be85-00144feab7de.html#axzz3e62 f5Bb2.

37. Ibid.

38. Jeremy Egner, "A Bit of Britain Where the Sun Never Sets: 'Downton Abbey' Reaches Around the World," *The New York Times*, January 3, 2013, LexisNexis Academic.

39. "Julian Fellows Q & A: The Inheritance Problem: The Heart of *Downton Abbey*," 2010, accessed February 12, 2015, www.pbs.org/wgbh/materpiece /downtonabbey/fellowes.html.

40. Ibid.

41. Matthew Philips, "Downton Abbey Has a Hidden Class Appeal to Americans," *Quartz*, January 4, 2015, accessed June 25, 2015, http://qz.com/320854 /downton-abbey-hidden-class-appeal-to-americans/.

42. Ibid.

43. Ibid.

44. Raymond Zhong, "The Anti-Snobbery of 'Downton Abbey'," *The Weekend Interview, The Wall Street Journal*, February 3, 2013, accessed June 25, 2015, http://www.wsj.com/articles/SB10001424127887323701904578273972 571512806.

45. Steven Mufson, "Eight Things 'Downton Abbey' Can Teach Us about the Modern Economy," *Wonkblog, The Washington Post*, February 10, 2014, accessed June 25, 2015, http://www.washingtonpost.com/blogs/wonkblog/wp /2014/02/10/eight-things-downton-abbey-can-teach-us-about-economics/.

46. Erik Kain, "Outside of Wonkland, 'We Are the 99%' Is a Pretty Good Slogan," *Forbes*, October 12, 2011, accessed June 25, 2015, http://www.forbes .com/sites/erikkain/2011/10/12/outside-of-wonkland-we-are-the-99-is-a-pretty -good-slogan/.

47. Joseph Stiglitz, "Of the 1%, by the 1%, for the 1%," *Vanity Fair*, May 2011, accessed September 30, 2015, http://www.vanityfair.com/news/2011/05 /top-one-percent-201105.

48. Carrie Budoff Brown, "Obama's 'Buffett Rule' to Call for Higher Tax Rate for Millionaires," *Politico*, September 17, 2011, accessed June 25, 2015, http://www.politico.com/news/stories/0911/63756.html.

49. Larry Elliott, "Thomas Piketty: The French Economist Bringing Capitalism to Book," *The Guardian Economics Blog*, May 2, 2014, accessed June 25, 2015, http://www.theguardian.com/books/2014/may/02/thomas-piketty-capital -in-the-twenty-first-century-french-economist.

50. Marc Tracy, "Piketty's 'Capital': A Hit That Was, Wasn't, Then Was Again: How the French Tome Has rocked the tiny Harvard University Press," *The New Republic*, April 24, 2014, accessed September 30, 2015, http://www .newrepublic.com/article/117498/pikettys-capital-sold-out-harvard-press -scrambling; Megan McArdle, "Piketty's Capital: An Economist's Inequality Ideas Are All the Rage," *Bloomberg Businessweek*, May 29, 2014, accessed June 25, 2015, http://www.bloomberg.com/bw/articles/2014-05-29/pikettys -capital-economists-inequality-ideas-are-all-the-rage.

51. Paul Krugman, "Why We Are in a New Gilded Age," *The New York Review of Books*, May 8, 2014, accessed June 25, 2015, http://www.nybooks.com/articles/archives/2014/may/08/thomas-piketty-new-gilded-age/.

52. Kim Peterson, "U.S. Is Minting Most of the World's Millionaires," CBS News MoneyWatch, June 10, 2014, accessed June 25, 2015, http://www.cbsnews.com/news/the-us-is-minting-most-of-the-worlds-millionaires/.

53. Pew Research Center, "5 Facts About Economic Inequality," January 7, 2014, accessed June 25, 2015, http://www.pewresearch.org/fact-tank/2014/01/07/5-facts-about-economic-inequality/.

54. Steven Mufson, "Eight Things 'Downton Abbey' Can Teach Us About the Modern Economy."

55. Matthew Philips, "Downton Abbey Has a Hidden Class Appeal to Americans."

56. Ursala Willis-Jones, "The Financial Crisis Explained, Via Downton Abbey," *Ursala Writes* (blog), September 25, 2011, accessed June 25, 2015, http://ursulawrites.blogspot.com/2011/09/financial-crisis-explained-via-downton.html.

57. Brett Arends, "10 Ways 'Downton Abbey' Servants Had It Better Than You," Slideshow, *MarketWatch*, March 2, 2014, accessed June 25, 2015, http://www.marketwatch.com/story/are-downton-abbey-servants-better-off-than-you-2014-02-26.

58. Brett Arends, "Inequality Worse Now Than on 'Downton Abbey'," *MarketWatch*, February 26, 2014, accessed June 25, 2015, http://www.marketwatch.com/story/welcome-to-downton-abbcy-america-2014-02-24.

59. Steven Mufson, "Eight Things 'Downton Abbey' Can Teach Us About the Modern Economy."

60. Kim Peterson, "U.S. Is Minting Most of the World's Millionaires," *MoneyWatch*, CBS News, June 10, 2014, accessed June 25, 2015, http://www.cbsnews.com/news/the-us-is-minting-most-of-the-worlds-millionaires/.

61. Brett Arends, "Inequality Worse Now Than on 'Downton Abbey'."

62. Terry Connelly, "America's *Downton Abbey* Economy," *The Blog, Huffington Post*, January 9, 2014, accessed June 25, 2015, http://www.huffingtonpost.com/terry-connelly/americas-downton-abbey-econmy_b_4569620.html.

63. Valerie Connors, "Downton Abbey Tours: Experience the Hit British Drama," *The Travel* Channel, accessed February 12, 2015, http://www.travelchannel.com/interests/arts-and-culture/articles/downton-abbey-tours.

64. Mary Hall, "Kohl's Offers Downton Abbey Inspired Jewelry," *The Recessionista*, January 28, 2014, accessed February 12, 2015, http://www.therecessionista.com/2014/01/kohls-offers-downton-abbey-inspired-jewelry.html.

65. Valerie Connors, "Downton Abbey Tours: Experience the Hit British Drama."

66. "An Evening Inspired by Downton Abbey," *WGBH*, February 27, 2012, accessed February 12, 2015, http://www.wgbh.org/articles/Scenes-from-An-Evening-Inspired-by-Downton-Abbey-7816.

67. Pew Research Center, "5 Facts About Economic Inequality."

68. Raymond Zhong, "The Anti-Snobbery of 'Downton Abbey'," *The Week-end Interview, The Wall Street Journal*, February 3, 2013, accessed February 12, 2015, http://www.wsj.com/articles/SB10001424127887323701904578273972571512806.

69. Jake Blumgart, "Justified at Home in Kentucky," *Oxford American*, April 30, 2013, accessed June 1, 2014, http://www.oxfordamerican.org/item/521-justified-at-home-in-kentucky.

70. Evan Smith, "Implementing Environmental Justice in Appalachia: The Social and Cultural Context of Mountain Top Removal Mining as Seen Through the Lenses of Law and Documentaries," *William & Mary Policy Review*, 170, no. 4 (2012): 170–209.

71. "The Land of Mountaintop Removal," Smithsonian Channel Web Series, n.d., accessed June 1, 2014, http://www.smithsonianchannel.com/sc/web/series/701/aerial-america/videos/title/20924/the-land-of-mountaintop-removal.

72. Smith, "Implementing Environmental Justice," 174–179.

73. Steve Fesenmaier, "Films on Strip Mining and Mountaintop Removal Mining," *The Ohio Valley Environmental Coalition*, September, 2008, accessed June 1, 2014, http://www.ohvec.org/links/mountaintop_removal/documentaries.html; "Celebrities and Public Join 'Mountain Heroes' Campaign to Stop Mountaintop Removal Mining," *EcoWatch*, May 31, 2012, accessed June 1, 2014, http://ecowatch.com/2012/05/31/celebrities-and-public-join-mountain-heroes-campaign-to-stop-mountaintop-removal-mining/.

74. "Justified," Season 2, Episode 7: Save My Love.

75. "Justified," Season 2, Episode 8: The Spoil.

76. Ibid.

77. Smith, "Implementing Environmental Justice," 176–177.

78. Ibid.

79. Ibid.

80. Ken Ward, Jr., "'Significant' Slurry Spill Blackens Kanawha Creek," *The Charlestown Gazette*, February 24, 2014, accessed June 1, 2014, http://www.wvgazette.com/News/201402110032.

81. "Justified," Season 2, Episode 9: Brother's Keeper.

82. Jake Blumgart, "Justified at Home in Kentucky."

83. Viviana Andreescu and J. Eagle Shutt, "Violent Appalachia: The Media's Role in the Creation and Perpetuation of an American Myth," *Journal of the Institute of Justice and International Studies*, 9 (2009), 62–75.

84. "Justified," Season 2, Episode 9: Brother's Keeper.

85. Kevin Kelly, "Better Than Human: Why Robots Will—And Must—Take Our Jobs," *Wired*, December 24, 2102, accessed July 1, 2014, http://www.wired.com/2012/12/ff-robots-will-take-our-jobs/.

86. Judith Aquino, "The Next Nine Jobs That Will Be Replaced by Robots," *Business Insider*, March 17, 2011, accessed July 1, 2014, http://www.businessinsider.com/9-jobs-that-are-already-being-replaced-by-robots-2011-3.

87. Carole Cadwalladr, "Are the Robots about to Rise? Google's New Director of Engineering Thinks So," *The Guardian*, February 22, 2014, LexisNexis Academic.

88. Ibid.

89. Noor Nazzal, "Robots May Replace Humans in 10 Years," *Gulfnews.com*, February 11, 2014, accessed July 1, 2014, http://gulfnews.com/news/uae/government/robots-may-replace-humans-in-10-years-1.1289791.

90. Carole Cadwalladr, "Are the Robots About to Rise?"

91. Verne Kopytoff, "For Google, A Leg Up in the Artificial Intelligence Arms Race," *Fortune*, February 5, 2014, EBSCO HOST (94326588).

92. Kevin Kelley, "Better Than Human."

93. Sherry Turkle, *Alone Together: Why We Expect More from Technology and Less from Each Other* (New York: Basic Books, 2011), 23–125.

94. Kyle Chayka, "As Military Robots Increase, So Does the Complexity of Their Relationship with Soldiers," *Newsweek*, February 18, 2014, accessed July 1, 2014, http://www.newsweek.com/2014/02/21/military-robots-increase-so-does-complexity-their-relationship-soldiers-245530.html.

95. Doug Gross, "Meet Pepper, The Emotional Robot," *CNN*, June, 6, 2014, accessed July 1, 2014, http://www.cnn.com/2014/06/06/tech/innovation/pepper-robot-emotions/.

96. Grame McMillian, "Intelligence: Like Chuck But with Magical Wi-fi and More Frowning," *Wired*, January 8, 2014, accessed July 1, 2014, http://www.wired.com/2014/01/intelligence-cbs-pilot-review/.

97. Mark Perigard, "'CBS' Cyber Warrior A Chip Off the Old Six Million Dollar Man," *The Boston Herald*, January 7, 2014, accessed July 1, 2014, http://www.bostonherald.com/entertainment/television/television_reviews/2014/01/cbs_cyber_warrior_a_chip_off_the_old_six_million.

98. "The Science of Singularity," *CBS video*, January, 2014, accessed July 1, 2014, http://www.cbs.com/shows/intelligence.

99. Sherry Turkle, *Alone Together*, 25.

100. Ibid., 56.

101. Henry Jenkins, "Why Do Humans Tell the Stories They Do: An Interview with Lily Alexander (Part Six), *Confessions of an Aca-Fan* (blog), April 14, 2014, accessed July 1, 2014, http://henryjenkins.org/2014/04/who-do-humans-tell-the-stories-they-do-an-interview-with-lily-alexander-part-six.html.

102. Ibid.

103. Graeme McMillan, "The Cult of *Orphan Black*," *Time*, April 21, 2014, EBSCO HOST (95738226).

104. "Join the Clone Club," *BBC America*, December 25, 2013, accessed May 1, 2015, http://www.bbcamerica.com/orphan-black/videos/join-the-clone-club/.

105. Emily Yahr, "'Orphan Black': Everything You Forgot from Season 1 That You Need to Remember," *Style Blog, The Washington Post*, April 18, 2014, accessed May 1, 2014, http://www.washingtonpost.com/blogs/style-blog/wp/2014/04/18/orphan-black-everything-you-forgot-from-season-1-that-you-need-to-remember/.

106. Jean Bentley, "An 'Orphan Black' Primer: The Neolutionists vs. The Pro-lethians," *Zap2it* (blog), April 16, 2014, accessed May 1, 2014, http://www.zap2it.com/blogs/an_orphan_black_primer_the_neolutionists_vs_the_prolethians-2014-04.

107. Matt Webb Mitovich, "*Orphan Black* Comic Books to Expand Sci-Fi Series' World," *TVLine*, July 23, 2014, accessed August 1, 2014, http://tvline.com/2014/07/23/orphan-black-comic-books/; Clone Club Book Club, August 2014, accessed June 27, 2015, http://discourse.cloneclub.co/t/cophine-fan-fiction-master-post/89.

108. Jessica Goldstein, "The Crazy Science of Orphan Black," *ThinkProgress*, May 20, 2014, accessed June 27, 2015, http://thinkprogress.org/culture/2014/05/22/3440331/meet-the-real-cosima-orphan-blacks-science-consultant/; Joelle Renstrom, "How Farfetched Is the Clone Conspiracy on BBC America's *Orphan Black?*" *Slate*, March 29, 2013, accessed June 27, 2015, http://www.slate.com/blogs/future_tense/2013/03/29/orphan_black_how_farfetched_is_cloning_like_on_the_bbc_america_show.html.

109. Sarah Hughes, "Orphan Black: A Worthy Heir to Buffy's Crown," *TV and Radio Blog*, *The Guardian*, June 2, 2014, accessed June 27, 2014, http://www.theguardian.com/tv-and-radio/tvandradioblog/2014/jun/02/orphan-black-worthy-heir-to-buffys-crown.

110. Kyle Hill, "Orphan Black Teaches You More about Science Than Any Other Show on TV," *The Nerdist*, June 20, 2014, accessed June 27, 2015, http://nerdist.com/orphan-black-teaches-you-more-about-genetics-than-any-other-show-on-tv/.

111. Mat Edelson, "Ask An Expert: How Close Are We to Cloning Humans?" *Johns Hopkins University Gazette*, September–October 2014, accessed June 27, 2015, http://hub.jhu.edu/gazette/2014/september-october/ask-an-expert-cloning-humans; Brenna Kass, "Tackling Ethics in Orphan Black," *Scholarblogs* (blog), November 3, 2014, accessed June 27, 2015, https://scholarblogs.emory.edu/ids216grimshaw/2014/11/03/tackling-ethics-in-orphan-black/; Carol Pinchefsky, "The Clone Wars: A Look at the Science of 'Orphan Black'," *Forbes*, May 31, 2013, accessed June 27, 2015, http://www.forbes.com/sites/carolpinchefsky/2013/05/31/the-clone-wars-a-look-at-the-science-of-orphan-black/.

112. Willa Paskin, "Nine Lives, at Least," *Slate*, April 17, 2014, accessed June 27, 2015, http://www.slate.com/articles/arts/television/2014/04/season_2_of_orphan_black_starring_tatiana_maslany_reviewed.html.

113. "Orphan Black," Season 1, Episode 10: Endless Forms Most Beautiful.

114. Ibid.

115. Robert Barnes and Brady Dennis, "Supreme Court Rules Human Genes May Not Be Patented," *The Washington Post*, June 13, 2013, LexisNexis Academic.

116. Ibid.

117. Kyle Hill, "Orphan Black Teaches You More about Science Than Any Other Show on TV."

118. Daniel Schorr, "A New, 'Post-Racial' Political Era in America," *NPR*, January 28, 2008, accessed June 28, 2015, http://www.npr.org/templates/story/story.php?storyId=18489466.

119. Ibid.

120. Anne Easton, "Oscar Winner John Ridley Discusses the No-Filter Race Relations of 'American Crime'," *Observer.com*, March 4, 2015, accessed June 26, 2015, http://observer.com/2015/03/oscar-winner-john-ridley-discusses-the-no-filter-race-relations-of-american-crime/.

121. Anne Easton, "Oscar Winner John Ridley Discusses the No-Filter Race Relations of 'American Crime'."

122. Hank Stuever, "'American Crime' Is the Rare Network Drama That Will Get Your Rapt Attention," *The Washington Post*, March 4, 2015, accessed June 29, 2015, http://www.washingtonpost.com/entertainment/tv/american-crime-is-the-rare-network-drama-that-will-get-your-rapt-attention/2015/03/04/bb84cbdc-c28c-11e4-9ec2-b418f57a4a99_story.html.

123. Kelly L. Carter, "'American Crime' Offers An Unapologetic Look at Race Issues in the U.S.," *Buzzfeed.com*, March 6, 2015, accessed June 26, 2015, http://www.buzzfeed.com/kelleylcarter/american-crime-race-in-america#.if2oY09J3.

124. Verne Gay, "'American Crime' Review: It's Like Nothing You've Seen on ABC," *Newsday*, March 3, 2015, accessed June 29, 2015, http://www.newsday.com/entertainment/tv/american-crime-review-it-s-like-nothing-you-ve-seen-on-abc-1.10000766.

125. Sonia Saraiya, "'American Crime': Oscar Winner John Ridley's New Prestige Drama Clinches ABC's Spot as America's Best Network," *Salon.com*, March 4, 2015, accessed June 26, 2015, http://www.salon.com/2015/03/04/"american_crime"_oscar_winner_john_ridleys_new_prestige_drama_clinches_abcs_spot_as_america's_best_network/.

126. Greg Braxton, "ABC's 'American Crime' Series Pushes Hot Buttons of Race, Culture," *Los Angeles Times*, February 27, 2015, accessed June 29, 2015, http://www.latimes.com/entertainment/tv/la-et-st-abc-american-crime-race-culture-20150301-story.html#page=1.

127. Anne Easton, "Oscar Winner John Ridley Discusses the No-Filter Race Relations of 'American Crime'."

Conclusion

1. Andy Greenwald, "TV Eats Itself," *Grantland*, November 6, 2013, accessed August 8, 2015, http://grantland.com/features/the-sopranos-walking-dead-end-tv-golden-age/?print=1.

2. David Hinckley, "With the Conclusion of 'Breaking Bad,' TV May Be Nearing the End of the Age of Ultradark Shows," *New York Daily News*, November 24, 2013, accessed August 6, 2015, http://www.nydailynews.com/entertainment/tv-movies/tv-age-dark-dramas-article-1.1525216.

3. Ibid.

4. "Fall Preview: 2015 to 2016 New Shows," *TV Guide*, accessed August 6, 2015, http://www.tvguide.com/special/fall-preview/gallery/2015-new-fall-shows/; Natalie Abrams and James Hibberd, "Fall TV Pilots 2015: The Full List," *Entertainment Weekly*, February 2, 2015, accessed August 7, 2015, http://www.ew.com/article/2015/01/26/tv-pilots-2015.

5. Ibid.

6. "Fall Preview: 2015 to 2016 New Shows," *TV Guide*; "HBO Teases Mick Jagger-Martin Scorsese Rock Drama 'Vinyl'," *Variety*, August 4, 2015, accessed August 7, 2015, http://variety.com/2015/tv/news/video-vinyl-mick-jagger-martin-scorsese-hbo-show-1201556445/.

7. "Fall Preview: 2015 to 2016 New Shows," *TV Guide*.

Selected Bibliography

Agresta, Michael. "'Girls', 'Mad Men', and the Future of TV-as-Literature." *The Atlantic*, accessed June 15, 2012. http://www.theatlantic.com/entertainment /archive/2012/06/girls-mad-men-and-the-future-of-tv-as-literature/258469/.

Akass, Kim and Janet McCabe. "Six Feet Under." In *The Essential HBO Reader*, edited by Gary Edgerton and Jeffrey Jones, 71–81. Lexington, KY: The University Press of Kentucky, 2008.

Al-Arian, Laila. "TV's Most Islamophobic Show." *Salon*, accessed December 15, 2012. http://www.salon.com/2012/12/15/tvs_most_islamophobic_show/.

Allister, Graeme. "How Mad Men Became a Style Guide." *TV and Radio Blog*. *The Guardian*, accessed August 1, 2008. http://www.theguardian.com/culture /tvandradioblog/2008/aug/01/youdonthavetowatchmadmen.

Alsultany, Evelyn. "24 Challenging Stereotypes." In *How to Watch Television*, edited by Ethan Thompson and James Mittell, 85–93. New York: New York University Press, 2013.

Anderson, Monica. "How Social Media Is Reshaping News." Pew Research Center, accessed September 14, 2015. http://www.pewresearch.org/fact-tank /2014/09/24/how-social-media-is-reshaping-news/.

Arends, Brett. "Inequality Worse Now Than on 'Downton Abbey'." *MarketWatch*, accessed February 26, 2014. http://www.marketwatch.com/story/welcome-to -downton-abbey-america-2014-02-24.

Arky, Beth. "Touch and Autism." *Child Mind Institute*, accessed January 31, 2012. http://www.childmind.org/en/posts/articles/2012-1-31-fox-show-touch -mixed-response-autism-advocates.

Bellis, Rich. "Which Great Literary Work Explains *Breaking Bad* Best?" *The Atlantic*, accessed October 2, 2013. http://www.theatlantic.com/entertainment/archive /2013/10/which-great-literary-work-explains-em-breaking-bad-em-best/280149/.

Bennett, Laura. "Against Antiheroes: It's Time to Retire Television's Most Overused Buzzword." *New Republic*, accessed August 17, 2013. http://www .newrepublic.com/article/114346/anti-antihero-against-cultural-buzzwords.

Bennett, Laura. "The True Anti-Hero of 'Breaking Bad' Isn't Walter White." *New Republic*, accessed August 8, 2013. http://www.newrepublic.com/article/114245/breaking-bad-review-walter-white-not-antihero.

Bethune, Brian. "Autistic Licence: Suddenly Asperger's Is the New 'It' Disorder on Screen and In Fiction." *MacLeans*, accessed July 13, 2009. http://www.macleans.ca/culture/autistic-licence/.

"Big Love's Creators Deconstruct the Show's Finale." *Fresh Air*. National Public Radio. Boston, MA: WBUR, March 21, 2011.

Billson, Anne. "Is True Detective Leading to an 'Undumbing of American TV'?" *Telegraph*, accessed April 9, 2014. http://www.telegraph.co.uk/culture/tvandradio/10721228/Is-True-Detective-leading-to-an-undumbing-of-American-TV.html.

Bingham, John. "TV Drama Is the New Literature, Says Salman Rushdie." *The Telegraph*, accessed June 12, 2011. http://www.telegraph.co.uk/culture/books/booknews/8571010/TV-drama-is-the-new-literature-says-Salman-Rushdie.html.

Bliss, Laura. "Previously On: In Praise of the Television Recap Sequence." *The Atlantic*, accessed February 4, 2015. http://www.theatlantic.com/entertainment/archive/2015/02/previously-on-in-praise-of-the-television-recap/385036/.

Blumgart, Jake. "Justified at Home in Kentucky." *Oxford American*, accessed April 30, 2013. http://www.oxfordamerican.org/item/521-justified-at-home-in-kentucky.

Bogado, Aura. "White Is the New White." *The Nation,* accessed August 16, 2013. http://www.thenation.com/blog/175786/white-new-white.

Braxton, Greg. "ABC's 'American Crime' Series Pushes Hot Buttons of Race, Culture." *Los Angeles Times*, accessed February 27, 2015. http://www.latimes.com/entertainment/tv/la-et-st-abc-american-crime-race-culture-20150301-story.html#page=1.

Buncombe, Andrew. "US Military Tells Jack Bauer: Cut the Torture Scenes . . . Or Else!" *The Independent*, accessed February 13, 2007. http://www.independent.co.uk/news/world/americas/us-military-tells-jack-bauer-cut-out-the-torture-scenes—or-else-436143.html.

Cadwalladr, Carole. "Are the Robots About to Rise? Google's New Director of Engineering Thinks So." *The Guardian*, February 22, 2014. LexisNexis Academic.

Carr, David. "Barely Keeping Up in TV's New Golden Age." *The New York Times*, accessed March 9, 2014. http://www.nytimes.com/2014/03/10/business/media/fenced-in-by-televisions-excess-of-excellence.html?_r=1.

Carr, David. "Giving Viewers What They Want." *The New York Times*, accessed February 24, 2013. http://www.nytimes.com/2013/02/25/business/media/for-house-of-cards-using-big-data-to-guarantee-its-popularity.html?_r=0.

Caumont, Andrea. "12 Trends Shaping Digital News." Pew Research Center, accessed October 16, 2013. http://www.pewresearch.org/fact-tank/2013/10/16/12-trends-shaping-digital-news/.

Clarke, Scott. "Created in Whose Image? Religious Characters on Network Television." *Journal of Media and Religion* 4, 3 (2005): 137–153, doi:10.1207/s15328415jmr0403_2.

D'Addario, Daniel. "This Is the Best Gay Character on Television: How 'Masters of Sex' Gets the Tragedy of 1950s Gay Life Right." *Salon*, accessed July 27, 2014. http://www.salon.com/2014/07/27/this_is_the_best_gay_character _on_television_how_masters_of_sex_gets_the_tragedy_of_1950s_gay_life _right/.

Dawn, Randee. "As TV Antiheroes Grow Ever Darker, Viewers Deal with Empathy Conflict." *The Los Angeles Times*, accessed May 29, 2014. http:// www.latimes.com/entertainment/envelope/tv/la-et-st-en-bad-triumphs-tv -antihero-20140529-story.html.

DeFino, Dean. *The HBO Effect*. New York: Bloomsbury Academic, 2014.

Delwiche, Aaron and Jennifer Jacobs Henderson. "What Is Participatory Culture?" In *The Participatory Culture Handbook*, edited by Aaron Delwiche and Jennifer Jacobs Henderson, 3–9. New York: Routledge, 2012.

Doherty, Thomas. "Storied TV: Cable Is the New Novel." *The Chronicle of Higher Education*, accessed September 17, 2012. http://chronicle.com/article /Cable-Is-the-New-Novel/134420/.

Douglas, William. "Subversion of the American Family." In *Television and the American Family,* Second Edition, edited by Jennings Bryant and Alison Bryant, 231–232. Mahwah, NJ: Lawrence Erlbaum, 2001.

Downing, John. "Racism, Ethnicity and Television." *The Museum of Broadcast Communications*, n.d. http://www.museum.tv/eotv/racismethni.htm.

Easterbrook, Gregg. "America's Creepy, Surveillance-Endorsing Love of NCIS." *The Atlantic*, accessed March 17, 2014. http://www.theatlantic.com/entertainment /archive/2014/03/americas-creepy-surveillance-endorsing-love-of-em-ncis-em /284453/.

Easton, Anne. "Oscar Winner John Ridley Discusses the No-Filter Race Relations of 'American Crime'." *Observer.com*, accessed March 4, 2015. http:// observer.com/2015/03/oscar-winner-john-ridley-discusses-the-no-filter-race -relations-of-american-crime/.

Egner, Jeremy. "A TV Series Winds Down, Portraying Characters Who Will Never Forget." *The New York Times*, July 1, 2010. LexisNexis Academic.

Elia, Eric. "Binge Programming: How Netflix's 'House of Cards' Changes the Game." *pbs.org*, accessed February 6, 2013. http://www.pbs.org/mediashift /2013/02/binge-programming-how-netflixs-house-of-cards-changes-the -game037/.

Engstrom, Erika and Joseph M. Valenzano III. "Demon Hunters and Hegemony: Portrayal of Religion on the CW's *Supernatural*." *Journal of Media and Religion* 9 (2010): 67–83, doi:10.1080/15348421003738785.

Everett, Anna. "Golden Age of Television Drama." The Museum of Broadcast Communications, n.d, http://www.museum.tv/eotv/goldenage.htm.

Feeney, Noah. "It Wasn't Bigotry Back Then: The Unsettling Message of *Masters of Sex*." *The Atlantic*, accessed November 18, 2013. http://www.theatlantic .com/entertainment/archive/2013/11/it-wasnt-bigotry-back-then-the -unsettling-message-of-i-masters-of-sex-i/281575/.

Friedersdorf, Conor. "Feminism, Depravity, and Power in *House of Cards*." *The Atlantic,* accessed February 20, 2014. http://www.theatlantic.com/politics /archive/2014/02/feminism-depravity-and-power-in-em-house-of-cards-em /283960/.

"Funny, Dirty, Sad: The 'Holy Trinity' for 'Transparent' Creator Jill Soloway." *Fresh Air.* National Public Radio. Boston, MA: WBUR, October 20, 2014.

Furlong, Maggie. "The Latest Trend on TV: Characters with Asperger's." *The Huffington Post,* accessed July 10, 2013. http://www.huffingtonpost.com /maggie-furlong/aspergers-on-tv_b_3574336.html.

"FX's 'The Bridge' Finds Authenticity in Spanish-Language Scenes." *Morning Edition.* National Public Radio. Boston, MA: WBUR, October 1, 2014.

Gan, Vicky. "How TV's 'Person of Interest' Helps Us Understand The Surveillance Society." *Smithsonian Magazine,* accessed October 24, 2013. http:// www.smithsonianmag.com/smithsonian-institution/how-tvs-person-of -interest-helps-us-understand-the-surveillance-society-5407171/.

Gilbert, Matthew. "Blurred Lines Between Good, Evil in Superb 'Homeland'." *Boston.com,* accessed September 30, 2011. http://www.boston.com/ae/tv /articles/2011/09/30/blurred_lines_between_good_evil_in_showtimes _superb_homeland/.

Gilbert, Matthew. "'Orange Is the New Black': Yuppie, Interrupted." *The Boston Globe,* accessed July 10, 2013. https://www.bostonglobe.com/arts/television /2013/07/10/orange-new-black-yuppie-interrupted/sfQieZah74YFAVWZYu- gu2O/story.html.

Gilbert, Matthew. "Stretching a Dollar with Roseanne? Or Scheming with Alexis?" *The Boston Globe,* accessed March 8, 2009. http://www.boston .com/ae/tv/articles/2009/03/08/stretching_a_dollar_with_roseanne_or _scheming_with_alexis/?page=full.

Graves, Lucia. "Frank Underwood and a Brief History of Ruthless Pragmatism." *National Journal,* accessed February 19, 2014. http://www.nationaljournal .com/politics/frank-underwood-and-a-brief-history-of-ruthless-pragmatism -20140219.

Green, Adam. "Normalizing Torture on 24." *The New York Times,* May 22, 2005. LexisNexis Academic.

Hardy, Jonathan. "Mapping Commercial Intertextuality: HBO's True Blood." *Convergence* 17, 1 (2011): 7–17, doi:10.1177/1354856510383359.

Heidkamp, Bernie. "New 'Mad Men' TV Show Uses the Past to Reveal Racism and Sexism of Today." *Alternet,* accessed August 23, 2007. http://www.alternet .org/story/60278/new_%22mad_men%22_tv_show_uses_the_past_to _reveal_racism_and_sexism_of_today.

Hendel, John. "10 Years After Its Premiere, 'The Wire' Feels Dated, and That's a Good Thing." *The Atlantic,* accessed May 31, 2012. http://www.theatlantic .com/entertainment/archive/2012/05/10-years-after-its-premiere-the-wire -feels-dated-and-thats-a-good-thing/257910/.

Hernandez, Bel. "Bridge Across the Border." *LatinoMagazine.com*, accessed Fall 2013. http://latinomagazine.com/Fall2013/the-bridge.html.

Holtzman, Linda and Leon Sharpe. *Media Messages, Second Edition*. New York: M. E. Sharpe, Inc., 2014.

"In 'The Americans', Art Imitates Real Life Lies." *All Things Considered*. National Public Radio. Boston, MA: WBUR, January 28, 2015.

Jenkins, Henry. "Seven Myths About Transmedia Storytelling Debunked." *Fast Company,* accessed April 18, 2011. http://www.fastcompany.com/1745746/seven-myths-about-transmedia-storytelling-debunked.

Jenkins, Henry. "Transmedia Storytelling 101." *Confessions of an ACA—Fan* (blog), accessed March 22, 2007. http://henryjenkins.org/2007/03/transmedia_storytelling_101.html.

Jenkins, Henry. "Why Do Humans Tell the Stories They Do: An Interview with Lily Alexander (Part Six)." *Confessions of an Aca-Fan* (blog), accessed April 14, 2014. http://henryjenkins.org/2014/04/who-do-humans-tell-the-stories-they-do-an-interview-with-lily-alexander-part-six.html.

Kassel, Michael. "Dramatic Family Genre." In *The Guide to United States Popular Culture*, edited by Ray Browne, 251–253. Madison, WI: University of Wisconsin Press, 2001.

Kelly, Kevin. "Better Than Human: Why Robots Will—And Must—Take Our Jobs." *Wired*, accessed December 24, 2012. http://www.wired.com/2012/12/ff-robots-will-take-our-jobs/.

Kerman, Piper. *Orange Is the New Black*. New York: Random House, 2011.

Keveney, Bill. "2nd 'Sleeper Cell' Gets into Torture." *USA Today*, accessed December 7, 2006. http://usatoday30.usatoday.com/life/television/news/2006-12-07-sleeper-cell_x.htm.

Keveney, Bill. "Amazon: Vote for Shows You Want Us to Make." *USA Today*, accessed April 14, 2013. http://www.usatoday.com/story/life/tv/2013/04/19/amazon-studios-releases-pilots/2095383/.

Khazan, Olga. "*The Americans*' Refreshingly Real Take on Russians." *The Atlantic*, accessed May 22, 2014. http://www.theatlantic.com/entertainment/archive/2014/05/the-americans-refreshingly-real-take-on-russians/371471/.

Kirsch, Adam and Mohsin Hamid. "Are the New 'Golden Age' TV Shows the New Novels?" *The New York Times*, February 25, 2014. LexisNexis Academic.

Kolodzy, Janet. *Practicing Convergence Journalism*. New York: Routledge, 2013.

Kurtz, Stanley. "*Big Love,* From the Set." *National Review Online*, accessed March 13, 2006. http://www.nationalreview.com/article/217027/big-love-set-stanley-kurtz.

Kurutz, Steven. "Russians: Still the Go-To Bad Guys." *The New York Times*, January 17, 2014. LexisNexis Academic.

LaPastina, Anthony. "Telenovela." The Museum of Broadcast Communications. http://www.museum.tv/eotv/telenovela.htm.

Leopold, Todd. "The New, New TV Golden Age." *CNN*, accessed May 6, 2013. http://www.cnn.com/2013/05/06/showbiz/golden-age-of-tv/.

Lewit, Meghan. "Bad Husband, Bad Wife, Good TV: The Fascinating Rise of Antihero Marriages." *The Atlantic*, accessed April 30, 2013. http://www.theatlantic.com/entertainment/archive/2013/04/bad-husband-bad-wife-good-tv-the-fascinating-rise-of-antihero-marriages/275347/.

Lyon, Margaret. "Can We Make Walter White Our Last Antihero, Please?" *Vulture*, accessed October 1, 2013. http://www.vulture.com/2013/10/let-anti heroes-end-with-walter-white.html.

MacInnes, Paul. "'Breaking Bad' Creator Vince Gilligan: The Man Who Turned Walter White from Mr Chips into Scarface." *The Guardian*, accessed May 18, 2012. http://www.theguardian.com/tv-and-radio/2012/may/19/vince-gilligan -breaking-bad.

Martin, Brett. *Difficult Men*. New York: Penguin Press, 2013.

McArdle, Megan. "Piketty's Capital: An Economist's Inequality Ideas Are All the Rage." *Bloomberg Businessweek*, accessed May 29, 2014. http://www.bloomberg .com/bw/articles/2014-05-29/pikettys-capital-economists-inequality-ideas -are-all-the-rage.

McMillan, Graeme. "The Cult of *Orphan Black*." *Time*, April 21, 2014. EBSCO HOST (95738226).

McNamara, Mary. "Amazon's Transgender Transition 'Transparent' Astonishes." *The Los Angeles Times*, accessed September 26, 2014. http://www.latimes .com/entertainment/tv/la-et-st-transparent-review-20140926-column.html.

McNamara, Mary. "Scandal Has Become Must-Tweet TV." *The Los Angeles Times*, accessed May 11, 2013. http://articles.latimes.com/print/2013/may /11/entertainment/la-et-st-scandal-abc-social-media-20130511.

Mendelsohn, Tome. "Is Breaking Bad's Ozymandias the Greatest Episode of TV Ever Written?" *The Independent*, accessed September 17, 2013. http://www .independent.co.uk/arts-entertainment/tv/features/is-breaking-bads-ozymandias -the-greatest-episode-of-tv-ever-written-8821985.html.

Mittell, Jason. "Strategies of Storytelling on Transmedia Television." In *Storyworlds Across Media: Towards a Media Conscious Narratology*, edited by Jan-Noel Thon and Marie-Lauie Ryan, 253–277. Lincoln: University of Nebraska Press, 2014.

Negron-Muntaner, Francis. "The Latino-Media Gap: A Report on the State of Latinos in U.S. Media." Columbia University, accessed June 2, 2014. https:// pmcdeadline2.files.wordpress.com/2014/06/latino_media_gap_report-wm .pdf.

Nikolas, Akash. "Where Is the Female Tony Soprano?" *The Atlantic*, accessed June 27, 2013. http://www.theatlantic.com/entertainment/archive/2013/06 /where-is-the-female-tony-soprano/277270/.

Nussbaum, Emily. "Primary Colors: Shonda Rhimes's Scandal and the Diversity Debate." *The New Yorker*, accessed May 21, 2012. http://www.newyorker .com/magazine/2012/05/21/primary-colors.

Nussbaum, Emily. "Shedding Her Skin, *The Good Wife*'s Thrilling Transformation." *The New Yorker*, accessed October 13, 2014. http://www.newyorker.com/magazine/2014/10/13/shedding-skin.

Nussbaum, Emily. "The Aristocrats: The Graphic Arts of Game of Thrones." *The New Yorker*, accessed May 7, 2012. http://www.newyorker.com/magazine/2012/05/07/the-aristocrats.

O'Connell, Michael. "The Highest Rated Broadcast Series of 2014—And How People Watched Them." *The Hollywood Reporter,* accessed December 30, 2014. http://www.hollywoodreporter.com/live-feed/highest-rated-broadcast-series-2014-760484.

"Orange Is the New Black in Federal Women's Prison." *Talk of the Nation.* National Public Radio. Boston, MA: WBUR, April 6, 2010.

Orr, Christopher. "*True Detective*: The Best Show on TV." *The Atlantic*, accessed February 11, 2014. http://www.theatlantic.com/entertainment/archive/2014/02/-em-true-detective-em-the-best-show-on-tv/283727/.

Ostrow, Joanne. "Jeffrey Tambor Is Brilliant in 'Transparent' Dramedy on Amazon Prime." *Denver Post*, accessed September 25, 2014. http://www.denverpost.com/television/ci_26599614/jeffrey-tambor-is-brilliant-transparent-dramedy-amazon-prime.

Paarlberg, Michael. "Breaking Bad Is a Middle-Class Horror Story." *The Guardian,* accessed September 9, 2013. http://www.theguardian.com/commentisfree/2013/sep/09/breaking-bad-middle-class-horror-story.

"Parents Beware of 24." *The Weekly Wrap*. Parents Television Council, accessed November 21, 2008. https://www.parentstv.org/PTC/publications/emailalerts/2008/wrapup_112108.htm#3.

Paskin, Willa. "Network TV Is Broken. So How Does Shonda Rhimes Keep Making Hits?" *The New York Times Magazine, The New York Times*, accessed May 9, 2013. http://www.nytimes.com/2013/05/12/magazine/shonda-rhimes.html.

Paskin, Willa. "Nine Lives, at Least." *Slate*, accessed April 17, 2014. http://www.slate.com/articles/arts/television/2014/04/season_2_of_orphan_black_starring_tatiana_maslany_reviewed.html.

Pinchefsky, Carol. "The Clone Wars: A Look at the Science of 'Orphan Black'." *Forbes*, accessed May 31, 2013. http://www.forbes.com/sites/carolpinchefsky/2013/05/31/the-clone-wars-a-look-at-the-science-of-orphan-black/.

Poniewozik, James. "Must-Read TV: *The Bridge*'s Elwood Reid on Getting America to Watch Subtitles." *Time*, accessed July 10, 2014. http://time.com/2966884/tv-subtitles-the-bridge-fx/.

Poniewozik, James. "Q & A: *Transparent* Creator Jill Soloway on Transgender Stories and Indie TV." *Time*, accessed September 25, 2014. http://time.com/3422038/transparent-interview-jill-soloway/.

Press, Andrea. "Gender and Family in Television's Golden Age and Beyond." *Annals of the American Academy of Political and Social Science* 625 (2009): 148.

Quay, Sara and Amy Damico, eds. *September 11 in Popular Culture*. Santa Barbara, CA: ABC-CLIO, 2010.

Robinson, James and Thomas Skill. "Five Decades of Families on Television: From the 1950s Through the 1990s." In *Television and the American Family, Second Edition,* edited by Jennings Bryant and Alison Bryant, 139–162. Mahwah, NJ: Lawrence Erlbaum, 2001.

Robison, John Elder. "The Bridge and the End of Asperger's on TV." *Vulture,* accessed July 12, 2013. http://www.vulture.com/2013/07/aspergers-tv-the-bridge-diane-kruger-sheldon-cooper.html.

Rose, Lacey. "Emmys: Good Wife Campaign Attacks 'True Detective' and Cable Rivals." *The Hollywood Reporter,* accessed April 16, 2014. http://www.hollywoodreporter.com/news/emmys-good-wife-campaign-attacks-696284.

Rosenberg, Yair. "'Homeland' Is Anything but Islamaphobic." *The Atlantic,* accessed December 18, 2012. http://www.theatlantic.com/entertainment/archive/2012/12/homeland-is-anything-but-islamophobic/266418/.

Rothman, Joshua. "'Person of Interest'": The TV Show That Predicted Edward Snowden." *The New Yorker,* accessed January 14, 2014. http://www.newyorker.com/culture/culture-desk/person-of-interest-the-tv-show-that-predicted-edward-snowden.

Ryan, Maureen. "Who Creates Drama at HBO? Very Few Women or People of Color." *The Huffington Post,* Huff Post TV, accessed March 6, 2014. http://www.huffingtonpost.com/2014/03/06/hbo-diversity_n_4899679.html.

Salinas, Brenda. "Is America Ready to Fall in Love with the Telenovela?" *NPR Code Switch,* accessed November 9, 2014. http://www.npr.org/sections/codeswitch/2014/11/09/362401259/is-america-ready-to-fall-in-love-with-the-telenovela.

Satell, Greg. "What Netflix's 'House of Cards' Means for the Future of TV." *Forbes,* accessed March 4, 2013. http://www.forbes.com/sites/gregsatell/2013/03/04/what-netflixs-house-of-cards-means-for-the-future-of-tv/.

Schatz, Thomas. "Workplace Programs." The Museum of Broadcast Communication, n.d. http://www.museum.tv/eotv/workplacepro.htm.

Schneider, Michael. "From *The Returned* to *The Bridge,* Viewers Adjust to Subtitles as TV Gets More Global." *TV Guide,* accessed December 5, 2013. http://www.tvguide.com/news/returned-bridge-viewers-1074256/.

Scolari, Carlos A. "Lostology: Transmedia Storytelling and Expansion/Compression Strategies." *Semiotica* 195 (2013): 45–68, doi:10.1515/sem-2013-0038.

Sepinwall, Alan. "How TV Shows Try (or Choose not) to Depict Asperger's Syndrome: Sepinwall on TV." *The Star Ledger,* accessed February 28, 2010. http://www.nj.com/entertainment/tv/index.ssf/2010/02/how_tv_shows_try_or_choose_not.html.

Sepinwall, Alan. *The Revolution Was Televised.* New York: Simon & Schuster, 2012.

Shire, Emily. "Finally, a Realistic Autistic Character on Television." *Salon,* accessed July 11, 2013. http://www.salon.com/2013/07/11/finally_a_realistic_autistic_character_on_television/.

Sifferlin, Alexandra. "Homeland and Bipolar Disorder: How TV Characters Are Changing the Way We View Mental Illness." *Time*, accessed October 9, 2013. http://healthland.time.com/2013/10/08/homeland-and-bipolar-disorder-how -tv-characters-are-changing-the-way-we-view-mental-illness/.

Sims, David. "*The Good Wife* Takes a Weak Swipe at Racism." *The Atlantic*, accessed January 12, 2015. http://www.theatlantic.com/entertainment/archive /2015/01/the-good-wife-stumbles-trying-to-confront-institutional-racism /384448/.

Smith, Aaron. "The Rise of the 'Connected Viewer'." Pew Research Internet Project, accessed July 17, 2012. http://www.pewinternet.org/2012/07/17/the -rise-of-the-connected-viewer/.

Smith, Evan. "Implementing Environmental Justice in Appalachia: The Social and Cultural Context of Mountain Top Removal Mining as Seen Through the Lenses of Law and Documentaries." *William & Mary Policy Review* 170, 4 (2012): 170–209.

Smith, Matt. "Are We on the Verge of Television's Third Golden Age?" *Lost Remote* (blog). *Adweek*, accessed October 27, 2014. http://www.adweek.com/lostremote /are-we-on-the-verge-of-televisions-third-golden-age/48194.

Smith, Murray. "Mad, Bad and Dangerous to Know: TV's Anti-Heroes." *Times Higher Education*, accessed July 17, 2014. https://www.timeshighereducation .co.uk/features/culture/mad-bad-and-dangerous-to-know-tvs-anti-heroes /2014483.article.

Smith, Paul Julian. "10 O'Clock Staying Power." *Film Quarterly* 64, 3 (Spring 2011): 10–11, doi:**10**.1525/FQ.2011.64.3.10.

Soraya, Lynne. "When Will ABC Get Asperger's Right?" *Asperger's Diary* (blog). *Psychology Today*, accessed February 10, 2009. https://www.psychologytoday .com/blog/aspergers-diary/200902/when-will-abc-get-aspergers-right.

St. John, Allen. "Why 'Breaking Bad' Is the Best Show Ever and Why That Matters." *Forbes*, accessed September 16, 2013. http://www.forbes.com/sites /allenstjohn/2013/09/16/why-breaking-bad-is-the-best-show-ever-and-why -that-matters/.

Stanley, Alessandra. "Wrought in Rhimes's Image." *The New York Times*, accessed September 18, 2014. http://www.nytimes.com/2014/09/21/arts/television/viola -davis-plays-shonda-rhimess-latest-tough-heroine.html.

Stuever, Hank. "'American Crime Is the Rare Network Drama That Will Get Your Rapt Attention." *The Washington Post*, accessed March 4, 2015. http:// www.washingtonpost.com/entertainment/tv/american-crime-is-the-rare -network-drama-that-will-get-your-rapt-attention/2015/03/04/bb84cbdc -c28c-11e4-9ec2-b418f57a4a99_story.html.

Summers, Lawrence. "American Risks Becoming a Downton Abbey Economy." *Financial Times*, accessed February 16, 2014. http://www.ft.com/cms/s/2 /875155ce-8f25-11e3-be85-00144feab7de.html#axzz3e62f5Bb2.

Tewksbury, David and Jason Rittenberg. *News on the Internet*. New York: Oxford University Press, 2012.

"The Polygamous Stylings of 'Big Love'." *Fresh Air.* National Public Radio. Boston, MA: WBUR, August 1, 2007.

Thompson, Clive. "From Anonymous to Bitcoin, *The Good Wife* Is the Most Tech Savvy Show on TV." *Wired*, accessed September 27, 2013. http://www.wired.com/2013/09/screen-smarts/.

Thompson, Robert J. *Television's Second Golden Age: From Hill Street Blues to ER.* New York: Syracuse University Press, 1997.

Turkle, Sherry. *Alone Together: Why We Expect More from Technology and Less from Each Other.* New York: Basic Books, 2011.

Weinstein, Shelli. "How 'Scandal' Paved the Way for ABC's Twitter-Based '#TGIT' Marketing Strategy." *Variety*, accessed September 22, 2014. http://variety.com/2014/tv/news/scandal-twitter-shonda-rhimes-tgit-abc-shondaland-120131 1282/.

"What's Empowering the New Digital Consumer?" *Nielsen Newswire*, accessed February 10, 2014. http://www.nielsen.com/content/corporate/us/en/insights/news/2014/whats-empowering-the-new-digital-consumer.html.

Whitney, Erin. "How Claire Underwood and 'House of Cards' Changed the TV Antihero Forever." *The Huffington Post*, accessed March 5, 2014. http://www.huffingtonpost.com/2014/03/05/house-of-cards-tv-antihero-archetype_n_4899440.html.

Wiegand, David. "'Rescue Me' Helped Us Deal with Sadness of 9/11." *SFGate*, accessed September 7, 2011. http://www.sfgate.com/entertainment/article/Rescue-Me-helped-us-deal-with-sadness-of-9-11-2310788.php.

Wu, Tim. "Netflix's War on Mass Culture." *New Republic,* accessed December 4, 2013. http://www.newrepublic.com/article/115687/netflixs-war-mass-culture.

Yaacobi-Gross, Tally and Amit Pinchevski. "Body of Evidence: *CSI*, the Detective Genre, and the Post Human Condition." Conference Paper, International Communication Association 2010 Annual Meeting, Communication and Mass Media Complete Data Base, Accession Number 59227364.

Yuhas, Alan. "The Walking Dead Is All about Blood, Gore—And Gun Control." *The Guardian*, accessed April 1, 2013. http://www.theguardian.com/commentisfree/2013/apr/01/walking-dead-blood-gore-gun-control-background-checks.

Index

About the Authors

AMY M. DAMICO, PHD, is a professor of communication at Endicott College in Beverly, MA, and is the faculty advisor to the Endicott College Scholars honors program.

SARA E. QUAY, PHD, is dean of the school of education at Endicott College in Beverly, MA, and is the director of the Endicott College Scholars honors program.

Their previous book, by ABC-CLIO, is titled *September 11 in Popular Culture*.